Women and kinship

DATE DUE

AP 2 9 03			
JE 8 05			

DEMCO 38-296

Women and kinship: Comparative perspectives on gender in South and South-East Asia

By Leela Dube

United Nations University Press

TOKYO · NEW YORK · PARIS

The views expressed in this publication are those of the author
and do not necessarily reflect the views of the United Nations
University.

United Nations University Press
The United Nations University, 53-70, Jingumae 5-chome,
Shibuya-ku, Tokyo 150, Japan
Tel: (03) 3499-2811   Fax: (03) 3406-7345
Telex: J25442   Cable: UNATUNIV TOKYO

UNU Office in North America
2 United Nations Plaza, Room DC2-1462-70, New York, NY 10017
Tel: (212) 963-6387   Fax: (212) 371-9454   Telex: 422311 UN UI

United Nations University Press is the publishing division of the
United Nations University.

Cover design by Joyce C. Weston

Printed in the United States of America

UNUP-922
ISBN 92-808-0922-9
02495 P

For S. C. Dube, 1922–1996
A fifty-year partnership in kinship and anthropology

Contents

Contents

viii

Acknowledgements

This study was born during discussions in workshops held at New Delhi and Penang in connection with the United Nations University Project "A Comparative Study of Women's Work and Family Strategies in South and South-East Asia," coordinated by Vina Mazumdar and Hanna Papanek. Owing to a succession of troubles with my health I have taken unusually long to complete this study. The wide canvas I had chosen and the complexities of social reality reflected in the material would in any case have caused some delay.

I am particularly beholden to Hanna Papanek for initiating the proposal, for her keen interest in this work, for providing me with useful contacts in South and South-East Asia, and for making very fruitful suggestions after several long discussions at different times. Vina Mazumdar and Malavika Karlekar of the Centre for Women's Development Studies, New Delhi, rendered much help. Other persons closely connected with the UNU's project who aided me with discussion and critical comment were Jean Illo, Wazir Jahan Karim, Karuna Chanana, Neera Desai, Maithreyi Krishna Raj, Narayan Banerjee, and Swarna Jayaweera. As a member of the steering committee of the UNU project, M. N. Srinivas was very receptive to my ideas. I also need to express my appreciation for the help I received from Kumiko Ishikawa of the UNU in the course of my work.

Many people helped me during my visits to Bangladesh, countries of South-East Asia, and the United Kingdom to collect material for this study. Here I thank a few of them in particular: Hameeda Hossain, Mahmuda Islam, Ishrat Shamin, K. M. A. Aziz, Salma

Sobhan, and Roushan Jahan in Bangladesh; Lynn Bennett and Bina Pradhan for the material on Nepal; Noeleen Heyzer, Jamilah Arrifin, Wazir Jahan Karim, and Cecilia Ng in Malaysia; Pat Lim, librarian at the Institute of Southeast Asian Studies, Singapore, and members of the Department of Anthropology at Singapore University; Koto Kanno of UNESCO; Chayan Vaddhanaphuti, Amara Pongsapich, and Napat Sirisamband in Thailand; Omas Ihromi, Pudjiwati Sajogyo, Sukanti Suryochandro, and Yulfita Rihartjo in Indonesia; P. M. Hobart, Andrew Turton, and Audrey Cantlie Hailey at the School of Oriental and African Studies, London, Naila Kabeer and Hilary Standing at Sussex University, and Patricia Kaplan and Deniz Kandiyoti – both friends of long standing – in the United Kingdom; and Joke Schrijvers, Carla Risseeuw, and Els Postel of the Netherlands.

When this project began I was a Senior Fellow at the Nehru Memorial Museum and Library, New Delhi. Later, as I continued to work on and finalize the manuscript, I was affiliated to the same institution, this time as a National Fellow of the Indian Council of Social Science Research. I express my gratitude to the Director of the Nehru Memorial Museum and Library, Ravinder Kumar, for his keen interest and for providing a congenial atmosphere for work. I would like to thank the two peer reviewers for their extremely useful suggestions. Following them meant additional labour, but I believe the work has been made significantly better.

Throughout my work on this study Kamala Ganesh's intellectual and emotional support has been invaluable. Rajni Palriwala's comments were useful. Rowena Robinson, in her characteristic unobtrusive manner, made a significant contribution to the preparation of the manuscript. Saurabh Dube helped with his incisive comments and through discussion, and Ishita Banerjee Dube provided constructive assistance. My sisters Usha Sant and Sumati Mutatkar gave me shelter at difficult times during periods of writing. Mukul Dube is one person without whom this manuscript would never have been completed. Besides looking after me in my ill health, he took the responsibility of editing and word-processing the entire manuscript.

S. C. Dube went through early drafts of the manuscript and made useful suggestions. He is not with us any more, but this book bears the imprint of his close association with my work and his rare acumen to sense the kind of help and support I needed at critical points. This book is dedicated to him.

1

Introduction

Gender relations are constructed differently in different cultures. A key area of cultural diversity is kinship. Kinship systems are an important context within which gender relations are located. In looking at gender in South and South-East Asia I focus attention on the complex of institutions that make up the structural and cultural dimensions of a kinship system.

My objective is to highlight certain issues that have remained largely neglected. It is my hunch that gender studies often leave out a consideration of kinship either because it is thought irrelevant or because it is viewed as an immutable given. The notion that it is irrelevant can be attributed to a deficient understanding of the influence of the organizing principles of kinship on the business of living – on the allocation of resources, on the constitution of production relations, on the immediate context of women's lives, and on sustaining a specific ideology of gender. The notion that it is defined for all time is derived from the belief that it is rooted squarely in Nature and from the conviction that men and women have different propensities, capabilities, and trajectories.[1]

Kinship systems often seem to contain the most change-resistant aspects of social organization. Whether this resistance is more apparent than real needs to be investigated. The persistent concern in both East and West with "family breakdown" suggests an ideology that holds that kinship systems *should* be stable; perhaps because our identities are rooted in our memories and in our images of family and kinship links. These ideas must be challenged, for they continue to affect the social sciences.

1

South and South-East Asia comprise countries from Afghanistan in the west to the Philippines in the east. In this study I look at aspects of family and kinship among some populations of Bangladesh, India, Indonesia, Malaysia, Nepal, Pakistan, the Philippines, and Thailand with a comparative perspective. (Because little material on it was available to me and because of its complex character, Sri Lanka is touched upon only occasionally.) Each of these countries is characterized by internal heterogeneity, although the extent of diversity varies among them. In choosing specific communities and geographical areas within them I have been guided by the availability of material and by their relevance to the issues I wish to explore.

Asia harbours a variety of kinship systems under the three main heads: patrilineal, matrilineal, and bilateral. South Asia is predominantly patrilineal, with two important matrilineal pockets in the south-west and the north-east. Although South-East Asia is predominantly bilateral, with both parents being relevant for reckoning kinship and for claiming rights to resources, there are also significant populations that follow matriliny or patriliny – to the last of which I have not given attention in this study.

The populations that I have taken up for comparison are Hindus, Muslims, and some Christians of India, high-caste Parbatiya Hindus and Newars of Nepal, Muslims of Bangladesh and Pakistan (the latter mainly from West Punjab), bilateral Malay Muslims of Peninsular Malaysia, the bilateral Javanese and matrilineal Minangkabau of western Sumatra and their offshoots in Negri Sembilan, the Buddhist Thai, and the lowland Christian Filipinos. I have left out all tribal groups of South-East Asia as well as populations of Chinese and Indian origin. Indian tribes have been touched upon at important points but not so tribes from the rest of South Asia.

I adopt a particular approach to grasp the differences and similarities in the character of gender relations among various societies in the two regions. My basic argument is that differences in kinship systems and family structures account for some critical differences among societies in the ways in which gender operates. The central concern here is to understand how gender roles are conceived of and enacted, the process by which women and men are turned into gendered subjects and thus implicated in the maintenance and reproduction of a social system. This can help us grasp the often bafflingly complex and subtle differences in the quality of gender relations.

It is not possible, however, to confine ourselves to the bare structural characteristics of these institutions – for then the significance of their interplay with religion and with wider political and economic structures and processes may remain hidden. In certain contexts, looking backwards to the historical or mythic past is also a necessity. Practices such as seclusion and segregation, the relative rigidity of the division of labour and of notions of the "naturalness" of males' and females' work, and many subtle aspects of gender relations all contribute to the shaping of – and are themselves shaped by – the texture and structure of family and kinship in a given society. Delving into these interplays poses problems; and the lack of parity in the data available for various countries and communities makes any attempt to deal with a common set of variables a formidable venture. The challenge is nevertheless worth taking up.

This work undertakes, then, to assess the relevance of the family and of the ideological and material aspects of kinship to the comprehending of the nature and quality of gender relations. Although caste and class are significant variables in the study of gender, their use must be informed by an awareness of the institutions and practices in the realm of kinship, marriage, and the family. And sometimes the norms and rules laid down by religion or by the state may differ from those prescribed by the kinship system, resulting in compromises, manoeuvring, and compartmentalization.

At any point in time the composition of a family is not just a function of demography. It reflects the rules of marital recruitment and residence as well as the normative and actual patterns of rearrangement of family structure in the replacement of one generation by the next. The actual composition of a family unit, moreover, with its configuration of role relationships and the specific contributions of its members to the business of living, is not all that determines the apportionment of resources, the gender-based and age-based divisions of work, and conceptions of the value of son and daughter, man and woman. Here we must enter also the arena of kinship, with its rules, norms, and ideology.

Indian nuclear or conjugal or modal five-member family households, for instance, cannot be equated with the nuclear family of the West. Their specificity in India is defined by the assumptions of the patrilineal and patri-virilocal kinship system, which are seen to have the authority of the laws of Nature. Nor can they be equated with households of a similar composition in South-East Asia, which function within a bilateral kinship system with a different set of assumptions. These assumptions concern the bases of the formation of households, the structure of a normal kinship group, and individual members' rights to nominally shared resources.

While emphasizing the necessity of looking at the various linkages between the individual household and the wider structures and processes of society, it is necessary to remember that the particularities of a system are crucial to an understanding of the complexities and subtleties of gender relations. At the same time, in looking at the bases of legitimation of the organizing principles of kinship as expressed through law, social patterns, behavioural norms, and judgements, we have also to look into cultural conceptions of biological processes and of the nature of female and male sexuality. This may take us to religious ideology, to the cultural conceptions of social reality, to the world-view of the people, and to patterns of production. I look upon kinship as significant and relevant to the understanding of women's lives, but I certainly do not wish to look at it exclusively and in isolation.

While contrasting patrilineal and bilateral kinship systems we should keep in mind that there is no uniform, undifferentiated pattern either for patrilineality or for bilaterality. This applies also to matrilineality. The historical antecedents of any variant of them need to be taken into account, for instance their roots in ancient or tribal cultures. So do their interaction and occasional confrontation with religions, particularly the newer ones for which more information is available.

A variety of marriage practices and specific principles of societal organization – such as caste in India, Nepal, and Sri Lanka – also deserve to be taken into consideration. Nor should we ignore the possible influence of environment and ecology and of the patterns of production that developed within their parameters. Encounters with colonialism and with powerful capitalist societies have also played a role.

There is some recognition of the dangers inherent in the use of a single overgeneralized Asian model, but we have still fully to understand the variety, diversity, and contrasts within the Asian social reality. Even when the activities of women at particular socio-economic levels in different societies are similar, the structure of rights in respect of these activities and the quality of gender relations can differ greatly. The apparent commonality in religious injunctions and basic legal codes – as among the Muslims of Bangladesh, India, and Pakistan and those in Indonesia and Malaysia – tends to obscure the interplay that has gone on between the cultural and structural matrices of societies and the religions practised in them. For instance, whereas there is corporate or individual control over female sexuality and a strong emphasis on seclusion and segregation among the patrilineal Muslim populations of Bangladesh, India, and Pakistan, the situation among the Muslims of Indonesia and Malaysia – and on the Lakshadweep islands off the south-west coast of India – is different. The differences between these two groups of populations are equally significant where women's participation in economic activities and their freedom of movement are concerned. Again, under the rubric of Hinduism there are considerable variations across regions, important ones being between north and south India, between castes and between patrilineal and matrilineal communities. I shall direct attention to some such differences and similarities.

In feminist anthropology the materialist approach (represented by a concern with relations of production and with division of labour) and the ideational or cognitive-oriented approach (which concentrates on the definition of conceptions of gender) are becoming increasingly interlinked (Schrijvers 1985). In my approach, kinship subsumes both material and ideological aspects of women's lives. In fact the two are so intertwined that they can be separated only analytically and notionally. The sphere of kinship cannot, of course, entirely explain them. As I have said earlier, part of their content and character obtain from religious ideology, various rules and codes, the production system or economy, and the polity. The linkages between kinship, religion, production system, and polity would be discerned, ideally, by adopting a historical perspective; but in this work I can merely point to them.

Kinship will not be viewed here only as a set of moral principles or explored in any of the more esoteric forms that are associated with its study. It will be seen as providing the organizing principles that govern the recruitment of individuals to social groups and their placement in them, the formation of the family and the household, residence at marriage, resource distribution including inheritance, and the obligations and responsibilities of members of the group in the business of living. The very notion of entitlement – whether to membership of a family, to access to strategic resources, to food and nutrition, to health care, to education, or to authority and decision-making – cannot be understood without accepting that the kinship system to a large degree provides the language for it and gives it legitimacy. A proper analysis of the ideology of the family is not possible without going into various aspects of the kinship system. Because many of them may not be clearly spelt out, it is necessary to search for the ideas and assumptions underlying the behaviour of people.

It is not my intention to seek to explain everything about women's lives in terms of the kinship system by which a society is governed. The thrust of my argument is that we need an awareness of the reach of the principles of kinship into human life and of the possible role of kinship in areas that ostensibly have nothing to do with it. This is especially important for South and South-East Asia, where kinship is a stronger force than elsewhere. I contend that, while trying to make greater sense of women's lives and grasp the quality of gender relations in these societies, it is necessary to keep in mind the many less or more subtle ways in which the ideologies, norms, and values rooted in the kinship system, as well as the jural rules derived from it, come into operation and make their impact. This task is best accomplished by adopting a comparative perspective.

When I associate a particular situation with a specific kinship and family pattern, I do not mean that this association is inevitable or that it implies any sufficient or necessary condition. I merely plead that the connections and associations that seem obvious to me be regarded as worthy of serious consideration. I believe that comparisons of a variety of patterns and configurations have the capacity to question notions of the "naturalness" of gender differences and of specific social patterns, the fairness of the social order, and the tacit belief in the immutability of a kinship system. As Papanek (1991) says, "notions of entitlement are both learned and taught – which means that they can also be unlearned." To unlearn such notions it is necessary first to go to their roots – to the principles of one's own kinship system. Only when these are seen in a comparative context can one disabuse oneself of the immutability of the kinship system in which one has grown.

Women in South-East Asia exercise an unusual degree of autonomy in economic and social life. Relative egalitarianism between the sexes appears to be a general feature of South-East Asian social organization. It is reasonable to assume that this peculiar quality of gender relations will have been established before the advent of Islam or Christianity and before the economic, political, and social impact of the West. Certain elements of these societies' kinship and family organization seem to be particularly relevant here: ego-centred bilateral kinship with variations in its inclination towards matrilineality and matrilocality that does not seem to have the compulsive character that the patrilineal, patri-virilocal pattern has; flexibility in the composition of households; no insistence on family continuity; equal rights of inheritance for sons and daughters; access to resources by both men and women; optation or choice in marital residence, which gives free play to expediency and individual initiative; respect for age and hierarchy of status as a cultural element, but a general ethos of non-authoritarian interpersonal relationships among kin and between affines; no great compulsion to remain married in the face of intense conflict and suffering; strong cultural approval of children's remaining with their mothers in the event of divorce, which keeps the mother–child tie intact and also permits a continuing relationship between children and their father.

In comparing these features with those of South Asian societies characterized by strong patriliny, patrilocality, male authority and control over resources, and what has been described as patrifocal family structure (Mukhopadhyay and Seymour 1994), I have been guided by the view that mechanically perceived superficial differences do not take us to the core of the problem. The material and the ideological must be explained, as well as their interplay. Starting with the perspective that kinship systems deeply affect the bargaining power of persons in dyadic as well as group relationships, I have tried to explore the implications of various kinds of kinship organization for women. The notion of bargaining power is important in this context, as is the closely associated one of negotiability. The key question is: What are the choices available to women? It is, after all, the existence of options that creates bargaining power and negotiability. South-East Asia seems to offer much choice in regard to marital partners, marital residence, household composition, divorce, and the adoption or fostering of children. Within limits set by economy and polity, women have choices and opportunities in regard to income-earning activities, and they are in a position to bargain and negotiate in interpersonal relations. Most South Asian women, rooted in patrilineal, patri-virilocal kinship, with limited rights over resources and virtually no inheritance rights, dependent, secluded and segregated, their sexuality managed by men, do not have choices or have only limited choices.

Some choices are built in to social structure and others have to be developed through investment in education and training. Women in whom such a long-term investment has been made have greater bargaining power. Investments depend on visions of the future and the needs of the present; and the making of them is itself determined to a great degree by the ideologies of cultures.

Choices curtail or reinforce one another. For instance, a woman may have the choice of ending a marriage; but if she has no earning power or kin's help with which to support herself, or if she cannot easily return to her natal home, this choice is devoid of meaning.

Another notion that suggests itself in the exploration of bargaining power is that of control. Control here refers to the power of directing, guiding, commanding, and restraining others and of unilaterally taking decisions that concern them. Ideology is used to exercise control over resources and over women's actions, bodies, and sexuality. The main mechanisms are the organization of work, space, and time; rules of avoidance and respect; modes of punishment; the distribution of resources; the withholding of love; the denial of knowledge and information; and, in general, the absence of opportunities to develop self-worth. Seclusion and segregation are among the most potent instruments of control. When we compare the two regions we see that South-East Asian women are weighed down and hemmed in by far fewer controls.

This is not an exhaustive overview of the region. Selected materials are presented in order to highlight certain contrasts. Besides the scrutiny of a mass of literature, intimate experiences of living in a culture, fieldwork in different geographical regions, and personal observations and communication with specialists as well as with common people in both the regions have also contributed to the structure and content of this study.

A brief outline of the kinship and family organizations of major communities of the two regions forms the background to what is dealt with later. Group membership and the inheritance and distribution of resources, which follow, may be seen as an extension, but they focus on contrasting the implications of different kinship systems for understanding gender. Along with these goes a brief discussion of women's economic and productive roles in the two regions. Their full import will become clear as we proceed further.

Management of female sexuality, differing patterns of seclusion and segregation, and the limitations imposed by females' bodily processes constitute another unit. The relationship of women to domestic and outside space forms a prelude to an extended discussion of the implications of marital residence for women's situation and gender relations. With these go examinations of the nature of marriage and divorce, conjugal relations, and rights over children. Issues such as the implications of intra-kin marriages, bride-price and dowry, marital violence and dowry deaths in South Asia are also taken up.

Finally, gender-based differences in the distribution of resources, in the division of work, and in short-term and long-term investments in children are broadly assessed in the contexts of the various kinship systems.

All these areas are hopelessly enmeshed. Many arbitrary decisions had to be taken about where particular points fit best and about the sequence of discussion. No arrangement suggested itself as perfectly logical, so I have followed what looked best to me. The most that I could hope to achieve was to avoid too many repetitions. I have concentrated on ethnographies of rural areas and small towns, for these depict the lives of the bulk of the people of the regions that this work deals with. Middle-class populations are not ignored, however. The highly educated, urban segments are only touched upon in a near-parenthetical manner. Again, relatively speaking, I have not given much attention to changes induced by modernity and economic and political upheavals – my focus has been on the *principles* of kinship systems.

2

Kinship and family organization

I begin with brief notes on kinship and family organization in the various societies covered by this study.

India

Of India's population of about 844 million, Hindus constitute over 82 per cent, Muslims about 12 per cent, and Christians 2.5 per cent. Others including Sikhs, Parsees, and Jains make up the rest, except that, of these, tribals make up 7.95 per cent. For Hindus, particularly for the upper- and middle-caste groups, the three-generational or four-generational, residential and commensal joint family is, broadly speaking, the cultural ideal. The cultural norm of the residential unity of close male agnates and the incorporation of in-marrying females is at the base of this kind of household. The care of the aged, the infirm, and the young and the raising of the young to adulthood are important functions of the family. However, there are regional as well as caste-linked and property-linked differences in the proportion that joint families form of all families (Kolenda 1987b). For instance, there seem to be more joint families, particularly among the upper castes, on the Gangetic plain than there are in Central India or in West Bengal. Most castes of north-western Mysore seem to have a large proportion of joint families. Many of them are rooted in land or are in business, where capital and close cooperation among kin are required.

Differences in the mores of family break-up, or what might be called patterned sequences of breaking up, might be demonstrably correlated with the proportion of joint families. Besides this, demographic factors such as life expectancy, age at marriage and at childbirth (R. Mukherjee 1969), the economic environment (especially access to ancestral land, property, or business as against dependence on individual resources), and migration are also relevant in assessing the viability of joint families. Cohn (1961) looks at these while discussing why the Chamar in the Gangetic plain have a very low proportion of joint families. Changes of occupation and employment away from the parental home, often in urban areas, also contribute to the establishment of independent conjugal households before the patterned or culturally expected time of break-up.

Research has indicated three different patterned timings of break-up, or what have been called patterned rearrangements of family structure through time. In one, a son may separate from the parental home within a few months or years of another son's marriage. Very often, older sons establish independent households as their younger brothers marry and form their conjugal units in the parental household. In another, married brothers break up upon or shortly after their father's death. In the third pattern the joint family breaks up at a much later stage, when it is headed by one of the brothers or even by a first-degree patrilateral parallel cousin. The break-up of hearth, dwelling group, land, and various kinds of property is a complicated process often completed in gradual steps.

The patrilineal, patri-virilocal joint family is more prevalent among communities engaged in business (Shah 1964) and among landed groups. Even when there is cultural sanction for sons to separate one by one from the parental home, the family does go through periods of jointness with different sons; and often a son, perhaps the youngest, continues to live with the parents. The Indian joint family must be looked at as a process. The cultural norm in regard to the cycle of the domestic group and the preferred time of break-up may vary among the different groups within Hindu society. This is related to the bargaining power of women as both cause and effect. The support of natal kin, relative ease in obtaining divorce, a growing emphasis on conjugality, education, and employment – or at least the capacity for independent earning – are some of the factors that can give women bargaining power.

Despite variations, some aspects of the Hindu kinship system can bring out the subtleties that are necessary for an understanding of the family in patrilineal South Asia. It is characterized by patrilineal descent, but the functioning units are mostly familial units in which

11

women have an important role to play. Lineages are significant mostly in jural and property matters and where issues of coparcenary and reversionary heirs are involved. A lineage also has an identity in the worship of its deity. Just as there are maximal, major, and minimal lineages, so there is a range from large-scale extended families (known as *kutumb* in most parts except Bengal) to very small-scale extended families. Even when a co-residential commensal joint family breaks up its members continue to belong to one "family."

The different levels of familial entities can be distinguished by co-residence and a common hearth at one end, close or distant ties of cooperation and obligations in the middle, and ties only of recognition at the other extreme. At this point there is fission, although recognition of the agnatic line often survives the break-up of the large-scale familial entity. Just as there is fission in the lineage, so there is fission in the extended family. A joint family, on the other hand, should be perceived as implying co-residence and commensality. Property helps in maintaining co-residence, although small-scale joint families are often seen to function without any property. The pooling of labour, the sharing of gains, and those several activities that are needed to run a household and to rear children, all are possible collectively in the absence of property. Such small joint familial households are commonly found even among artisans, small traders, and agriculturalists, as well as among the urban service class. Their tenure is variable.

The three-generational – or sometimes four-generational – familial entity, even when distributed across more than one domestic group, is expected to maintain close contact. Very often it may function as one entity in relation to affines and uterine kin, sending representatives to attend ceremonies and rituals and to give prestations, and also in relation to agnatic kin outside its limits. Between the units within this "family" there are generally obligations to render assistance of various kinds, and there are also expectations of cooperation and sharing of responsibilities in family rituals and ceremonies.

It is into this patrilineal, patri-virilocal family that a bride is ushered. Her entry is marked by rituals of incorporation, but this conversion of an outsider into an insider is a continuing process, not an event. In rural as well as urban areas the patri-virilocal joint family organization exists in the minds of people far more strongly and far longer than it does in reality.

The survival of the joint family ideology against all odds cannot be overlooked. A nuclear family may become a supplemented nuclear family or a joint family with the addition of a widowed parent or orphaned siblings, or with the marriage of a son, at least for a short period. Wadley and Derr (1988), in their study of Karimpur families over 60 years, have shown a preference among the people for joint families and an increase in their number. Many micro- and macro-studies point towards an increase in the proportion of joint families (Palriwala 1994, Caldwell et al. 1988). It is difficult to say whether this is happening in spite of dilution of ideology and is dictated by practical considerations, and to what extent new adjustments are being made and flexibility is being sought in terms of interpersonal relations, devices of separation of space and lifestyles within a joint family household, and greater freedom of interaction with women's natal kin. A new consciousness of the advantages of pooling re-sources may also encourage joint living. At the same time, stress on conjugality has become an accepted feature of today's family.

However, it seems a reasonable observation that in terms of genealogical complexity the character of joint families has changed and is changing. Lineal small joint family households are sustained while lateral extensions are arrested. Norms concerning the time of break-up are also changing in different groups. The well-known pattern that had emerged among prosperous and moderately well-off agriculturalists in northern India, who expected one or more sons to work in urban areas to provide the cash needed by modern agriculture, is no longer functioning well. The expenses of an urban lifestyle, consumer items, and children's education, an emphasis on con-jugality, and sometimes wives' assertiveness – these tend to wean men away from their rural kin and responsibilities, yet they still expect their shares in ancestral property.

The depletion or shrinking of the family, its expansion, and partic-ularly its fission are conceived of in terms of the cultural ideal of the unity of agnatic kin and the incorporation of in-marrying females. The propriety of the composition of the "supplemented nuclear fam-ily" – in which around one cohort and its unmarried children there live other kin such as an old parent, a brother or a sister – is assessed in terms of the cultural understanding about who are its rightful members and therefore entitled to residence, resources, and support (Dhruvarajan 1989, Shah 1973, L. Dube 1974, Kolenda 1987a). In this setting virilocality connotes patri-virilocality. As I emphasized in the introduction, the nuclear family embedded in patrilineal patri-virilocal kinship needs to be distinguished from those that are rooted in matrilineal or bilateral kinship or have only weak cognatic and agnatic kinship links.

A few illustrations will illuminate the variety of patterns in Indian family organization. The average generational depth of the joint family household, making for a smaller or larger presence of collaterally related conjugal units, may differ between the landed or propertied groups of north and south India; but joint living, in which young women are placed in the same unit as their parents-in-law and other members of their husbands' immediate families, is quite common in south India also. In *The Family Web*, the family whose story Sarah Hobson (1978) narrates belonged to the Gowda agriculturalist caste of Karnataka. It was rooted in the land and had six married sons living with their parents along with their wives and children. According to the villagers' perception, the younger women were bound to quarrel over petty things, while their mother-in-law would make sure that they lived in peace. The mother-in-law told the author that when she scolded her daughters-in-law they would shout at her in return, even abusing her; but she would remain firm and pull up those who did not do their work.

In her description and analysis of Smartha Brahmin kinship, Kathleen Gough (1956) pointed towards the strength and unity of the extended family, with its basis in the corporate rights of the lineage in land, and emphasized that this strength and unity depend upon solidarity among the males and upon the subordination of the women to their husbands. Women's assimilation to men was seen in various forms, such as in the rituals for ancestors, where the dead wife of an ancestor did not have to be mentioned separately, and in that a dead woman could not be incorporated among the ancestors while her husband remained alive. This seems to be the general pattern of Brahmin ancestor rituals in other parts of the country as well. A wife's assimilation to her husband and her incorporation into his family are corroborated by my personal information and experience.

A patrilineal joint family or a cluster of agnatically related families do not exhaust the world of kinship even in northern India. Formal and informal visits and contacts are an important feature of affinal and cognatic relations. A marriage establishes an alliance between two families and networks of kin. Affines in one generation mean consanguineous or cognatic kin in the next. For children, the mother's parents' home or that of a maternal uncle is the favourite place to go to. Personal accounts collected by me from women in Bangladesh include nostalgic memories of visits to their natal homes. Much has been written about such kinship networks and the utilization of affinal and cognatic links in the economic and political spheres. The tenor of relationships and behaviour depends on factors such as the degree and nature of asymmetry between bride-givers and bride-takers, regional or village exogamy, and the presence or absence of a preference for intra-kin marriages. Thus the extent to which a woman can expect support in crises from her natal kin is variable.

A few Hindu caste groups in Karnataka and Kerala are known for matrilineal descent and kinship organization. The Bants in Karnataka, a landowning caste, have followed matriliny with virilocal residence. The Tiyas of north Kerala, traditionally toddy tappers, coconut pluckers, tenants with inferior rights, and labourers, have also been known for matrilineal descent with virilocal residence. Their women have had secure rights in their matrilineal property. With diversification of occupations, education, and legal changes, they have moved towards bilaterality.

As Saradamoni (1992a) says, a wide spectrum of Hindu castes, including low castes and even tribes with not much property to inherit, followed matriliny, where women had a special place in their natal homes. But the caste group – divided into sub-castes – best known for matriliny is the Nayars, landowners and retainers as well as tenants with superior rights (Gough 1961). The Nayars of north Kerala followed matrilineal descent and inheritance but men brought their wives to live with them on their corporate *taravad* land, which they shared with their matrilineal kin. The maternal uncle wielded authority. A conjugal unit generally lived in a conjugal household but was surrounded by the man's matrilineal kin and their conjugal families. Women retained their right to property and residence in their own matrilineal units and returned there on divorce, widowhood, and often in old age. Adolescent or adult male children moved from the father's *taravad* to the mother's, where lay their rights to membership and property.

The Nayars of central Kerala (south Malabar, Cochin, and middle Travancore) had a different system of *taravad* organization and marriage. Owing to visiting marriage, polyandry, and the absence of nuclear families they have been the subject of detailed anthropological investigations and debates. As Gough (1975) says, traditionally the "ideal-typical" household was a segment of a matrilineage with a depth of three to six generations, of which both male and female members were permanent residents. The eldest male was the head and legal guardian. Both men and women were permitted more than one spouse at a time. Marital relationships were effected through husbands' visits to their wives, generally at night. Many of these unions were hypergamous, between Nayar women and Nambudiri or other Brahmin or Kshatriya men.

Polygamy was made illegal under the law in 1920. Two decades later both men and women were permitted to claim individual shares of their *taravads'* property, but the *taravad* system survived. Accounts from the 1950s and 1960s make this clear (Gough 1961, Karve 1965, Mencher 1962, Nakane 1963, Unni 1956). Gradually, however, household composition changed in terms of the degree of genealogical complexity. Gough's data show a shift from matriliny to bilaterality. Fuller (1976) offers another account depicting the Nayars' history as well as the changes that came about. Saradamoni (1983) has discussed the relation between the passing of various laws, encouraged by the mainstream culture and Nayar men's keenness to change the patterns of kinship and marriage, and the movement towards distinctly unequal relations between the sexes.[1]

Women in Nayar matriliny were hemmed in by restrictions stemming from their being part of the caste system. Comparing them with the Khasi, a matrilineal tribe of north-eastern India, makes this clear. This will be taken up later, as will the Khasi and Garo women's situation under their respective matrilineal systems.

The matriliny of the Muslims of the Lakshadweep islands is in a way an extension of Nayar matriliny and is not yet a thing of the past. It is mentioned here before coming to the patrilineal Muslims spread all over India. It is described mainly with the help of the ethnography of one island. Variations on other islands are ignored.

Kalpeni is one of the coral islands of the Lakshadweep group off the south-western coast of India. The people of these islands – except those of Minicoy, which belongs to the Maldives group – are descendants of migrants from the Kerala coast. They were converted to Islam in the thirteenth or fourteenth century, about four centuries after the major migrations. These islands have all along maintained themselves through trade with the Indian mainland. Their products, mainly coconut and coir, are carried to the coast in sailing craft, which bring back essential goods for consumption, including rice. The islanders are a matrilineal people within the fold of Islam. Descent is traced through the mother and property is divided equally among a woman's children. A person has an inalienable right of use over the matrilineal group's property; but whereas a woman's share automatically devolves on her children, a man's share reverts to the matrilineal group after his death. The distribution of individually acquired property, however, is governed by the Islamic law of inheritance (Kutty 1972).

The traditional pattern of residence at marriage ordinarily excludes the possibility of husband, wife, and children living in one domestic unit. Groom and bride do not leave their respective residences upon marriage. The socially approved sexual relationship that the marriage establishes between the spouses is effected through a pattern of nocturnal visits by the husband. In the early 1960s, 515 out of 670 married men were visiting husbands. Of the others, 124 lived uxorilocally, 23 lived neolocally, and the wives of 8 had moved to live with them (Kutty 1972, L. Dube 1969a).

Christians in India belong to a variety of churches. The influence is visible of those Hindu groups from which the converts came, of church teaching, and of the kinship and family organization of the cultures to which the missionaries belonged. There is thus no uniformity among Christian groups in India where kinship and family organization are concerned.

Christianity has spread among many tribal groups, but barring the insistence on monogamy, which created problems, the basic nature of kinship did not change after conversion. Thus we have matrilineal Khasi and Garo Christians, patrilineal Mizo and Naga Christians, and a host of tribal groups – essentially patrilineal – in central India. There are also the Toda of the Nilgiris, known for polyandry.

Those who were converted from Hinduism may be divided broadly between peninsular and non-peninsular India. The Christian groups of non-peninsular India are essentially patronymic, with the expectation that the family name will continue through sons. The union of spouses is viewed as the basis of the formation of a nuclear family, which is considered the normal unit. The idea that is clearly expressed at weddings – that from the beginning of creation God made man and woman and for this reason a man shall leave his father and mother and cleave to his wife, the two being one flesh – justifies nuclear families. We do often see a married son living with his parents for convenience, or two brothers' families living together, but a bride's entry into such a family is ordinarily not ritualized and a daughter or sister may also join the group without difficulty.

The patrilineal, patri-virilocal joint family does not seem to be the ideal anywhere. Cognatic links are important, but not because they represent alliance and affinity. These are mostly urban people, for the rural areas of this region have hardly any Christians. The poorer sections in urban areas seem more inclined towards Hindu customs; for example, they are emphatic that parental property must go to sons and not to daughters (P. S. Dwivedi, personal communication).

In southern and south-western India the situation is different. Groups such as the Catholics of Goa and the Orthodox Syrian Christians of Kerala are landed communities who live in rural areas and have the patrilineal, patri-virilocal family as the ideal. A bride is ceremonially ushered into this family.

Jointness is still the ideal among Goan Catholics. They hold that brothers should live together and share everything, and that their wives should cook together. That this does not happen often is understandable. Whereas the eldest son generally lives with his parents, his brothers and their conjugal families take up separate residence. If the house is large enough it may be partitioned.

At marriage a daughter is transferred from one family to another. The crossing of the boundary of the natal village, a ceremony known as *shim*, expresses this well. Sons continue the name of the lineage and the family. Daughters are entitled only to dowry and, later, to gifts. They have no right to parental property. Married daughters and their children do not have free access to their parental or brothers' households because they are no longer full members there. The proportion of supplemented nuclear family households in a Goan village clearly indicates the norm of caring for the aged and the young of the larger patrilineal family. Goan Christians are divided into castes. Rooted in the land, they follow many Hindu customs, and the structure and process of the patrilineal, patri-virilocal joint family closely resembles that of the Goan Hindus (Rowena Robinson, personal communication).

The Orthodox Syrian Christians of Kerala are primarily landowners, which influences their cultural consciousness. Patriliny and patri-virilocality are the basis of the ideal family. A son brings his wife to live with his parental family and it is customary for a younger son and his conjugal family to live with his parents to look after them in their old age and inherit the house; a certain proportion of households are always joint. The possibility of a widowed father or mother and younger siblings joining a brother's nuclear household points to the complex composition of households. Although people may live in nuclear families, the ideal is the three-generational household. Even when residence is not shared, brothers commonly live in a contiguous area and in terms of quality of relationships constitute extended families.

As for the timing of fission, a son sets up a separate household when he becomes a father or the brother next to him marries. Even after separation, however, production may be joint and the authority of the father is respected. Children are under the care of their fathers' mothers, leaving their mothers free to participate in different activities (Visvanathan 1989).

Dowry is looked upon as pre-mortem inheritance, though in middle-class families what is spent on a daughter's wedding may be more than what a son will eventually get. We shall take up *streedhanam* (also known as *streedhana*) and its ramifications in our discussion of dowry.

As regards the Protestants who belong to the Church of South India, Caplan (1984) does not directly speak of the existence of patrilineal, patri-virilocal families; but the way he describes the utilization of what he calls bridegroom price, which is paid by the bride's father, points towards the authority and leadership of the groom's father. This seems to indicate that the joint family is a phase, howsoever brief, in the cycle.

This discussion of kinship and family organization among Indian Christians points to a strong influence of patrilineal South Asia along with a seeping in of some of the ideas and practices of the Mediterranean. It reminds one of the statement by Leach (1975) that, although in bilateral societies there is no possibility of unilineal descent groups, among the property-owning sections the practice of marriage and the rules of inheritance have been so contrived as to create notionally permanent property-owning corporations that are conceived of as patrilineal descent groups. He gives two examples: the bilateral Kandyan Sinhalese and the landed gentry of eighteenth-century and nineteenth-century England. Devices were introduced to prevent the inheritance of landed property by a female who had male siblings. These included primogeniture, entailment, and dowry in cash and jewellery rather than in land. The general ideology becomes strongly patrilineal and the use of patronymic surnames is an important feature.

Muslims in India are not one homogeneous community. They are divided by ethnic group, high and low ancestry, caste-like groups in many areas, a variety of occupations carrying unequal statuses, and a baffling array of customs and practices. That they follow the *sharia* (the sacred law of Islam) cannot be denied; but it is not clear to what extent, in what manner, and with how much blending with Hindu social structure and beliefs and practices. On the basis of varied accounts spread across the ethnographic literature and observations carried out in different parts of the country, we can say that Indian Muslims are entrenched in patrilineal kinship organization and patri-local residence. Joint or extended family living is a part of their culture. For instance, the joint family is found among small industrialists in Delhi, in Dharwar in Karnataka, in eastern Uttar Pradesh, in Madhya Pradesh, and in Assam (Ahmad 1976).

As among Hindus, the normative time of break-up differs from group to group and between urban and rural areas, but a bride begins her married life in patri-virilocal residence. The custom of *rukhsat* (sending the bride to live with her husband in his parental home) is the same as among the Hindus. If one-fourth of households are lineal or collateral joint, as mentioned in the study of Assam (Ahmad 1976), surely the principle of residential unity of patrikin and their wives, with a view of the family as a process, is operative. People may express a desire to establish nuclear households and may be conscious of domestic politics and lack of freedom in a joint household, but it is only after a year or two of marriage that couples establish independent households. Further, there is a general tendency to have three or four domestic units in a single compound. If the landholding is small, pooling of resources seems more reasonable than fragmentation. Thus, even with separate hearths, production may be undertaken jointly. The weavers of Banaras, for example, see a clear advantage in collective living and cooperative occupational activity.

That the family has to be seen as a process cannot be overlooked, but lineages or sub-lineages have their role to play even when households separate. The care of the old and the bringing up of the young are considered a family's duties. In Old Delhi areas joint families predominate. The norms favouring joint family living are widely held. Owing to marriages among close kin and because families live close together, there is likely to be greater contact with women's natal kin and the two groups may converge to some extent. This is similar to what obtains among Hindus in parts of southern India.

About joint family living in the Nizamuddin area of Delhi, Patricia Jeffrey (1979: 69) says that "the average size is just over ten persons, with one household consisting of over twenty persons and around three quarters clustering between eight and sixteen." Again, "it is rare for a *pirzada* woman to be the only domestically competent female in the household.... Brides often move directly into an extended household and are surrounded by a mother-in-law, the wives of their husband's elder brothers, and his sisters who are not yet married." According to her account the extended household is the common form among the Pirzada (custodians of the shrine of saint Hazrat Nizamuddin Aulia). Generally, one aged couple live with their married sons in the same house and cook and eat together. After the parents die the brothers tend to separate and form nuclear families, which eventually grow into extended ones. Further, these related households, including some affinal ones, are close by.

Whether among the Gujar Bakarwals of Jammu and Kashmir or among the Meos of Rajasthan, patrilocality is common (Ahmad 1976). Among the Meos the joint family is the ideal type, desirable, and prestigious. It prevents division of land and increases the influence of the family. After the death of the father, however, brothers tend to separate.

Where sons separate one by one, at least one usually remains with the parents to look after them. The supplemented nuclear family has the same connotation as among Hindus. Where there is a strong sense of patrilineage or *gotra*, agnatic kin have an important role to play; but relations with cognatic kin are also generally strong.

Among most tribal groups of India, nuclear family residence is very common and is culturally approved. It is achieved through the practice of setting up separate hearths for sons when they marry or when they have had one or two children. In many groups, though, one son is expected to continue to live with his parents. It is also customary for the families of brothers and close male agnates to live in contiguous areas. Sometimes, even after the separation of hearths, production may be joint or there may be a pattern of cooperation and help at critical points. A woman thus leaves her parental home on marriage to live among affines.

Nepal

Among the Parbatiyas, of whom Brahmins and Chhetris are important, each caste consists of discrete exogamous groups. Descent is patrilineal. Women are relevant "as wives who serve as *links* between groups and the means by which these groups *perpetuate* themselves" (Bennett 1983: 41). The cardinal value and first organizational principle of the patrifocal model is, according to Bennett, the solidarity of male agnates. Two principles of hierarchy are constantly articulated through speech and behaviour: that males rank above females of the same generation, and that age ranks above youth. These ranking principles hold true for nuclear as well as for extended families.

The extended family, consisting of married brothers living together, working jointly held property, and sharing its produce under the authority of their father, is the cultural ideal. (Here "extended family" is used to refer to what we called "joint family" in the context of India.)

Chhetri and Brahmin are divided horizontally into agnatic units called *thar* and *gotra*. *Gotra*, which traces ancestry back to one of the ancient sages, is rarely operative in actual social relations. *Thar* traces ancestry back seven generations, but it appears that membership of a *thar* is also only nominal. A man is a member of his father's *thar* and *gotra*, whereas women's membership of these categories after marriage derives from their husbands.

The *parivar* (family or household), spanning between two and four generations, is the operational kinship group. It holds property jointly and observes most life-cycle and calendrical rituals. Members of a *parivar* are under an obligation to observe pollution rituals for 10 days for a birth and for 13 days for the death of a member. They share a single hearth and live under the same roof. Formal authority is vested in the males and property is transmitted in the male line. The care of aged parents, the performance of funeral rites, the production of patrilineal heirs, and the maintenance of ritual continuity are all the responsibility of the sons of the lineage.

Under Nepali law sons can ask for the partition of the joint family estate at any time, and that they do this is evident from the large proportion of nuclear or supplemented nuclear households in the population (Bennett 1983). Agnatic solidarity is greatly valued and it is women, outsiders to begin with, who are blamed for these separations of joint families. It is recognized, however, that there can be considerable competition and rivalry between brothers. Both Lynn Bennett (1983) and John Gray (1982) have described the dynamics of joint family fission graphically. Gray has argued that the Chhetri household structure is inherently paradoxical. Ideally the *parivar* or domestic group is a patrilineal joint family consisting of a three-generational or four-generational agnatic descent group of males, their wives, and unmarried daughters. At the same time, the joint *parivar* is an unstable group ever liable to division into nuclear families. Much that has been said about the family in India is applicable to Nepali Hindus. Old people live with a married son. Migration leads to separate living. So also does an improper marriage. Temporary migrants leave their families behind with their parents.

The Newari castes of Nepal are divided into patrilineal descent groups called *dewali*. The collective performance of ancestor worship or the *dewali puja* of the *degu dyas* serves to reaffirm the identity of a *dewali*. Descent and inheritance are from father to son. A daughter ceases to be a member of her natal *dewali* upon marriage and is incorporated into her husband's *dewali* by a special ritual. Marriage within the *dewali* is proscribed. Members are placed in a hierarchy based on generation and age. Decision-making is vested in the head, the *nayaa*, and another seven members stand in order of seniority. The female counterpart of the *nayaa* derives her position as *nakii* from her husband's as head. On the death of her husband she relinquishes her position in favour of the wife of the man next in seniority.

On occasions of worship and during feasts connected with the *dewali*, the positions taken by the members of each family indicate their seniority and relative status. *Phukii* is the relationship between the members of a *dewali*. There are well-defined social obligations between *phukii* families. Birth and death pollution in one family is binding upon all families in the *dewali*. On a birth all *phukii* families join the celebration and give offerings to mother and child. In the case of death, all the families must take offerings of food to the bereaved family. When a *dewali* splits, a splinter family forms a separate *dewali* – although the ancestral deity remains the same.

Bangladesh

In Bangladesh there is a preponderance of nuclear families: micro-studies give evidence that 60–70 per cent of domestic groups are nuclear. The cultural norm, however, is the patrilineal, patri-virilocal joint family in which three generations live together. Children take their social identity from their father. A male child continues his father's *bongso* (lineage) while a female child is eventually incorporated into her husband's *bongso*. Sons remain in their father's house and on marriage bring their wives to live there. A joint family is thus likely to be experienced by the younger generation at least for a few years. Studies show that the incidence of joint families is markedly higher at the higher levels of income and landholding. Poverty and a consequent inability to look after its vulnerable members may lead to a family's breaking up.

Where obligations, responsibilities, and rights to resources are concerned, joint family organization remains on the mental horizon of the people. With any demographic change a nuclear family can acquire new members: a widowed mother or father; a widowed sister and her children; or a deceased brother's widow and children. This process is similar to that in India. Parents also look forward to being supported in their old age by their sons.

A necessary corollary to these cultural norms of a patrilineal, patri-virilocal kinship organization is the attitude towards daughters, which is unfavourable to making investments in their future that would raise their earning capacity and give them self-reliance. Moreover, agnatically related families tend to be spatially close, and those that have common resources are tied together even after the separation of hearths. The *bari*, or homestead, which consists, ideally and to a great extent actually, of patrilineally related households, controls cooperation and interaction among women.

"The newly married woman frequently comes as an unknown individual to reside permanently in her husband's house" (Aziz 1979: 116) and remains there unless divorced. If a widow does not marry she continues to live with her husband's family or in his agnatic *bari*, particularly if she has children. When a widow or a divorcee remarries, her children are accommodated in her previous husband's family.

Upon marriage a woman is "transferred" to her husband and family and is not expected to identify any longer with her father's *bongso*. Her right to inherit half a brother's share of patrimonial property is more formal than real. Seclusion and a widespread preference for village exogamy do not allow women to retain control over their shares of patrimonial land; and a considerable number waive their right to ancestral property in favour of their brothers, in a kind of bargain in which they retain the right to visit the natal home, where they can relax, and by which they seek to ensure the continuation of support and protection in times of crisis (Kabeer 1985b: 88). As among most patrilineal Muslims in South Asia, marriages between certain kin are permitted and often preferred, but their incidence is not high.

Pakistan

Although the patrilineal, patrilocal extended family as a unit of residence and consumption was never the universal or dominant pattern in many regions of Pakistan, it has been culturally the ideal form.

In rural areas, patrilineally related nuclear or supplemented nuclear families tend to live in close proximity, facilitating constant interaction. Thus the sources of social control and socializing agents are not restricted to the nuclear household.

Naveed-i-Rahat (1990) reports that the village of Meharabad near Rawalpindi had a nucleated residential area surrounded by its lands. There were 158 (75 per cent) nuclear families and 52 (25 per cent) extended or extended–joint families. In the category of nuclear family were included 71 units of mother and children, the husband being away from the village. She claims that the dominant pattern of residence in the village was the extended or extended–joint family, but male emigration affected this.

Donnan (1988), however, writing of the Dhund in northern Pakistan, argues that there is no clear historical evidence to demonstrate that the vitality of the joint family was greater in the past than it is at present. He says that at least in Punjab the joint family seems to have been no more widespread in the nineteenth century than it is today. Among the Dhund, normally a household remains intact only so long as its children remain unmarried. Ideally, a new household should be established at marriage or shortly thereafter, this ideal being found throughout western Punjab. The exception to the rule is the youngest son: the Dhund believe that he has to take care of his parents in their old age. This results in a certain number of lineally joint families. A few families are also found of two brothers and their wives and children. Responsibility for the aged, orphans, and widows of the larger family always results in the formation of some supplemented nuclear families.

Most Dhund households are composed of nuclear families comprising a husband, wife, and unmarried children; and this is consistent with the trend in Pakistan as a whole. Of the 122 households in the village studied, only 8.7 per cent were lineally or collaterally joint families. While 59.5 per cent of families were nuclear, 25 per cent were supplemented nuclear. Supplemented nuclear families clearly represent the norm of the family embedded in patrilineal kinship. Other ethnographic accounts and statistics indicate that Pakistani communities differ in respect of the normative time for the break-up of families.

Authority depends on the stage of development of a household. An old father may relinquish his authority if a son is living with him. Wakil (1991) also insists that behind the averages of household size lies a rather variegated pattern of size of family, attitudes towards fertility, and desired family size. He quotes some studies to show how older respondents had families of six or more children, while younger ones had fewer children.

The value accorded to male children is closely linked to patrilineal descent and inheritance. The continuity of the family name, the preservation of family property, the retention of land in the family, and the value of sons in production and in caring for elderly parents are all factors.

Malaysia

Barring matrilineal Negri Sembilan, parts of Melaka, and some southern and central areas, Malay kinship is bilateral and ego-centric, with theoretically equal recognition to the relatives of both parents. There are no separate sets of terms for paternal and maternal relatives. Studies of Malay kinship and family have noted a bias towards matrilocality, particularly in the first few years of marriage, and a tendency for the females on the wife's side to cooperate closely, particularly when family conflicts occur (Djmour 1959, Chee 1979). Property acquired jointly by a couple is divided between husband and wife either equally or, following Islamic law, in the ratio 2:1. In *adat* or customary law, brothers and sisters have equal shares in inheritance. "There is a tendency for comparatively prosperous people to choose Islamic law, but it is not always strictly applied and the continuing tendency to equal divisions between male and female children shows that the principle of fair division is common" (Tsubouchi 1977).

Chee (1979) regards the Malay family as extended, saying that typically a family would comprise a couple and their children, of whom one daughter would be married. According to Tsubouchi there are no fixed rules of marital residence, and the compound of either the wife's side or the husband's side may be chosen, or else an entirely new one. In some villages there appears to be a tendency to choose parents-in-law who are richer in paddy fields or rubber trees. According to Strange (1981), whenever newly-weds live with parents the "choice of family tends to be expedient, based on ... economic opportunities and the personal preferences of those concerned, a pattern referred to as ambilocal residence. Because of the close affective tie between mothers and daughters, a young wife usually prefers to live with her parents because she and her mother have well-established cooperative patterns."

An uxorilocal bias is reported by many. Even when a young married couple want their own home, they prefer to settle near parents and relatives: independence is thus combined with basic security. In the rural areas a young bride feels insecure if she has to go away from amongst her kin and set up a household entirely on her own. It is often said that marital adjustment is easier if a bride is not thrown in alone with her husband. This may not apply, of course, to educated urban brides. The extended bilateral kinship network is important in the people's perception. A tendency to marry within a small radius is often motivated by the confidence that relatives will offer help and consideration. The kindred, again, is not a bounded group and leaves much to the choice of the individual.

A fact of special interest is that, even when she lives virilocally or neolocally, in situations of conflict, divorce, or widowhood a woman and her children are readily accepted by her parents. A woman thus has the continuing support of her parents and other kin.

Statistics show a preponderance of nuclear households centred on married couples, but such a household may include – often temporarily – relatives from the network of kin. Thus aged parents may be taken into their children's homes, or grandchildren may go to live with their grandparents. The lineally extended family that is created when one of the children gets married is often only an interlude, for residence does not remain fixed. Depending on circumstances a conjugal family may move from one extended family, or one locality, to another; and it may be joined by supplementary members, young or old.

The Javanese

Among the Javanese no fixed rule governs the residence of a newly married couple. From the use of the term *emah-emah* ("to set up a household") for marriage, Koentjaraningrat (1985) infers that the ideal is to set up an independent neolocal household. He adds that, since in rural areas people marry fairly early, they are usually considered incapable of managing an independent household; and they therefore reside with either's parents for some time. Initial residence with parents is an accepted pattern.

Most often the wife's parents' home is chosen because she prefers to learn about household management from her own mother. After this the couple move into a newly built house, which is, however, in the compound of the parental house. If the parents can, they may

27

assign the use of a garden plot and a few fruit trees to the young couple. If there is not much space, the married children's houses may be attached to the dwelling place of the parents. After some time a couple may leave the parental compound to live in another hamlet, village, or city. At any point in time there are some uxorilocal, some virilocal, and even some ambilocal extended families. When children move out, one married daughter usually remains behind to care for the parents in their old age; and she generally inherits the house.

The quality of transience of a household is reflected in the variously composed household types found in Javanese villages. The situation in one village has been graphically described by R. R. Jay (1969: 51–60). In his terminology, there were nuclear families, some containing retired elderly parents; multiple nuclear families, consisting of a couple and their married children; and joint family households of siblings and their spouses. The terminology is different, but both lineally joint and laterally joint households appear to be a reality. However, more often it would be sisters with their husbands and children rather than brothers who choose to live together. It is not unusual for a married couple moving out of the parental house to leave their first child with its grandparents.

On divorce each spouse retains personal property. Communal property, which includes all that was acquired by the couple during their marriage, is divided between husband and wife in the ratio 2:1. This is identified with Islamic law, and the principle of equal division with the Javanese style. In actuality neither principle seems to be strictly followed. The concept of *rukun* or social harmony plays an important part in negotiations and settlements (Jay 1969).

There are variations in the placement of children in the event of divorce. Koentjaraningrat (1985: 46) reports that, whereas young children go with the mother, other children are to be distributed equally between their parents; and they also have the right to decide where they want to go. Jay reports that in the event of divorce the children go with the mother: "The dominance of 'mother right' in fact may be viewed as one of the main organizing principles of Javanese kinship" (1969: 68).

The kinship network differs for every individual and varies according to circumstances. Broadly speaking, it includes members of the nuclear family of orientation and procreation, parents' siblings and their children, grandparents, siblings' children, and affinals. This is an occasional bilateral kin group. According to Koentjaraningrat, this group is not exactly ego-centric but centres around a couple or a nuclear family. The other kind of bilateral kin group is the *trah* or *alur waris*, an ancestor-oriented, ambilineally defined group whose members share the obligation of caring for their ancestors' graves and of meeting the expenses of the ceremonies and feasts involved (Koentjaraningrat 1985: 150–151; see also Geertz 1961, Jay 1969, Sairin 1982).

The Minangkabau

The Minangkabau of West Sumatra follow matrilineal descent and inheritance. *Merantau* (out-migration) takes men away from home with periodic returns there. Since kinship ties are reckoned through the maternal line, females are crucial to the continuity of the matri-line. Houses and land are held corporately by the kin group, not individually. Any sale of land must have the sanction of all members. A long-house is often divided into smaller units where couples and their children live. Husbands' periodic migration for earning is a standard practice. The smaller units may have the woman's close kin, particularly her mother, staying with her.

A woman has life-long rights to specific pieces of land, irrigated and unirrigated. She cultivates this land with the help of her husband when he is present. Her brothers' help in land management is customarily expected. Earlier, a man of the lineage could also have access to its land, but this is no longer possible because even women's shares are becoming inadequate. A man may share-crop a female relative's land. Rights of use are inherited from their mothers by daughters, not by sons. Men do not inherit tangible property, but they do inherit kin-group titles. They function as kin-group leaders and as representatives to deal with outsiders. Decisions are taken largely by consensus.

The Philippines

Lowland Christian Filipinos constitute about 85 per cent of the population of the Philippines. In spite of the Spanish political and cultural subjugation for 300 years and the United States' colonization for 50 years, followed by the Japanese conquest, the Filipino family has retained its Malay characteristics. It is embedded in the bilaterally extended kinship system. Broadly speaking, it is characterized by an age-based hierarchy of authority, a highly egalitarian relationship between spouses, monogamous marriage allowing only for separation, marriage based on individual choice with parental approval, and a tendency to marry within one's locality, class, and linguistic-ethnic and religious grouping; but there are no strict positive or negative rules for marriage and no set rules for residence after marriage.

There is an emphasis on blood ties, which theoretically can extend the kin group to enormous size, but recognition of consanguineous ties does not normally extend beyond third cousins. And, more than structural closeness or distance, factors such as physical proximity, personal compatibility, and the social position of relatives play an important part in interpersonal relationships. Scholars of Filipino kinship and family life emphasize that there is mutual cooperation and fulfilment of obligations and responsibilities among relatives. Kin expect and get assistance in daily life as well as in crisis situations. The importance of relatives is emphasized in socialization. At marriage the spouses acquire each other's relatives. There is a broad tendency, however, for individuals to depend more on their own relatives.

The term *mag-anak*, which is commonly used to refer to the family, indicates the centrality of offspring in the formation of a family. It is perceived as a social unit composed of a father, a mother, and their unmarried child or children, whether biological or adopted. It is viewed as a unit of production and consumption. Such a unit may also have house-helps; additional members may come and go. Besides nuclear family households, there are also extended families where parents and their married children live together, or the families of two siblings. In a study by Mendez and Jocano (1974), 236 families out of 708 were extended and 432 were nuclear. The remaining units contained an assortment of kin. The typical Filipino household was an extended family arrangement although not necessarily in the classical three-generational sense of the term. Unmarried siblings, children of siblings, siblings of parents or their children constituted the most common type of lateral extensions. There were also lineally extended families where parents and married children lived together (1974: 263–265).

The point emphasized about the Filipino family is the fluidity of its membership. There are no rigid rules of residence for the newly married couple. For a period after their marriage they can stay with the family of either. Jocano (1972) reports that newly married couples frequently lived in the wife's parental household until the birth of the first child. Even where residence is not joint, the responsibility of caring for children tends to be shared by grandparents, aunts, and uncles. It is important to note that a disgraced member, particularly if female, is always welcomed back to the fold of the family. The sibling relationship is emphasized strongly (Illo 1990). It is not circumscribed by gender or social class and not altered by distance or marriage. Brothers and sisters are both socialized to nurture and protect one another. Age demands some respect, and an older sibling generally assumes parental authority when parents are dead or absent (Jocano 1969).

Thailand

Thai kinship is bilateral but matrilocality is the predominant type of post-nuptial residence among most of the rural population. A husband comes to live with his wife but maintains ties with his parents and other relatives. Marriage tends to start off with an initial stay at the wife's natal home.

There are significant differences among the kinship systems of north-eastern, northern, and central Thailand. In the villages of the north-east there is a tendency towards the co-residence, in compounds, of married female siblings, daughters, and matrilateral parallel cousins. This is owing to uxorilocal residence and a tendency towards the inheritance of the right of residence by daughters rather than by sons. The normal acting unit in the village is the household. Although residence and inheritance have a matrilateral bias, kinship is bilateral and ego-oriented. There is a wide range of kin ties within the village.

There are a number of multi-household compounds, with those of one or more daughters (and, in a few cases, of sons) cultivating jointly with the household of the parents, who own the rice fields. This association is only a phase in the family cycle and does not continue beyond one generation. Thai multi-household compounds do not function in the politico-jural realm, being purely domestic.

Tambiah (1970) also speaks of compounds of multiple households, two to six in number, whose key linking members were close kin who derived their rights to residence from a common ascendant or set of ascendants. In these compounds there was usually a core of females and their families, but there were also instances of only brothers and of siblings of both sexes together with their descendants (Pongsapich 1992). Although men are officially heads of households, women have been controlling household activities.

According to Podhisita (1984), matrilocality in north-eastern Thailand presents an interesting mode of intergenerational succession to land and authority. Although women are the key members of the household through whom the majority of households are formed and regulated, jural authority lies with the men of the house. It passes from father-in-law to son-in-law rather than from father to son or from maternal uncle to sister's son.

Northern Thai kinship is characterized by effective matrilineality and the structural centrality of women. Membership of the kin group is symbolized by membership of the spirit cults. Inheritance divides property equally among children of both sexes, with two corollaries: that the house goes to the youngest daughter and that it is customary for men to sell their rights to their sisters or to their sisters' husbands. Sulamith Potter (1977) argues that Thai social structure, particularly in the north, is conceptually female centred. Unlike structures in which the significant blood relationships are between men – father and son in the patrilineal system and mother's brother and sister's son in the matrilineal system – the relevant consanguineous ties are those between women. She also makes a distinction between female-centred and matrifocal social systems and says that in northern Thailand the social system is female centred but not matrifocal. Women do not play a leading role psychologically. They do not have more authority, influence, and responsibility than their husbands. Davis (1984) states that northern Thai matrilocal ideology is closely linked to a matrilineal mode of descent. They are organized into matriclans.

Family types in the villages of northern Thailand also have to be viewed as a domestic cycle. Three stages may be discerned: (a) family consisting of father, mother, and their young unmarried children; (b) in addition to parents and unmarried children, the spouse of the married daughter and her children; and (c) that form, with the older daughter having gone to settle in another household in the same compound on the marriage of a younger sister. Even in its new household the daughter's family continues to depend on her parents. They still work the land, use the common rice granary, or share the crop. But they also begin to accumulate wealth and land for cultivation.

The social position of women in central Thailand is reported to be powerful. It is they who control the money of the entire household. Kaufman's (1960) description of a central plains village distinguishes three kinds of family group: the household, the spatially extended family, and the remotely extended family. The household is run by the mother, who raises the children; the father is only a "putative head." The general pattern of residence is matrilocal for the first year of marriage. Sons and daughters inherit equal shares of land; but the youngest son or daughter, or the one who stays with the parents, receives the home and the equipment. The spatially extended family has relations of mutual help and cooperation but does not form an economic unit. "There are no prescribed consanguineous obligations concerning the various aspects of the household economy." Extended kin demonstrate relationship by contributing to funerals. Some comments made casually by Kaufman indicate that authority over a family's property passes from father-in-law to son-in-law.

A similar kind of family cycle as in the northern region can be visualized for central Thailand. As Jacques Amyot (1976) says of three villages in Ayutthaya, in the traditional pattern of residence when a young couple marry they stay with the bride's parents for an initial period. Until they are able to start a household of their own they farm the parental land and look after the livestock. The formation of a separate household may coincide with the marriage of another daughter. Traditionally the women receive the land, the men receiving cash or kind. For the new household the wife's father provides land close to his own house as well as land to cultivate, although this is not universal. Many couples start new households immediately after marriage or go to live with the husband's parents, particularly when the husband's parents are wealthier or when the husband is an only child or the only one left to help his parents.

According to Jack Potter (1976), in rural Thailand, with cooperative labour exchange and collective life, kinship relations play a very important role. According to Pongsapich (1992), bilateral kindred is indeed the overt pattern of kinship in rural Thailand; but it also needs to be emphasized that the role of kinship and kin relations is closely connected with land and other resources. Hence the inheritance of land is a very important aspect of kin relations, and since land passes largely in the female line, it seems that the pattern may not be bilateral. However, the inheritance of land seems to be guided by residence and finally by the care of aged parents. There is greater flexibility in the Thai pattern than in patriliny and even matriliny.[2]

3

Group membership, inheritance, and resource distribution

Group membership

The basic difference in the statuses of male and female children between the patrilineal societies of South Asia on the one hand and the bilateral and matrilineal societies of both regions on the other is in the nature of membership of descent groups and familial and kinship units. In the former, at birth both boys and girls take their social identity from the father and are placed in his agnatic group and familial unit. Whereas a son is a permanent member of these units, a daughter is a transient or impermanent member. A son has the potential to continue the patriline; but a daughter enters the family for only a short sojourn. A Hindi folk song puts it poignantly:

> *O father, I am a sparrow taking shelter*
> *in a tree in your compound.*
> *I shall fly away one day.*

In South Asia the cultural emphasis is on marriage as *the* destiny of a girl. A daughter's transfer to another home upon marriage is seen as inevitable. In contrast to Hinduism, Islam does not seem to have any injunction making marriage compulsory for women; but, perhaps due to the religious and social unacceptability of sex out of wedlock, Muslim patrilineal communities in South Asia live under almost the same cultural compulsions as do Hindu communities. In the Matlab area of Bangladesh surveyed in 1974, never married women formed 0.1 per cent of women in the age group 45–49 (Aziz 1978: 32). The possibility of intra-kin marriage, which is available to certain communities in southern India and to most Muslim communities in the region, does not do away with the element of compulsion in respect of transfer from the natal home: at the most, marriage may not mean going to the home of complete strangers. Except in matrilineal communities, for a daughter marriage implies loss of membership of the natal home.

A female child's membership of her father's agnatic unit is neither permanent nor complete. She is spoken of as someone born into such and such family or *gotra* or clan, but she is not seen as a member in perpetuity. Her rights to maintenance and residence must necessarily be transferred from her natal family to her husband's family. She is destined to change her social identity; unlike her brother, she is incapable of carrying forward her patriline. If a girl remains unmarried she continues to bear the name of her natal family or her father, but she cannot represent it as a full-fledged member.

In the patrilineal communities of Bangladesh, India, Nepal, and Pakistan, a woman is therefore a fringe or peripheral member of her descent group. In both kinds of unilineal descent there is a deliberate underplaying of the place and contribution of one parent; and only the other parent is considered relevant to group placement and the continuity of the lineage. In patriliny, however, the mother cannot be ignored beyond a point, being the necessary instrument for carrying forward the patriline, and special efforts are therefore made to incorporate her into her husband's group. It is also considered necessary to watch her behaviour.

Patrilineal descent in South Asia tends to be unusually harsh on women, with mechanisms for the management of their sexuality and for control over their procreative powers. It severs them from the natal group and leaves them to struggle through the process of becoming insiders in the husband's group. The material dependence of women and a strong ideology of gender contribute to their struggle.

In bilateral societies a child is reckoned to be the child equally of both its parents. There is no attempt at underplaying the importance of either parent, but the mother's biological role tends to make her more important. Children of neither sex are made to feel that they are temporary or peripheral members of the group of birth. Ego is at the centre of the bilateral kinship system. In post-marital residential arrangements there is some choice and flexibility. Social identity is derived from both parents. (In Malaysia and to a degree in Indonesia, the naming pattern is derived from Islam, in which individuals are identified as the sons or daughters of their fathers; and in the Philippines it comes from Christianity – but this has no effect on social identity.) In the Philippines, for instance, both parents are acknowledged and a loosely knit bilateral kinship network functions. Marriage does not obliterate an earlier identity.

Marriage and legitimate paternity do have significance, but a child born out of wedlock is not discarded. In Islamic countries such as Malaysia and Indonesia, marriage is necessary so that a man can own up to paternity and prevent the child from getting the status of *haram*; but the kind of fuss and outrage over a baby's birth out of wedlock that is seen in patrilineal communities is absent here. In Thailand and the Philippines, children with unidentified paternity are often brought up by their maternal grandparents. Thailand is perhaps more liberal than others because of Buddhism, which traditionally has few specific prescriptions and proscriptions in respect of family matters. Catholicism condemns women for bearing illegitimate offspring, although not unpardonably, but it does not reject children born "in sin." Even orphans can be brought into the fold through baptism, for which no parent is necessary.

In Malaysia, many people have adopted a patrilineal Arabian naming system in which an individual's personal name is accompanied by a patronymic. A woman does not ordinarily adopt her husband's name. The Catholic influence is seen in names in the Philippines. The wife generally adopts her husband's last name and a child, its father's. Neither in Indonesia nor in Thailand need a woman change her name to align it with her husband's. The Western influence is apparent only in small sections of the population.

In Malaysia and Java, marriage may be looked upon as an honourable and natural course of life, but it does not imply loss of membership of the natal family or the total transfer of a girl to another kin group. There are no discrete and distinct kin groups in these bilateral societies, and post-marital residence is flexible.

In South-East Asia generally, both son and daughter have the potential to augment the kin group. The bilateral Malay kinship system gives equal significance to male and female sides of a family, ego being at the centre. There are no family names and no unilineal kin groups whose continuity is at stake. The range of kin depends upon a family's or an individual's recollection and recognition. Expanding and activating or discarding kinship links for personal reasons is easier, but there is a certain value associated with kinship in these societies.

In patrilineal Hindu South Asia different naming patterns are seen;

but whatever combination is chosen – from among territorial (town or village) name, lineage name, father's name, family name – to accompany the personal name, it is the link with the father that is demonstrated. A married woman is expected to adopt her husband's personal or family name as a suffix to her personal name; although in Maharashtra and Gujarat it is customary for her to add both. Among upper-caste Hindus in many parts of India it is still the custom to give a woman on her marriage a new personal name as well, thus entirely obliterating her identity – although this is generally only a ritual. In the rural areas and small towns of northern and middle India, in her affinal home a woman may be referred to as so and so's wife or mother, or as coming from such and such village. In Bangladesh too, according to many observers, a woman in the rural areas is hardly ever identified by her own name.

A custom of Garhwal in cis-Himalayan India is worth mentioning here. An unmarried girl does not generally carry the family name of the father, using only her personal name. I was told that, since a girl has to adopt her husband's family name on marriage, it is best that she remain without a family name until then.

In matrilineal communities, in South Asia as well as in South-East Asia, children of either sex acquire permanent membership of the unilineal descent group into which they are born. To establish social identity, the name of the lineage is generally used together with personal names. Thus, among the Lakshadweep Muslims and the Nayar of Kerala, individuals belong to the mother's *taravad* or lineage. As a result of social change the Nayar have begun to use the father's name or initial letter along with that of the *taravad*; and sometimes they even drop the *taravad* name. In the Lakshadweep islands, however, the use of the *taravad* name along with the personal name continues.

In Lakshadweep, residence does not change at marriage; the marital relationship is effected through a pattern of visits by the husband. Among the matrilineal Khasi of north-eastern India a man may move to live with his wife and her kin, or to a neolocal residence on the land of his wife; but his lineage or clan membership do not change. After his death his bones must be sent to his mother's or sister's place to be placed with the others of the matrilineage. Among the Garo, also in north-eastern India, a man joins the *nok* or house of his wife but remains a member of his unilineal group. In northern Thailand a man joins the group identified by his wife's ancestors, but he is not thereby separated from his own group. In Negri Sembilan in Malaysia and among the Minangkabau of Sumatra, women are firmly rooted in the land and descent identity of the matrilineage. Men are travellers and have conjugal relationships with women of other clans; but they retain their lineage and clan memberships with the right to return whenever they want.

Inheritance and resource distribution

Gender differences in group membership and social identity are closely connected with patterns of inheritance and resource distribution. In the following discussion the major forms of property and resources for living – principally land – are considered. Along with women's economic roles, this is a crucial area for the theme of this study. Patrilineal South Asia offers a clear contrast to bilateral South-East Asia and to the matrilineal communities of both regions.

In much of Hindu South Asia, property is inherited by male heirs and transmitted through them. Traditionally, daughters have had only the right to maintenance and to a marriage in keeping with the status of their natal families. Male children have coparcenary rights in ancestral property. They acquire a share in such property at birth and are entitled to ask for their shares even during their father's lifetime. This is in keeping with the Mitakshara school of law, which was operative in large parts of India. The Dayabhaga school gave sons a right not at birth but only upon the death of the father. A law passed in 1956 abolished this distinction, although the ethos of the second pattern is retained among the Bengali *bhadralok* (the largely urban middle class).

According to the law of 1956 daughters are still not coparceners but along with sons are entitled to a portion of the father's share of ancestral property as inheritors. More often than not, however, a daughter's dowry and the expenses on her wedding are viewed as a substitute for her share in her father's property. In fact the same logic is applied to a daughter's share in her father's individually acquired property as well.

A father may make a will leaving some of his self-acquired property to his daughters; but very often he might be guided by traditional ideas and leave little or nothing to them. If he dies intestate his property is to be divided equally among his widow and children of both sexes. But daughters hesitate to claim their shares, to which their brothers tend to feel they have no right. A woman who demands her share of her father's ancestral or self-acquired property risks ruining her relationship with her brothers. She may no longer be invited to her natal home on special occasions and may no longer receive periodic gifts. Often women succumb to their brothers' suggestions to give up their rights in parental property. The general belief is that, whereas an unmarried daughter may be given a share, a married daughter has no right to one unless she is particularly badly off. The argument is that, whereas brothers' shares remain in the family, giving shares to sisters leads to fragmentation of property. The belief is deeply ingrained that sons, who continue the line and perform the father's last rites, have an exclusive right to the patrimony.

It is only among a few educated people that daughters receive their shares without reservations. By and large the new law remains ineffective so far as daughters are concerned. Sometimes sons-in-law press their wives to claim their shares, leading to disputes and bickering.

More or less the same situation prevails among the Parbatiyas of Nepal. Only a daughter who remains unmarried until the age of 35 is legally entitled to a share. Otherwise only sons are entitled to shares in patrimony. The notion persists that daughters have a right only to gifts, not to shares.

In south India a few communities give pieces of land as dowry to daughters. Carol Upadhyay (1990) has recorded this custom in detail for landed castes such as Kammas, Velmas, and Reddys. The Kammas of coastal Andhra Pradesh are particularly well known for it. This dowry, people argue, is in lieu of the daughter's share in the patrimonial property. In Nellore District the piece of land gifted to a daughter on her marriage is called *posupu kumkum* (turmeric and vermilion), meaning perhaps that it is intended to meet the personal expenses of the married woman. In Maharashtra, resources gifted to a daughter are meant for her "bangles and blouse."

If a daughter is married into a nearby village, she and her husband can look after the gifted land; or else her father and brothers till it and give her the produce or proceeds. Owing to intra-kin marriages (mother's brother and sister's daughter or father's sister's daughter and mother's brother's son) it often happens that a piece of land keeps moving between two families for generations. But what a daughter is given is still not strictly by right of inheritance; in Telugu, for example, it is called *bahumanam*, meaning gift, not *bhagam*, share. In Tamil society a woman would (this practice is still prevalent to some degree) customarily be given some land upon her marriage. Known as *manjal kani* (*manjal* meaning turmeric), this land was meant to afford her an independent income. Such land was supposed to pass from mother to daughter, but this did not always happen. A woman could also get land from her father's mother (Mukund 1992). Again, this did not represent real inheritance.

It must be mentioned that in some states, such as Andhra Pradesh, Karnataka, Haryana, and Maharashtra, recent legal measures have given daughters equal rights in ancestral property, but their efficacy remains to be proved. Wherever there are only daughters they tend to get their fathers' self-acquired property. This does not apply to ancestral land. There are regional and caste variations and others that depend upon the strength of the patrilineage and the consequent claims of close male patrikin. The adoption of a son for the sake of lineal continuity is an accepted practice.[1]

Among Christians a daughter is entitled to a share equal to a son's, but there are regional variations. In Travancore-Cochin, the home of the Syrian Christians, the Travancore Christian Succession Act of 1916 gave a daughter only one-fourth of a son's share or Rs 5,000, whichever was less. Dowry effectively disinherited a daughter, so this applied only to unmarried daughters. This unfair Act was struck down by the Supreme Court as being unconstitutional and void as a result of the case of Mary Roy. However, recent happenings show that even their church has come to the support of those Syrian Christians who do not want to lose their rights to property to the daughters of the house with retrospective effect (Jacob 1986, Joseph 1993).

A community that has been following its own rules and practices of inheritance is the Goan Christians. According to the law applied to the converted Catholics of Goa from the sixteenth to the nineteenth centuries, a daughter was entitled to inherit her father's property along with her brothers. A widow, however, had the right only to maintenance from her husband's estate. But daughters' right to inherit contravened the patrilineal norms of inheritance. In the late nineteenth century Portugal formulated a new set of laws for its converted colonies. According to these laws, which still exist, women continue to have the right to inherit but they can be given a dowry or trousseau instead. In theory the dowry may consist of both movable and immovable property, but daughters usually get only the first. Land is the major component of property, which needs to devolve in the male line to avoid fragmentation.

In the absence of a son, the marriage of a daughter with a son of her father's brother is looked upon as a device for keeping property within the patriline. But such a marriage with close kin requires special dispensation from the church, which can be obtained by making a donation.

Streedhana – a woman's movable property in the form of various kinds of gifts – has been common all over India; but the woman's control over it has varied. Sadly, in recent years dowry seems to have replaced the traditional *streedhana*. The values and contents of dowries have increased many times over, because bridegrooms and their parents treat marriage as an easy method of accumulating wealth and acquiring capital or consumer goods. The absence of inheritance rights for daughters certainly gives an impetus to the practice, as does the caste system with the restrictions that it places on marriage.

In practice the Muslims of patrilineal South Asia have radically deviated from Quranic rules of inheritance. Daughters are completely deprived of shares in their father's property in the interest of keeping the patrimony intact (Ahmad 1976, Government of India 1974). A daughter's husband may force his wife to claim her share, but again this leads to dispute and to a rift between the woman and her brothers. In rural Bangladesh women usually neither get nor claim their legal right to paternal property. Researchers have noted that many daughters notionally exchange this right for the right periodically to visit the natal home, where they get a respite from the strict code of conduct enforced in the marital homestead, apart from gifts and better food (S. Ahmed 1984, Kabeer 1985b). This periodic "going home" is known as *nayor*, which connotes warmth, care, the absence of critical eyes, and so on. In Pakistan too, women wish to retain the right to visit the natal home and the support of their brothers to get through the ordinary difficulties of life as well as through the possible problems of divorce and widowhood (Pastner 1971, 1978). There is also a sense of impracticality attached to honouring a married daughter's right to a share in immovable property owing to physical distance and women's seclusion. Indeed, in patrilineal South Asia, with a few exceptions, a daughter's right to a stipulated share in land tends to go unhonoured.

Among both Hindus and Muslims in urban areas, rich fathers are often inclined to leave property and movable resources to their daughters. But again, when considerable expenses have been incurred upon their weddings, their brothers try to stop such moves. Among people with limited means, daughters can expect hardly anything. In business communities sons have to be alert to retain resources within the family.

This may be contrasted with the practice in matrilineal Muslim Lakshadweep by speaking of coconut trees, the main form of property. There are two kinds of property: that of the *taravad* or matrilineage, which is shared and transmitted through female links alone, and individuals' property, whose transmission is governed by Islamic law. *Taravad* property has traditionally been considered impartible, although it may be divided for usufruct. Both male and female members have inalienable rights in this property; but through females they extend to their children, who are permanent members of the matrilineage, while male members enjoy their shares only as long as they live.

Men gift their individual property to children and wives. Interestingly, however, they tend to deviate from Islamic law under the influence of matrilineal values. More often than not, sons and daughters will receive equal shares of disposable property rather than shares in the ratio 2:1. There is also a distinct preference for turning the property given away under the authority of the *sharia* into collective indisposable property after the matrilineal manner. The argument is that the property would be fragmented among different *taravads* if it were to be given as individual property to sons (L. Dube 1991b, 1994).

In Peninsular Malaysia *adat* or customary law requires that property be divided equally among sons and daughters, while according to Islamic law a male heir should get double the share of a female. There is a distinct inclination to follow *adat* rather than the *sharia* in this connection. Tsubouchi (1977) writes that, although there is a tendency among comparatively prosperous people to choose Islamic law, it is not strictly applied; the principle of equal division between the sexes is considered more fair. Shares are individually owned, which is in keeping with both *adat* and *sharia*.

Among the bilateral Javanese too, the Islamic division of property in the ratio 2:1 between sons and daughters does not find as much favour as the *adat* pattern of equal shares. There is no real conflict with Islam in the notion of individual property. Koentjaraningrat (1985: 156–157) has described the inheritance pattern among the Javanese. He says that Islamic rules for the division of property between sons and daughters are not always followed and that the complex process of division of property among heirs should be seen as one of gradual transmission. Different kinds of property, movable and immovable, are conceptually classified separately, and children are often given their shares of the parental property at an early stage.

Agricultural land is inherited by children of both sexes. A daughter who sets up an independent household may be given a new house with a garden plot and the right of use over agricultural land. Her husband cultivates this land, often as a sharecropper; he does not get the title to it.

Patterns of allocation of resources between sons and daughters in different areas of Thailand have already been described when dealing with kinship and family organization and will be taken up again when discussing residence. Gender parity, flexibility in kinship, and the overall absence of discrimination between brothers and sisters in the allocation of resources and in the transmission of property – in fact, the favouring of daughters or one daughter, depending on residence – are characteristic features of the Filipino and Thai cultures.

This outline of contrasting inheritance rules and practices brings out an important point, which will become clearer when I take up shelter, residence, and conjugal relations: that the dependence of women in South Asia is rooted both in materiality and in ideology.

This brings us to another contrast. In South Asia a woman's right to property and resources during an extant marriage is ineffective or almost non-existent. In principle she has control over household resources – she is the giver of food, the caretaker, and is responsible for rituals and for perpetuating the traditions of the family. She ought to have control over jewellery or other forms of property she may have received from her parents. In some communities it is also recognized that a woman owns what she has received as *streedhana* from her in-laws at the time of marriage. But very often all valuables and cash may be taken away from her; or they may be drawn upon in times of difficulty, for after all the honour of the family depends on her.

The household is a woman's domain of power, not just the arena of her work and responsibility. In terms of control over strategic economic resources the women of South-East Asia enjoy a high status. They are free of the feeling of dependence that a wife in a South Asian marriage harbours. In South Asia even those women who participate in productive activities, working in the family's fields or in its occupation, do not have control over resources or earnings. Those who earn wages may have to spend all that they earn on running the household. In practice they may have control over their income but in terms of ideology they are still dependent; they may be reminded that they live in the houses of their in-laws, whose food they eat.

It is only after she becomes a widow that a South Asian woman is entitled to a share of her husband's resources. She may inherit part of his self-acquired intestate property along with her sons and daughters. Daughters' rights may be side-tracked, but a widow generally gets her share. If this is immovable property, it is very often looked upon as not disposable. In the relatively recent organizational structures, an employee's provident fund, gratuity, and so on are paid to his widow, who can use her discretion in disposing of them. However, if the cash received is converted into immovable property such as land, the nature of her right to it is likely to change, particularly in north India. Land is traditionally viewed as a male form of property (U. Sharma 1980), and her sons are likely to be named as co-owners. Daughters are unlikely to be included, and after a time the woman's own right may come to be regarded as usufructuary, without the right of disposal. Such things often happen when widows are barely educated and, without any experience of legal transactions, must depend on male kin.

The South-East Asian situation poses a sharp contrast to what has been described above. In South-East Asian countries there is an understanding of conjugal property that gives the wife rights over what her husband earns. Wife and husband each have an individual right to what they bring to the marriage, and what is acquired during the marriage belongs to both. The possibility of one spouse's withholding information about his or her income cannot be ruled out, but it remains a fact that women in South-East Asia are more or less free of the feeling of dependence that a wife in South Asia harbours.

Explanations have to be sought also in the contrasting attitudes towards female sexuality, in patterns of segregation and seclusion, in differences in post-marital residence, and also in the nature and character of marriage. At this juncture, however, it is necessary briefly to examine the economic roles of women.

Women's economic roles

Considerable economically valuable work by women remains invisible in South Asia. Women at the lower economic levels have always been engaged in labour of some kind. The agricultural sector has a large female labour force that works in the fields and also looks after the storage of grain and the preservation of seeds, kitchen gardening, and care of livestock. Poultry raising and a great deal of craft work are also done by women. In the rural areas of India and Nepal, women of the poorer sections work in the fields as wage labourers and render various kinds of service to those better off. Women's work in agriculture is much more important in paddy-growing areas. Older experienced women in southern India often supervise labour. In other parts of the country women generally work under men's supervision.

At the lower levels, *parda* (purdah) does not prevent women from working in the fields either among Hindus or among Muslims. At the middle level it might do so, depending on the status and tradition of the community or caste. There is also a distinction between working in the family's own fields and working in the fields of others for wages or as contract labour. Women in many places undertake the selling of milk and milk products, vegetables, and fruits.

In the villages of Bangladesh *parda* usually prevents women from participating directly in productive activities outside the home. Men work in the fields and do the marketing and shopping. Women do all the work that can be carried out inside or around the home. This includes wage labour in others' houses (Chaudhury and Ahmed 1980). With poverty, women are being drawn into various kinds of labour such as road construction.

In Pakistan *parda* obstructs women's entry into the urban labour force for all but the poorest sections of society. However, in settled villages such as those of West Punjab, women of tenant or subsistence farmer families work in the fields whereas those of the higher classes do not. Throughout Pakistan economic market-places are reserved for men, admitting only a handful of the poorest women who must work when they can.

In India women have been working in factories of various kinds for decades. There is segregation within the labour market – factors responsible for it include responsibility for domestic work and child care and the difficulty of travelling long distances and at odd hours. Avoiding interaction with strange men is a consideration mainly for younger women, but perhaps it is not so important as it is in Pakistan. Certain factories in Pakistan either employ only women or restrict them to segregated sections. The status of a family is affected if its women work outside the home. The position of man as provider is undercut if his wife has to take up employment.

In South Asia women participate in the family occupation. They remain invisible and do not have independent incomes although they contribute substantially to their families' enterprises. Women are also engaged in different kinds of cottage industries and handicrafts. A wide variety of crafts and skills comes under home-based production.

The informal sector absorbs women in all these countries, but in most cases they are separated from the market and do not enjoy the benefits of direct participation in it, except in the small number of instances where their work is in cooperatives or similar organizations (Mies 1982, Singh and Kelles-Viitanen 1987).

Educated women's employment in the tertiary sector has increased many times over during the past few decades. There is a variety of jobs carrying salaries ranging from the low to the very high. Teaching and medicine are perhaps the most favoured professions for women in South Asia. They are valued because they provide education and health care to females. In India women now work in a variety of jobs and enterprises. In Pakistan, though, *parda* gets in the way of women's taking up secretarial jobs, for example. There is no doubt, however, that South Asian women, particularly those who observe seclusion or segregation or are hemmed in by low mobility and constraints of space and time, have to face many handicaps. Especially in Pakistan and Bangladesh, it is at the top, upper-middle and lower levels that women engage in economic activities without many restrictions. In these countries educated middle-class women are becoming visible in the economic sphere only gradually. India is in a better position in this respect, but there too the status of a job and its requirements in terms of working hours, travel, and possible neglect of household duties have to be weighed.

The extent to which a job and an income give economic and general independence and respect and identity to a South Asian woman is a moot question. Her income certainly contributes to running her household and to maintaining a standard of living for her family, but does it give her control over resources? Further, what an unemployed woman does by way of looking after the household, supporting her husband in his social mobility, and undertaking the socialization of her children is also status production work. Does she get recognition for it?

Whereas the women of South Asia have traditionally been home-bound, their roles as wife and mother emphasized, South-East Asian women are known for their vital economic roles. Besides being wives and mothers they have always engaged in income-earning activities. Their undertaking of a wide range of tasks has contributed to their economic independence and to a large measure of autonomy and power. This is true of most Thai, Peninsular Malaysian, Javanese, and Filipino women. In societies such as the Atjehnese, where men are away for much of the time, women manage both agricultural work and family affairs.

In general, women are integral to the peasant economy. Speaking of Malaysia and Indonesia, Manderson (1983) emphasizes that women alone are responsible for establishing and tending nurseries, transplanting seedlings, weeding, harvesting, and winnowing and thrashing the paddy. She mentions women's share in the cultivation of other crops such as rubber and in the production of copra. Women are almost entirely responsible for the commercial production of vegetables, for domestic animals, and for silviculture.

The Javanese household is a woman's domain, where her control over strategic resources is near complete. She also takes most of the decisions in household matters.

Unlike women in many parts of South Asia, who also contribute substantially to productive activities, South-East Asian women retain control over what they produce and earn. It appears that, besides rules of inheritance, the institutionalization of conjugal property in this region also encourages women's control over resources.

All over South-East Asia women are known for their important presence in trading. They trade surpluses and make and sell food, clothes, and a variety of other items. Women's presence is over-whelming in rural and urban markets. This role has in places been carried over into the modern economy. In Thailand, for example, women are deeply involved in the ownership and management of businesses.

That South-East Asian women engage in all manner of income-earning activities is certainly related to their freedom of association, their ability to migrate (often leaving children behind), the support of their kin, their hold over resources, and their rights over space. Some of these points will be taken up in subsequent chapters of this book.

In the new capitalist economy rural women are being employed away from their homes and in unusual circumstances are losing their sense of proportion. Many of them migrate to towns and adopt the lucrative professions of massage girls and sex workers.

Women often bear alone the burden of rearing their children and supporting their parents and siblings. Their economic contribution cannot just be seen as augmenting those structural features of kinship that favour them. We can agree that their contribution, the near-parity with men that is given to them in bilateral societies, and the residence pattern there all combine to give women a distinct value.

It is agreed throughout South-East Asia that women are good with money (Papanek and Schwede 1988) and that they are superior to men in financial management and business dealings. What a woman actually gains from these qualities depends on her resources and the class to which she belongs. Many are at least assured of the regular income that is necessary to meet their families' needs. About the power and autonomy that they might derive, Stoler (1977: 84) observes, in relation to Java, that while among poor households women's earnings give them a position of considerable importance, for wealthier women incomes provide a material basis for acquiring social power. Inheritance, conjugal property, and rights over space tie up well with women's economic roles and what they gain through them. Their position is in contrast to that of women in South Asia, who may gain some bargaining power because of their earnings but whose economic roles do not seem to sit well with the ideologies of their kinship systems.

South-East Asian women's control over finances and their authority within the household have been stressed in different ways in various ethnographic studies (Jay 1969, Dewey 1962, Djmour 1959, Firth 1966, Koentjaraningrat 1985, Geertz 1961, Karim 1987, n.d., Jocano 1969, Illo 1990, Hollnsteiner 1981, Maneevone 1974, Stoler 1977, Tanner 1974, Ward 1963).

In conclusion I might point to one commonality between women in the two regions. Women are to be found at the middle levels in various professions; not many women reach the top.

4

The management of female sexuality

There is a marked contrast between South Asia and South-East Asia in the management of female sexuality. We have to look at the combined influence of ideological and institutional factors. It is necessary to try to grasp how the ideological evaluation of women compares with their actual behaviour in the familial, economic, and reproductive spheres. Although symbols and ideological definitions are not in themselves sufficient to explain the status of women in South and South-East Asia, they must be included in any discussion of the subject.

Placement in groups is essentially a function of paternity in patrilineal South Asia, and in the culture of this region sexuality and reproduction cannot be separated. Unlike in parts of Africa, rights *in uxorem* and rights *in genetricem* are merged (Gough 1971, Tambiah 1989). Women's sexuality therefore needs to be rigidly controlled. Virginity at first marriage is a value cherished both in Hinduism and in Islam. Concern with it takes a variety of forms: *ihi*, or pre-pubertal ritual marriage with a *bel* fruit representing the god Narayan, among the Newar of Nepal (Allen 1982a); child marriage; pre-pubertal marriage with delayed consummation, widely prevalent in Rajasthan, Uttar Pradesh, and Madhya Pradesh (Government of India 1974, Palriwala 1990, T. Patel 1991, L. Dube 1996); and the widespread practice of marrying off a girl as early as possible after puberty. Laws specifying the lowest permissible age at marriage exist, as in Bangladesh, Pakistan, and India, but they are ignored. Elsewhere in this work we discuss the preoccupation with a daughter's marriage and the marking of puberty as an important point in a girl's life. These are clearly associated with concern over the management of female sexuality. A girl must be guarded properly during the liminal period between menarche and marriage. Sexual desire is believed to awaken at puberty and to need control and harnessing.

Women need to be guarded even after they are married. Owing to the unrepudiable character of maternity and the crucial importance of paternity for group membership, in people's perception women's sexuality tends to be equated with their reproductive power. Linked to this is the notion that a woman's purity is fragile: the pollution she incurs through sexual intercourse is internal, whereas that incurred by men is only external. One should add here that the presence of caste as a factor defining status makes the notion of female purity stronger among Hindus than it is among Muslims – although an overwhelming concern with paternity is common to all patrilineal groups in South Asia. Marriage establishes a husband's right over his wife's person. In fact, *nikah* (Muslim contractual marriage) is supposed to establish a man's exclusive right to his wife's vagina. *Mahr* (an agreed payment to be made to the bride's dowry) has the significance of conferring a right over the wife's sexuality.

The principle of protection is basic to considerations regarding female sexuality. The responsibility for protecting an unmarried girl lies with her natal or patrilineal male kin, particularly fathers and brothers. The "honour" of males and of the larger family vests in that of their women. Pakistani brothers' vigilance over the honour of their sisters is well known: even a semblance of encroachment on it through a chance remark or gesture is liable to trigger off a fight. In Andhra Pradesh a brother will scold his sister for standing in the doorway, particularly at dusk, for that smacks of inviting outsiders in the manner that prostitutes adopt. In the subcontinent, control over women's sexuality is so strong that brothers have been known to kill a sister guilty of illicit love or wanting to marry against their wishes or those of their parents.

This responsibility for protection gives males the right to exercise power over the females in their charge and often to dictate every facet of their behaviour. A proper demeanour is essential for remaining safe and above reproach. Downcast eyes and a shrinking body, almost creating a private, sacrosanct space for oneself within a public space such as a road, constitute part of this demeanour. Girls prefer to move in groups rather than singly. It is not only the fear of molestation but also that of being maligned as "bad" that make a girl follow a strategy that Johanna Lessinger (1990), describing the movements of women petty traders in Madras, calls "public chaperoning."

The provision of an escort for maintaining *izzat* (personal as well as collective honour) is common. Correspondingly, unescorted females are considered fair game, depending on where they are encountered and on how they comport themselves. This is well expressed in the saying, "A standing cot and a standing girl may be laid down first by whosoever wishes" (Krishna Sobti, personal communication). Protection, chaperoning, and unobtrusive movements on the part of a girl are all implied in this. This protection continues, to a greater or lesser degree, until a woman reaches menopause. Both seclusion and segregation, which are discussed separately, are parts of it.

The perennial fear of misbehaviour on the part of women and the fear of assault are expressed in the imposition of controls over their physical movement and their association with males. There are a number of terms of abuse that cast aspersions on women's purity and character. The most common abuse in Hindi, "*sala*" (meaning "wife's brother"), hits at the recipient by implying that his sister is a sexual object for the abuser. Similarly "*harami*" (bastard), "son of a widow," "son of a whore," "mother-fucker," and "sister-fucker" are abuses hurled at males, but in point of fact they are meant for the women on whom they cast aspersions.

The minds of girls and women are sought to be kept occupied with the cultivation of feminine skills such as needlework and culinary art. Participation in religious rituals and festivals is encouraged with the same objective. Working with the cattle and processing milk products and other activities are designed to keep them from mischief.

South Asia shows a special kind of male control over female sexuality, rooted in patrilineal ideology and in a consciousness of territoriality and group solidarity, which may be called *corporate control*. In a village in Bangladesh, for instance, although poor men may not impose restrictions on their wives, the village elders – the real decision makers – decide what work women should do and where (M. Chen 1990). It is well known that a male-dominated village *panchayat* (council or adjudicatory body, notionally five in number) or caste *panchayat* can decide on matters of separation, divorce, and compensation, and can take note of the adulteries and illegitimate pregnancies of unattached women.

An incident in a caste of vegetable growers in central India powerfully portrays one kind of corporate control over female sexuality. A beautiful girl was married by her step-father to a poor boy

51

who could not pay the bride-price but was prepared to live and labour at his father-in-law's house. He was sturdy and hard-working but of small build and unprepossessing appearance. The couple were married in childhood, and when they grew up they realized that they did not suit each other. The young man became peevish while the young woman grew more and more attractive.

The arrival of a distant cousin of the husband triggered off a conflict. The woman was attracted towards the handsome young man, and soon the two began to think of marriage. The woman asked her step-father to call a meeting of the caste council and get her a divorce. The step-father was against this because his son-in-law was a hard-working fellow. He ignored his daughter's claim that the man was impotent.

When nothing seemed to be happening, the lovers decided to elope. The step-father sent a few strong youths after the couple. They brought the young woman back and she was locked into a room. The man then approached the *panchayat* elders (the *panch*) and said that his daughter was out of her mind and not fit to be presented before the *panchayat*. He therefore proposed to present the case himself. After hearing the case the elders asked the husband whether the charge of impotence was true. He flatly denied it, arguing that his wife's infatuation with the other man had induced her to make it. One of his friends then came forward and argued that because of her entanglement the young woman had become sexually excited. He said that her infatuation and consequent excitement needed to be controlled.

The *panch* then argued that the woman must be controlled well in time or else she would set a pernicious example to the other young women of the village. But how were they to force her to live with her husband? She might elope again. The headman said that he knew of one remedy that had been tested by their ancestors. The young woman should be treated as a cow or she-buffalo in heat. The young men of the village supported this, arguing that the woman had no need to go to a stranger for sexual satisfaction while they were there.

The young woman's mother sought without success to prevent what followed. One after another seven men were sent into her daughter's room. When the seventh emerged he reported that the young woman was absolutely still, and that she might well be dead. Nobody believed him, being certain that this treatment would set her right. The next morning she was found dead. This was justice delivered by a *panchayat* of men (Tambe 1991).

Another kind of corporate control over women's sexuality relates to rights of access to it. Where there is a strong sense of the patrilineal principle and a belief in the commonality of the blood of agnates, a woman may be regarded as sexually accessible by the brothers of the man to whom she is married. The fraternal polyandry of the Khasa of Jaunsar Bawar in the cis-Himalayan region is well known (Majumdar 1962, J. Gupta 1990). The Jats, an agriculturalist caste with tribal origins who live mainly in Rajasthan, Punjab, Haryana, and western Uttar Pradesh, have been known to follow this practice, although not very openly. Among them, women's contribution to the household economy is substantial. Owing to an adverse sex ratio it is often difficult to obtain a wife. A study by Chowdhry speaks of this sharing of a woman by a number of brothers and even agnatic cousins, and of the compulsion on a widow to marry a brother of her deceased husband. The objective is to keep the woman within the family or lineage and to ensure that any children retain their rights in their father's land and remain available as labour. There is a strong feeling of ownership over the woman, her labour, and her procreative power. "The importance of the reproductive role of women can be gathered from this local proverb from Amritsar: 'A Jat woman, a Persian wheel, are never superfluous: One populates the villages, the other waters the fields'" (Chowdhry 1990).

There are differences among castes and regions as regards the rights of the husband's family over an in-married woman's sexuality. What was true of the Jats does not necessarily apply elsewhere. For instance, even where there is the custom of a widow's marrying her deceased husband's younger brother, this may not be compulsory. Elsewhere a divorced or widowed woman's natal kin may take the responsibility for her remarriage or may leave the choice to her.

The South Asian sense of rights over the sexuality and the reproductive capacity of an in-marrying woman is closely tied to the sense of common agnatic blood, to patrilineal, patri-virilocal family solidarity, and to the understanding that the woman now *belongs* to the family and clan. This sense is stronger in some communities than in others. Where one agnate (brother or parallel cousin) is regarded as a substitute for another, we see the phenomenon of corporate rights of use over the sexuality of a woman married into the family; but where a husband has an exclusive right over the sexuality of his wife, rights over her labour – and to an extent over her children – may be shared by the agnatic family. Children belong to the father and his kin group, which can retain them even when their mother gets a divorce or remarries as a widow. Even among Muslims a woman may keep a son only until he is seven years old and a daughter until she attains puberty.

In practice a man's rights over his children may be exercised only when it suits him to exercise them, often when he wants to torment his wife. Among the poorer sections in urban areas it is common for a man to abandon his children or to leave their care entirely to their mother.

It is often observed that in secondary marriages women may choose their partners by themselves. A married woman who participates in productive, service, or marketing activities outside the home has opportunities to move around and also a greater freedom of association than unmarried girls do. However, if the woman is a divorcee her new husband may be required to pay compensation to her previous husband or a bride-price to her parents. Thus, even in a situation of relative freedom, a woman does not have complete control over her own sexuality.

Another, uncommon, kind of right over a woman's sexuality involves its use by the husband for earning money. Individual instances can probably be encountered everywhere, but among the Doms of Uttarkashi in the cis-Himalayan belt it is an established practice. Men borrow from landlords and others to finance their marriages, which involve the payment of bride-price, and then send their wives into prostitution in cities. Their husbands are deemed to have fathered the children born to these women (J. Gupta 1990).

In looking at female sexuality it becomes essential to examine the implications of caste for women. Caste imparts a special character to the control exercised over female sexuality and constrains women in specific ways. The fact that membership of discrete and hierarchically graded groups is defined by birth entails a concern with boundary maintenance through the regulation of marriage and of sexual relations. The onus of boundary maintenance falls on women because of their role in biological reproduction. There are innumerable sayings that emphasize the difference between male and female sexuality, in the context of caste as well as otherwise: sexual intercourse with a person of another caste pollutes a man only externally, but it pollutes a woman internally; whether a petal falls on a thorn or a thorn falls on a petal, it is the petal that is hurt; nothing can happen to buttermilk – it is only milk that can go bad; an earthen pot is permanently defiled if touched by a person of a lower caste, whereas a brass vessel can be purified; and so on.

Hypergamous unions (where the man is of higher caste than the woman) are not entirely disapproved of, provided that the social and ritual distance between the castes is not too great; but not so a hypogamous union. There is a strong reaction to an upper-caste woman marrying a man of inferior caste; and any entanglement of a high-caste or middle-caste woman with an untouchable man is intolerable. An incident that occurred in Mehrana near Mathura in Uttar Pradesh in March–April 1991 was a harrowing illustration of this. A 15-year-old Jat girl eloped with a Jatav (an inferior caste, originally leather-working) boy whom she had met while he worked in her father's fields. Another Jatav youth helped in this venture, and the trio soon returned to their homes. The girl was adamant that she would marry the untouchable boy.

The Jats, who dominated the village *panchayat*, decided to inflict a punishment so severe that no Jatav male would dare to touch a Jat girl again. The two Jatav boys were brutally tortured and finally hanged. The Jat girl was also hanged. The Jatav parents had been coaxed and bullied into agreeing to this proceeding, but the Jat parents wished both to take revenge on the Jatavs and to be rid of a daughter who had "blackened their faces" (*India Today*, 30 April 1991). A number of cases are reported in which young girls who form or are suspected of forming relationships with men of different castes or religions are beaten or even killed by their own brothers.

When it is possible to hush up such entanglements or elopements, the parents of the girl try to bring her back and marry her to a man of their own caste as early as possible. This may be at some distance, where the exploit is unknown, or it may have the support of a huge dowry. A young man of "unclean" caste involved with a girl of "clean" caste is viewed as a criminal, to be punished severely or even physically eliminated. This is what is reported to have happened to a Harijan boy in one of the eastern districts of Andhra Pradesh, not the only incident of its kind in that region (G. Lakshmi, personal communication).

Irrespective of the system of descent followed, the caste affiliations of both parents are relevant in the attribution of caste to a child. This becomes clear if we compare two matrilineal communities: the Khasi of Meghalaya, who are a tribal group, and the Nayar of central Kerala, who have been part of the caste system. Traditionally Nayar women married men from among the Nambudiri or other Brahmin groups, from Kshatriyas, from castes or sub-castes that were at least equivalent to their own, and from among their own sub-caste. Being supported by *taravad* property and living in the *taravad* house, their children could be brought up without fathers being present. However, their paternity had to be identified with an appropriate group. A pregnant woman who could not offer this was excommunicated or killed (Gough 1959, 1961).

Among the Khasi, who are not part of the caste system, a person's group identity is derived solely from the mother. The word "Khasi" itself means "child of one's mother." A Khasi woman's child was recognized as a Khasi even when known to have been fathered by a British soldier or a caste Hindu man. Children born out of wedlock are automatically absorbed in their mothers' matrilineal groups. They do suffer some loss of status in as much as there is a specific term for them that signifies that the father is unknown (Tiplut Nongbri, personal communication), but they are otherwise unaffected. Khasi women have always participated in productive and marketing activities and have had much freedom of movement. It must be mentioned, though, that adultery on the part of either spouse is unacceptable and can easily lead to divorce.

Under matriliny and duolocal residence, the Nayar women enjoyed a high status as perpetuators of the matriline, as links for inheritance and succession, and as permanent members of their respective *taravads*. Mothers and sisters were greatly respected. Often elderly women were efficient supervisors in productive activities. Within the accepted limits of connubial relations women must have had considerable freedom to marry and to divorce (for a somewhat different view see Chapter 9, p. 121). They were not dependent on their husbands and their children belonged to them. At the same time, in contrast to Khasi women, Nayar women, particularly when young, had to live under vigilance and their lives were hemmed in by many constraints. The restrictions on movement protected them from contact with lower castes and other religious and ethnic groups. The point here is that even a kinship system that may be considered favourable to women in many respects cannot transcend the effects of the presence of caste.

I have not yet directly referred to the denial to women of sexual gratification as a means of "protecting" their sexuality. Public opinion serves as an important medium of control here. When the system of controls fails or when women either succumb to temptation or become victims of sexual violence and this in turn becomes known, they cannot easily remain within the fold of respectability. India's large number of orphanages have their basis in the complete unacceptability of illegitimate births: social workers estimate that 85 per cent of the babies who arrive in orphanages are illegitimate.

A woman who has been raped is not easily accepted even by her own family. Often the only course open to her is prostitution. During the war that gave birth to Bangladesh as a nation, many Bengali women were raped by Pakistani soldiers and for that reason became unacceptable to their families. A very large effort was needed to provide them with shelter, to carry out risky abortions, and to take care of the babies that were born.

The violation of women's sexuality is essential if superiority over their menfolk is to be demonstrated. Women routinely suffer when there is caste or communal violence or when there are struggles between landowners and tenants or labourers. It is taken for granted in urban slums as well as in rural areas that poor or low-caste women are available for sexual abuse by those who have economic, political, or merely physical power. The paradox here is that women who are relatively less subordinated to their menfolk are more vulnerable to sexual abuse outside the home.

Analytical studies of the phenomenon of rape show that this predicament of women has ideological and material components. If women who are raped are not acceptable in what are ordinarily described as their homes, one must ask whether these homes are in fact their own.

In South-East Asia female sexuality is not placed under such severe restrictions as it is in South Asia. Besides the absence of caste, the system of descent, inheritance, and group membership, as well as residence and the nature of conjugal relations, all contribute to this. Women cannot be driven out of their homes for sexual offences. The notion of protection of women and control over them by men seems alien to the bilateral kinship system and to the ethos of the region, which is egalitarian in respect of gender. In a matrilineal system, too, men are not looked upon as the custodians of women's sexuality as they are in the patrilineal systems of South Asia. The idea that men are the *users* of women's sexuality seems to be alien to these cultures. The placement of children is not as acute a problem as it is in South Asia. In Malaysia the Islamic influence has caused young girls to be somewhat constrained, but it has been pointed out that both sexes are subject to more or less the same codes of sexual behaviour:

Although a young girl is expected to remain chaste and virtuous till she is ready for marriage and the term used for a young woman meaning unopened flower indicates greater emphasis on the virginity of women than men, male youths too are bound by strong rules of social decorum and propriety; sexual promiscuity in men is greatly condemned; a quiet demure male is much preferred as a husband or son-in-law [to] one who is known to have had sexual experiences with other women. (Karim 1987)

Once they are married, women may be much freer. They participate in economic and productive activities and are not seen as being under the control of men. Divorce and remarriage do not carry a social stigma. Behaviour appropriate to one's class is important, but there is much less differentiation based on gender than there is in South Asian societies.

In Indonesia, too, there are greater restrictions on unmarried women than there are on married women, but they are nowhere near as great as those that are placed on South Asian women. Women at the higher levels of society are demure and take care to behave in an appropriate manner, but that is true of men as well. Restrictions on physical movement are negligible. Very often women migrate to towns, leaving their husbands behind to manage the land and look after the children (Hetler 1990).

In the Philippines, despite the influence of the notions of the macho male and the feminine female taken from Spanish culture, the women are quite capable of looking after themselves. Theoretically virginity and chastity before marriage are valued, but monitored courtships and dating after engagement are quite common. As we note elsewhere in this book, children born out of marriage do not carry any strong stigma. Prostitution, which is common, is not approved of, but it is looked upon as a means of making a living. A woman is not made a permanent outcast because of it: she may leave it for a "proper" family life. There is no uncrossable dividing line between women who earn by their bodies and respectably married women.

Thailand has come to be known for the commercialization of sex. There are massage girls, others rendering personal services to foreigners, and prostitutes. A less extreme system of gender relations, where the purity of women is not fragile and where a child's social identity does not depend entirely on known paternity, may have contributed to the commercial exploitation of sex. However, this does not represent men's use of female sexuality or their control over it. No doubt there are compulsions of poverty. Many young women support their parents and siblings by taking to these professions; but they leave them after a time to get married and settle down.

58

Often their parents back in the villages may not know what their real profession is (Phongpaichit 1982). The spirit cults of northern Thailand do indicate a concern with the protection of female sexuality, particularly of young girls (Cohen and Wijeyewardene 1984), but surely the notion of sullied sexuality, a sharp distinction between virtuous women and "bad" ones, does not obtain.

South-East Asian women suffer from a lack of sufficient help from men, who, they complain, are irresponsible. But by and large they do not have to live under the tutelage, protection, and control of men. Nor do they face scandals of the kind that haunt South Asian women. The two regions differ widely in their attitude to female sexuality and in their view of women's reproductive power. This seems clearly related to the contrasting situations of women in the two regions in respect of their economic and productive roles and the avenues of earning open to them.

5

The seclusion of women

Parda (purdah) or the seclusion of women is closely related to the concern over the management of female sexuality characteristic of South Asia. In regard to the seclusion and segregation of women this region poses a sharp contrast to South-East Asia. We could compare the strongly patrilineal Muslim populations of South Asia with the bilateral and matrilineal Muslim populations of South-East Asia. Among Hindus the mechanisms are somewhat different in both form and purpose, but they do impose constraints on women, restricting movement and participation in many important areas of life.

The observance of *parda* is not uniform among all the Muslim populations of South Asia. Class is an important variable in this respect. In rural areas women who work in the fields do not generally observe *parda*. Only the women of landed and well-to-do families are confined to their houses away from the gaze of strangers. The separation between *zanana* (women's quarters) and *mardana* (men's quarters) is an important mechanism for keeping women segregated and secluded. Interestingly, as observed by Farida Shaheed (1985) in Pakistan, communities have evolved complicated sets of rules defining public and private space. These rules differ from class to class and from one social setting to another. In settled villages the fields are out of bounds for all upper-class women but not for the women of tenant or subsistence farmer families. And even among the Pathans the washing area or water-well, although situated outside the family compound, has been incorporated into the private or female domain. Throughout Pakistan economic market-places are reserved for men. Only a handful of the poorest women come into the bazaar areas.

All over South Asia *parda* among Muslims is justified by reference to Islam. Although interpretations of Quranic verses vary, and intellectuals and progressive and feminist elements argue that Islam does not prescribe seclusion for women, the common understanding is that *parda* has religious sanction.

Besides agricultural workers, other working women too may not observe *parda*. But among artisan groups such as the weavers of Varanasi, women are confined to their homes and carry on their work there. Similarly, the *chikan* (special hand embroidery) workers of Lucknow are not involved in direct communication with the contractors who buy their work. At most they may speak from behind curtains. Poor women who must work in others' homes or go to the market use the *burqa* (veil) or other form of covering while in public places.

The practice of *parda* varies according to region, community, class, and education. The women of the Pirzada community of Nizamuddin village in Delhi observe strict *parda*, because their men's status as religious functionaries would suffer otherwise. Shame and honour are associated with women's seclusion. Although ordinarily the observance of *parda* is strict among the middle classes, it is relaxed among educated families in urban areas. However, in the older parts of cities such as Bhopal, Lucknow, and Delhi, as also in Pakistan and Bangladesh, the *burqa* is still prevalent.

There is a distinction between people in whose presence the norms of seclusion have to be followed and complete strangers among whom one can remain unrecognized. This is particularly applicable in a plural society such as India. School and college girls come out of their homes properly covered but tend to discard the *burqa* once they are out of their own locality (Roy 1979, Anjum 1992).

A distinction has been made between strict, partial, intermittent, and absent *parda* (Vreede-de Stuers 1968). *Parda* of the eyes is achieved by lowering the eyelids and not looking men straight in the face. *Parda* of the voice involves remaining silent or speaking in low tones.

Shopping can be done while properly covered and moving in covered vehicles, chaperoned, but by and large women do not venture into markets. It is only groups such as the vegetable growers and sellers of central India whose women can freely sit and sell their produce. Saiyed (1976) has described the Muslims on the western coast of India, whose women lead far less circumscribed lives. Men are absent for long periods and women have to manage household affairs and take important decisions.

It would thus be wrong to assume uniformity in the observance of *parda* among the Muslims of South Asia. It is understandable that enlightened, well-informed Muslims should protest against the projection of a depressing undifferentiated picture of Muslims. It remains a fact, though, that seclusion and segregation are associated with female modesty and chastity and are symbols of status.

According to the Quran, although man and woman have similar rights over each other and are equal before God, their roles and work are different. Men are the providers. As such they are the protectors of women and in charge of them. If a man cannot provide for his household and does not control its women, his honour suffers. Women's behaviour reflects men's honour.

The ideology of *parda* with its attendant code of behaviour permeates all spheres of life (Shaheed 1985). *Parda* segregates men and women and confines women to household activities. Girls face elders' reluctance to send them to school and college. Low literacy, low participation in the labour force, restrictions on middle-class women's taking up employment where they may have to encounter strangers, women's inability to look after their own property, resulting in dependence on men, their lack of knowledge stemming from lack of exposure to the world – all these can be attributed to segregation and seclusion. It is difficult for women who live in seclusion to fight for their rights relating to resources and property, shelter and children. Nor can they interact in dyadic relations with confidence.

The physical mobility of Javanese women is a sharp contrast to the seclusion and the confinement to the homestead of Muslim women in rural Bangladesh, who have traditionally not participated in paddy cultivation, and to that of women in rural Pakistan, who work in the family fields but are restricted in their movements, having to veil themselves when outside the village. The same applies to rural Muslims in India. Trading, a common activity among the women of Java, is unthinkable for these women because it involves dealing with strangers and moving unescorted amidst them.

In the villages of Bangladesh and Pakistan there is a sharp segregation of the sexes, with women coming out into public spaces only when men are absent, or else with the prescribed covering. Women among the matrilineal Minangkabau in Indonesia, in Negri Sembilan in Malaysia, and on the Lakshadweep islands have not been thus constrained by strict segregation or seclusion. They take part in economic activities outside the home and the homestead and interact with men.

Women in other parts of Malaysia that follow the bilateral pattern of kinship have also been known for freedom of movement, the absence of seclusion, and independent involvement in economic activities. Attending educational institutions does not pose problems of chaperoning and protection. The relatively recent social movement demanding conformity with Islamic injunctions has brought in a special cloak that covers the hair, neck, and arms and also covers the bust with a double thickness of fabric. A similar cloak is being adopted by women on the Lakshadweep islands, if only for special public occasions.

Malaysian men who complete the Haj pilgrimage are often converted to the desirability of the veil for women, but their wives may remain unconvinced. Women argue that they will adopt the veil only if the Quran in the original asks them to do so (personal information). Older women are particularly opposed to the use of the cloak and argue with their sons-in-law in defence of their daughters' right not to take to the portable *parda*. One of their arguments is: "This is not our custom. We have never done it. Have we not been good Muslims?" Again, "My daughter is going to find it extremely uncomfortable and inconvenient."

But the pressure to cover the head and to use the cloak continues to grow. In Kedah, for instance, recorded messages are broadcast through loudspeakers telling men that their prayers to Allah will go to waste if their wives, mothers, and sisters do not take to the cloak. A compromise has evolved in the form of a scarf that covers the hair; but even this is used by many women only when they go out with their husbands or other male relatives who insist on the observance of a certain degree of *parda* for the sake of Islam.

We may note, however, that the Malaysian cloak does not seem to impose constraints and disabilities comparable to those imposed by the *burqa*, the *chadar*, and other measures of keeping women invisible in South Asia. The latter symbolize seclusion in no uncertain terms. They also represent a "symbolic shelter" (Papanek 1982b) for women, who are believed to need protection, care, and control. Moreover, women's sexuality is seen as a threat to men, who find it difficult to control themselves in their presence (see articles in Papanek and Minault 1982). By contrast, Malaysian women who wear the cloak do not cover their faces; and they move about with confidence and do not seem to hesitate in carrying on necessary interaction with men. Educated women in Kuala Lumpur who wear the cloak do so out of a conviction of its appropriateness to religious

63

injunctions. The assumptions that underlie the seclusion of South Asian Muslim women are not apparent in the Indonesian or Malaysian contexts. A comparison of the childhood experiences of women from the two regions and of their perceptions of themselves would bring out the difference clearly.

How can we explain the great differences that exist among followers of Islam in the two regions in respect of seclusion and the mobility of women? It seems to me that, although there are many ramifications to be worked out, in the final analysis it is the principles and ideology of kinship that need close examination. Can it be a mere coincidence that women in bilateral and matrilineal Muslim communities do not observe seclusion whereas for women in patrilineal and patri-virilocal kinship organization it has become a mark of identity?

Islam assumes patriliny to be the natural form of social organization and lays down a code of conduct and a system of law in keeping with it. The notions of male superiority, a father's rights over his children, and his obligation to support his wife and children, and an emphasis on woman's dependence and obedience all fit well into patrilineal descent and patri-virilocal residence. A man's right over a woman's sexuality is established by *nikah*. Virginity and marital fidelity become necessary virtues for a woman. Seclusion, which firmly controls women's sexuality, is a useful device, even if not always successful (D. Jacobson 1982), to ensure their virginity prior to marriage and the identification of the paternity of their offspring. It creates circumstances that make a woman entirely dependent on the men of the family. In South Asia, *parda* has drawn its legitimacy both from the kinship organization and from religion and has served to sustain a strongly patriarchal family structure as well as unequal gender relations.

It should be reiterated here that, in most of India, Muslim women involved in agricultural or other productive or selling activities do not observe strict *parda*. It is also not generally necessary to observe *parda* within one's own village. However, sexual segregation and a demeanour befitting it constitute an essential aspect of women's lives. *Parda* is a mark of status and is indicative of upward mobility. At the same time, higher education, employment, and high family status make women free of strict *parda*.

Here I shall not dwell very extensively on *parda*. Some communities among South Asian Muslims follow very strict *parda* while others – for instance the Khoja Ismailis, followers of the Aga Khan –

have almost discarded the veil. *Parda* may not be practised among the educated élite, but segregation of the sexes is visible at ostensibly mixed parties. Among the middle and lower classes the *burqa* is often replaced by a *dupatta*, which covers the head and the chest.

What does the imposition of a veil mean to a girl who looks towards the world with eagerness and expectation? "The Library Girl," a story by Vishwapriya Iyengar (1990, 1991), describes the first time that Talat, a girl fond of books and a regular visitor to the library, goes there in a *burqa*. To her horror she finds that none of those whom she greeted on her way to the library can recognize her. To them all she has become a stranger, just a woman clad in a *burqa*.

Within the veil, a darkness seized Talat. It had bandaged her mouth, her eyes, and sealed her voice. Today her smiles had lit nothing.... She had wanted to lift the veil and say, "Look – it's me, only me in a Persian robe. It is a joke". Aziza [the librarian] had seen a woman in a *burqa* waving her hands, falling down and weeping; she did not realize it was Talat eagerly coming to borrow the book which Aziza had promised her. All communication with the outside world had snapped. Talat had become unrecognizable.

Papanek (1982b: 14) has stated that women in *burqas* are experienced as non-persons by those who are not used to such a sight, particularly Westerners. It remains to be explored further whether such women themselves feel depersonalized and whether they are perceived as less than persons by those who interact with them.

Against this background the total or relative absence of seclusion in South-East Asia and in the Lakshadweep islands needs to be viewed as a function of the bilateral and matrilineal forms of kinship organization found there. Marriage has a different texture and character in terms of the relationship between spouses, rights over children, choice of residence, and also access to and rights over strategic resources. Certainly kinship organization, which makes for relatively egalitarian relations between spouses and between the sexes in general, women's rights over resources and children, and active participation by women in production, pre-dated the adoption of Islam in these societies. Given this, the ideology of seclusion could not take root. The institutions of marriage and divorce and the forms of rites of passage are ostensibly Islamic but their texture is different. These societies offer institutionalized choices in such matters as entering and leaving marriage, marital residence, and the nurturing of children. The absence of seclusion has enabled women to use these choices and assert their bargaining power.

65

Parda among the Hindus needs to be distinguished from that among the Muslims of South Asia both in respect of its meaning and in respect of the details of its practice. The notion of women as *fitna*, signifying danger, and the concern with protecting men from temptation by keeping women unseen and unheard are essentially a part of Muslim *parda*. The physical invisibility of women achieved through the organization of space into interior and exterior and through the use of cloaks and covered vehicles is indicative of the conceptions of the seductive female and the vulnerable male. The aim is to protect the male by making women silent and invisible. Women, on the other hand, are allowed to see men through veils and curtains and to hear their voices. Women's sexuality, also vulnerable, is controlled through their very invisibility.

Segregation among the Hindus perhaps aims not so much at protecting men as at protecting female sexuality. The difference is subtle: it is not denied that men are attracted towards women, but this attraction poses a grave risk for female rather than for male sexuality. Restraints on behaviour and movement are particularly stringent for unmarried post-pubertal girls and pre-menopausal widows.

Seclusion among Hindus varies across regions, communities, and classes. Muslim *parda* seems to have influenced communities such as the Rajputs and Charans (bards) of Rajasthan, the Marathas of Maharashtra, and high-class Reddis and Velmas of Andhra Pradesh. The Oswals of Rajasthan are known for strict *parda* (Mehta 1982). In southern India, interaction between the sexes is controlled through the segregation of spaces within the house, either absolutely or for specific purposes and particular hours. Many languages make a clear distinction between inner and outer spaces. Age is an important factor in determining which spaces a person may enter, as is kinship status to some degree. The entry of outsiders is very strictly controlled. Even in the absence of veiling, a proper demeanour, the maintenance of physical distance, and proper modes of speech serve as mechanisms for the management of female sexuality. They also help in the preservation of kinship norms, an important component of north Indian Hindu *parda*.

As I explain elsewhere, the phenomenon of boundary maintenance characteristic of caste society places special responsibilities on women. This objective is served by patterns of segregation and by controlled physical mobility and social interaction even without seclusion or veiling. Caste as a bounded group is generally stronger in southern India, where there is a correspondingly greater concern with the purity of blood and hence with the purity of women. Everywhere the concern that women do not mate with men of lower caste is stronger among the higher castes.

One of the indicators of position in the caste hierarchy is strictness over women's movements and social contacts. Women immured in the home, women working in their own fields, women working in others' fields, and women working for wages outside the village tend to be graded in that order. Women's behaviour thus becomes the concern of men. Uncontrolled female sexuality is a danger to the purity of both the agnatic group and the caste group. The theme of female chastity, with its miraculous powers, and that of the dangers of uncontrolled female sexuality are prominent in mythology as well as in folk literature (Wadley 1980, Beck 1974).

Although there is no *parda* in southern India except in a few castes, segregation and social and physical distance – seen very clearly, for instance, in public transport – serve the same function to some extent. Although women are to be seen in the market-place as sellers and as buyers, they have far less freedom of movement than women in South-East Asia. Johanna Lessinger's (1990) study of women vegetable sellers in Madras city brings this out clearly.

Although not as distinct or as rigid as among Muslims, the practice of *parda* has formed part of the way of life of the Hindus of northern and central India. It has decreased enormously over the past few decades, but it still exists on a large scale in the old quarters of cities, in small towns, and in villages.

The division of domestic space and the veiling of women's faces are important features of Hindu *parda*. To my mind the control of female sexuality – vulnerable and therefore in need of protection – forms one aspect of Hindu *parda*. However, whereas Muslim *parda* is directed towards keeping women out of the sight of strangers and outsiders, among Hindus segregation and veiling are strongly linked to rules of kinship and marriage.

A clear distinction is made between natal and affinal kin. A woman does not have to observe *parda* with her kin in her natal home, but for a married woman there are strict rules to be followed in relation to affinal kin senior in generation or in age to her husband. They are to be avoided so far as is possible, and in their presence her face and body must be properly covered. To quote Doranne Jacobson (1982), who worked in a village in central India:

Ideally, a man never sees a daughter-in-law's face, nor does he ever converse with her. When a man enters a courtyard or house, he makes coughing or throat-clearing noises to warn the women within of his approach. The women can identify individual men by these noises and act accordingly. At the approach of an elder brother-in-law or father-in-law, a woman stops talking and quickly pulls her sari down low over her face, keeping the cloth loose so that none of her features may be distinguished (*ghunghat karna*). At the arrival of a seldom-seen elder male affine, some young women retire to an inner room of the house and do not show even their veiled forms to the visitor.

She says further that young brides of high castes observe the most stringent *parda*. It is only with years of living in the family and with a rise in kinship status and age that *parda* is relaxed. The *parda* of the women of lower castes is less stringent. That Hindu rules of seclusion and veiling go beyond sexual concerns and into the realm of relations within a family or kin group and between affinal kin groups is evident from the fact that women observe *parda* even in the presence of certain women such as the mother-in-law, the grandmother-in-law, the husband's elder sister, and other classificatory relatives of a similar kinship status.

Anthropologists who have written on Hindu *parda* have made a clear distinction between natal kin and village and affinal kin and village. A woman, married or unmarried, is free to move about in her natal village; whereas a married woman in her affinal home must observe strict segregation and seclusion (Minturn and Hitchcock 1963, D. Jacobson 1982, Luschinsky 1962). The contrast is sharper in regions that have practised village exogamy.

In the presence of elders a young wife has to veil herself and refrain from communicating with her husband. Sexuality and special bonds of interest and affection must not be made apparent. This is a mark of respect for elders and also keeps under control the possible conflict between mother-in-law and daughter-in-law over the affections of the same man. Such *parda* – avoidance based on respect – helps maintain a certain harmony in a joint family by keeping in line with relations of authority and hierarchy. Although this is not openly expressed, the veiling of younger women is also meant to avoid disruption in the family by keeping control over sexuality and avoiding situations in which the husband's male kin might be tempted by the young wife's attractions. This does not mean, of course, that Hindu *parda* restrictions effectively prevent extramarital sexual activity (D. Jacobson 1982, U. Sharma 1980).

In Nepal no *parda* is observed by women, but, as Lynn Bennett (1983: 173) says, "the idiom of *parda* is used to express a woman's respect–avoidance relationship with senior affinal males. A daughter-in-law usually pulls the end of her sari up to cover her head in front of her father-in-law and she is expected to always do this in the presence of her husband's elder brother."

Parda among Hindus is thus viewed as a mechanism for maintaining the solidarity of a joint family or an agnatic kin group in the face of the entry of outsiders. Affinal women are necessary for the perpetuation of the lineage, but they must be kept under control so that they cause no disruption. The practice is a clear reflection of the deep distrust in which an agnatic group holds affinal women. It also reflects on the fickle nature of males and the possibility of the use of power on their part. Incorporated women try to control the new entrants. As Jacobson has pointed out, the various expressions of respect expected of a young wife restate and reaffirm her subordinate status, her alienness, the dangers associated with her entry, and the need to control her sexuality and possible rise in her power and influence.

Respect–avoidance practices by women towards their affines are not completely alien to many Muslim communities in South Asia (Vatuk 1982, Jeffrey 1979, Vreede de-Stuers 1968). At the same time, in stressing the contrast between natal village and affinal village, anthropologists have ignored the use that is made by Hindu women in northern and central India of degrees of *parda* with outsiders and in public places. These rules are applied, as Vatuk (1982: 60) has said, selectively according to a woman's age, marital status, and position in the life cycle, besides her rank and social status.

Finally it must be said that for both the concerns that form the basis of *parda* – the protection of women from potentially threatening outsiders and the observance of relationships of respect within the family and kindred (Vatuk 1982: 62) – patriliny and patrilocality provide fertile soil. *Parda* aggravates the disadvantages and disabilities that are women's lot in such kinship systems. It reinforces and perpetuates their dependence and denies them opportunities for development.

6

Bodily processes and limitations on women

For Muslims the association of *napak* (impure) for menstrual and parturient blood has a religious basis. Menstruation and parturition are polluted states during which women are forbidden to pray, fast, or touch the Quran. This basic belief is common throughout South and South-East Asia, but there are distinct differences between the two regions. The acknowledgement of menarche as a coming of age, demanding special circumscription, is more marked in Bangladesh, India, and Pakistan. Among the matrilineal Muslims of the Lakshadweep islands the onset of puberty used to be celebrated, but that seems to have been a legacy of the people's distant Hindu past. It fitted well with the matrilineal ideology, in which fertility has a special significance.

Among the Muslims of South Asia menarche signals a girl's vulnerability and requires mechanisms to protect her from the opposite sex. If not already begun, segregation and seclusion have to be implemented. Even where strict *parda* is not observed, a certain demeanour has to be acquired and physical and social distance have to be maintained. Restrictions are imposed on a pubescent girl's movement, particularly outside the home, and greater care is taken over chaperoning and escorting. Within the kin group, interaction with male cousins is controlled or altogether forbidden. In Blanchet's (1984: 38) words, "it is her initiation to the restrictions a woman must observe, it is the beginning of her *purdah*."

"A significant symbol of gender distinction in Bengali society is ritual pollutability of females" (Aziz and Maloney 1985: 79–80). Blanchet (1984: 38) dwells at some length on the rituals of the first menstruation in village Miyapur in Bangladesh. "Menstruation is impure but, if properly contained, it is also auspicious as it symbolizes and announces in a positive way a woman's generative potential." In Miyapur the rituals of the first menstruation are minimal and private. The event is regarded as auspicious. It is discreetly handled by the women of the household, without any big display or much expense. A married woman briefs the girl about the danger of her polluted condition. She is told that she must not endanger anyone by preparing or serving food, or go barefoot lest she pollute the earth, or touch anyone with a skin or eye infection lest she make it worse. The pollution of the first menstruation is especially severe and demands great caution. It is believed that, if the necessary precautions are not observed, Lokkhi (Lakshmi), the goddess of wealth and good fortune, will forsake the unfortunate girl, who will then be unable to bring *unnoti* (prosperity) to her husband.

The newly mature girl observes the rules relating to pollution and all the necessary prescriptions so as not to anger spirits such as *bhut*, *jinn*, Kwaz, Kali, and Lokkhi. All these beings are believed to react to pollution. Blanchet (1984: 40–41) observes: "They may be god-protector of another *jati* [caste or religious group], but they have power over Muslims. They are considered as 'spirits of the land' and every woman who dwells on their territory must mind their power." And the threat is great: "Women's pollution is a danger to cows, field, grain and river, which are not only symbols of fertility but the very elements on which the traditional rural economy of Bangladesh is based" (1984: 48).

With Blanchet's Bangladeshi Muslims we may also take note of the Pirzada women near Delhi studied by Jeffrey (1978), who are forbidden during the period of pollution to carry on those activities that connect them with their husband's means of livelihood: they are forbidden to sew curtains for the saint's tomb or prepare sweets for the pilgrims.

According to Mahmuda Islam (personal communication) and others, observances relating to menstruation and menarche are not uniform throughout Bangladesh. For instance, Aziz and Maloney (1985: 79) write that "often [a menstruating woman] can work in the kitchen after taking a bath.... But avoidance of the cowshed and of fields with standing crops is widely observed. Almost all our respondents said she cannot visit a sick person, and all agree that she cannot say prayers or touch a holy book."

Despite these variations, it becomes abundantly clear that there are many restrictions on menstruating women, with their bases in the beliefs of the people, and that this particular bodily process makes women distinctly inferior to men. By and large, though, restrictions on cooking and other household work are not a feature of South Asian Muslims' way of life. Dangers to menstruating women from ghosts and spirits are believed in by some groups, depending on region and socio-economic level. The prohibition on religious activity during menstruation is of course universal.

Among the Malays menarche is not a ritual occasion and is not marked by any celebration or rejoicing. Nor do there seem to be any prescriptions or proscriptions attending the first menstruation. Instead it is childbirth that is thought a significant event, changing a girl into a woman (Laderman 1983). Of course, in preparation for her future role and for her own dignity, a girl's behaviour becomes somewhat circumspect after puberty. The people's perception that Islam requires a first-time bride to be a virgin causes restrictions to be placed upon young girls. In Java as well, although unmarried girls are expected to be modest and cautious in their behaviour, the onset of puberty is not marked as a distinct stage.

Another difference between South Asia and South-East Asia is also striking. In Bangladesh, menstrual blood as well as the blood of parturition are believed to attract evil spirits, ghosts, and even some Hindu deities, as we have seen. In Malaysia, on the other hand, the somewhat more realistic belief is that menstrual blood is so dirty and smelly that it does not attract the Earth Spirit and his company. A new mother, however, requires care and protection – for the blood of parturition is sweet and dangerously attractive.

These bodily processes do not seem to be regarded as strong sources of pollution by the Tagalog or the Thai. Christianity and the bilateral ethos together keep the Tagalog away from notions of pollution caused by bodily processes. For Theravada Buddhism, however, it is women's involvement in the bodily processes, including procreation and the nurturing of the young, that makes them unfit for ordination. As van Esterik (1982b: 77–78) observes,

Women are viewed as being more rooted in the world and are the center of household stability.... In contrast to monks who are less attached to this world and should be following the path of increasing detachment and ultimate extinction, all women are "tied to" the opposite process of becoming, through their reproductive capacities. As convenient symbols for fertility, women are the specialists in the "becoming" – the production and nurturance of children.... The attachment that individual women feel for their children means that women do not meet the conditions for ordination as monks.

Among the Sinhala people "the biological potential of women to become mothers is ... at the core of their cultural degradation and restriction: their supposed impurity makes women especially vulnerable to evil spirits; it circumscribes their behaviour and defines their bodies and minds as being inferior to those of the male" (Schrijvers 1985: 125).

Schrijvers asserts that this ideological discrimination is supported by the way in which villagers in the North Central Province interpret Buddhism, the religion of the majority. She quotes AmaraSingham (1978: 104), who relates the representation of women in Sinhalese Buddhist religion to their maternal functions:

Women represent involvement in life because they are the ones who give birth and thus perpetuate the *karmic* round.... In the great tradition certain meanings are given to women: sensuality, desire, and attachment. And most importantly, because women embody birth, they become a metaphor for the *karmic* energy that maintains suffering in the world.... only as a man can one achieve *nirvana* (transcendence).

Kinship among the Sinhalese is not strongly patrilocal. Its base is bilateral, both sons and daughters being entitled to receive land. However, residence is crucial in determining a daughter's right to land. A daughter who marries the *diga* way, leaving the natal home for virilocal residence, is entitled to a movable dowry; whereas one who marries the *binna* way, adopting uxorilocal residence, is given immovable property such as land. It is said that if a *diga* married woman returns to her natal home she is entitled to a share of land there (for variations and details see Palriwala 1994). It appears that it is not kinship but religion that devalues women and that the institution of caste has made the Sinhalese particularly concerned about the purity of women (Yalman 1963). This point needs further exploration, for special rituals at menarche have traditionally been practised both among the matrilineal Muslims of Batticaloa and among the Christians of Sri Lanka (McGilveray 1982, Winslow 1980).

There appears to be a contrast between the Thai and Sinhala traditions, Buddhist though they both are. The view of the first menstruation as a turning point, deserving of rejoicing as well as the placing of restrictions, seems to be related to the presence of castes.

In its recruitment, caste is essentially a principle of bilateral affiliation, and women's role in biological reproduction puts on them the onus of boundary maintenance. In caste societies there is thus a special concern for the purity of women. Special note is taken of menarche, which signifies emergent sexuality (Yalman 1963).

Among the lowland Catholic Filipinos, pollution is not associated with menstruation and childbirth nor is there any special importance attached to menarche. Girls may be asked to be careful in their relations with the opposite sex, but segregation and seclusion of the kind that is seen in India are unthinkable.

Menstruation and childbirth are strong sources of pollution among the Hindus of South Asia, where they make women intrinsically less pure than men (L. Dube 1996, Ferro-Luzzi 1974, Krygier 1982). Thus there is, within a caste, a hierarchy based on gender. It is well known that the ritual and existential concerns of purity and pollution underlie the hierarchy of castes. There is a pervasive notion that women never attain the level of purity of men of their own castes, essentially because of the self-pollution that they incur through bodily processes. They are therefore regarded as unfit for many roles in the sphere of rituals and worship. Priestly functions and the worship of certain deities are not permitted to them.

Food constitutes a critical element in the ritual idiom of purity and pollution. The ritual impurity of menstrual blood prohibits women the use of specific spaces and the handling of certain kinds of food. Brahmin and Chhetri women in Nepal say that during the first three days of menses they become like female dogs: untouchable. During this time a woman may not enter the kitchen or touch food or water of which others are to partake. Nor may they worship the gods or the spirits of ancestors (Bennett 1983: 215). Similar taboos apply to women in Hindu India.

Such observances vary, however, with caste level. Broadly speaking, women of the higher castes are expected to follow stricter rules of behaviour (Ferro-Luzzi 1974, Dhruvarajan 1989, L. Dube 1996). Ethnographies of castes and of villages bring this out clearly. Thus, whereas menstruating women among the higher castes keep out of ordinary circulation and household activities, those of many middle and low castes consider a bath and the washing of their hair sufficient to make them fit for ordinary cooking and most household work. Many urban, educated families even among the higher castes have done away with restrictions on routine activity during menstruation.

But menstruating women at all caste levels everywhere still keep away from participation in rituals and worship.

In India and in Nepal, women observe a special *vrata* (vow or ritual observance) each year on Rishipanchami to expiate any sin that they may have accumulated, even inadvertently, by not observing menstrual taboos. The mythological recitation made on this day clearly indicates that the defaulting woman's husband also has to suffer for her sin (Bennett 1983: 218–234, Carter 1983).

Parturition makes a Hindu woman untouchable only briefly. For some time thereafter she is subject to a very few constraints, being only partially excluded from work. (In a different way, childbirth affects the entire agnatic familial grouping: minor pollution attaches to females as well as to males and imposes restrictions on entering temples and on participating in rituals.)

Patriliny and caste combine to create a perception of menstrual blood as particularly threatening, as I discuss in the chapter on women's sexuality. This is clearly expressed in the special ritual value accorded to females in the pre-pubertal phase, which is looked upon as one of intrinsic purity and celebrated in a number of ways. The custom of worshipping and feeding virgin girls is widespread in India. They are given special recognition in life-cycle rituals. This phase contrasts sharply with the next one, that of puberty, menstruation, and emergent sexuality.

Puberty introduces dramatic changes into the life of a girl. In many Indian languages menstruation is likened to the process of flowering or blossoming – the necessary stage before fruit can appear – and expressions such as "her body is ripe," "it is ready," "it is full" are common. References to her having become a woman, "knowledgeable," and so on all express the fact of a girl's change of status at puberty. In southern India this change of status is marked by rituals and ceremonies. Common features are the seclusion of the girl for a certain number of days in recognition of her polluted state; *arti*, the waving of a lamp to signify the auspiciousness of the occasion and to ward off evil; and special food and gifts for the girl (Kolenda 1984, L. Dube 1988a,b). In many communities in Orissa and Maharashtra we see the essential features of puberty rituals. Elsewhere in India the event is taken care of unobtrusively.

Although the details differ from place to place and from caste to caste, the core is the same and the message is clear: the girl has become a sexual being. This calls for restrained behaviour on her part and for protection and vigilance by others. An unrelenting control over a woman's sexuality begins at puberty and ends only with the menopause, which is unsurprisingly seen as a point of liberation. The most critical period is between menarche and marriage, the point at which she obtains a legitimate seed-giver (L. Dube 1986).

In Nepal the puberty of a girl is marked by confinement and special rituals. The Newar, who celebrate *ihi* (pre-pubertal mock marriage to the deity Narayan), take special note of menarche (Allen 1982a). Among the upper-caste Parbatiyas the event is marked by the immediate removal of the girl from her home and her seclusion in a dark, windowless room described as a cave. She may not see or be seen by Surya, the Sun God, or her male natal kin. At the end of her seclusion she takes a purificatory bath and receives from her father and brothers a red *sari*, a blouse, and the accessories of a married woman, signifying "a complete transference of the daughter's nascent sexuality away from her natal group and to another patriline" (Bennett 1983: 240). Bennett also makes the point that her sexuality is culturally asserted through her strict avoidance of her male natal kin during the period of seclusion.

A brief reference to ethno-reproductive beliefs will not be out of place here. They tell us about notions concerning the roles of the two sexes in procreation and provide the rationale and the justification for rights – or lack of rights – over children and in inheritance and succession.

Almost all over patrilineal India the process of biological reproduction is described with the metaphorical use of the terms "seed" and "earth" (or "field"). The seed symbolizes the father's contribution and the earth represents the part played by the mother (Inden and Nicholas 1977, L. Dube 1986). The seed is of the essence, because it determines the variety: the child's identity for placement within a kinship group is derived from its father. The seed is contained in semen, which is believed to come from the blood; hence a child shares its father's bloodline, which is how a patriline is viewed. Males are the transmitters of the blood of a patriline. The mother's role is to nourish and augment what her womb has received. Milk is also derived from blood, but a mother's blood does not give social identity to her child.

From ancient times the process of human reproduction has been visualized in terms of a male seed germinating in a female field. There is also the idea that male and female both have reproductive fluids whose mingling is essential for conception to occur, but the seed–field metaphor is much more important. References to it are found in marriage rituals, books of law, the deliberations of village councils, and popular sayings. The notion is part of literate traditions as well as of people's consciousness. Besides Hindus, patrilineal tribal communities as well as Muslims subscribe to it (L. Dube 1986, Jeffrey 1981). The metaphor of seed and field is recorded in a series of well-known ethnographies (quoted in L. Dube 1986), but its implications for the situation of women and for gender relations are not elaborated.

Nature is thus seen as having assigned unequal roles to the two sexes in procreation. Although the mother–child bond is emphasized, in the final analysis a woman is only a receptacle, an instrument for the perpetuation of the line of her child's father. Thus the mother's role is explicated in a manner that excludes her from the line of sharers of blood and property. The metaphor provides a clear rationalization for a kinship system that alienates women from productive resources and denies their rights over their own labour and their offspring (L. Dube 1986).

This view is found throughout patrilineal India. Even in the south, where elements of bilaterality can be seen and where patriliny is claimed to exist in a reluctant form, particularly among non-Brahmins, it applies to group affiliation. Even in justifying cross-cousin marriage, it is argued that the partners after all do belong to different patrilines.

Among matrilineal communities, on the other hand, the mother's blood gives a child its social identity. It is said that the womb "dyes" the baby. A child shares its blood with its mother and her matrikin. "A maternal uncle is one's own blood, while a father provides only pus," say the Khasi (Tiplut Nongbri, personal communication).

Beliefs about conception differ between South Asian and South-East Asian Muslims. In Bangladesh and India it is common for patrilineal Muslims to think, as the Hindus do, in terms of the seed–field metaphor, in which man is the active agent (Jeffrey 1978, Blanchet 1984, Aziz 1979, Aziz and Maloney 1985). A woman's blood is not completely ignored, for consanguinity is taken into account: those who claim descent from Fatima, the Prophet's daughter, are held to be higher in status than others. The logic of marrying within a *khandan* (extended family or kin group, patrilineal descent group) also takes into account the quality of woman's blood. But, by and

77

large, the father's contribution – determining a child's social identity within patrilineal descent and his rights over his children – is deemed to be far greater than the mother's.

For Malaysia various sources including personal interviews indicate the presence of the belief that the father will have been pregnant for 40 days before conception takes place in the mother's womb. A baby's existence begins in the father's brain, and having experienced his rationality and emotions it descends to the penis. In its mother's womb, according to midwives and most of the people to whom Laderman (1983) spoke, the baby finds a resting place, like a seed planted in nourishing earth. "Already formed from the four elements of which the world is made, it will develop in the darkness of its mother's body until it can emerge, like a flower, into the light" (Laderman 1983: 92). Laderman adds that this theory is not acceptable to all in its totality. According to *bomoh* (Malay indigenous medical practitioners), who are acknowledged to have more learning than midwives, the baby is incomplete as it makes its way through its father's body; and it needs the addition of its mother's earth, air, fire, and water before it can develop into a human being (Laderman 1983).

When pregnancy is induced by the falling of the seed, the opening of the womb is thought to close, glued shut by a mixture of reproductive fluids.[1] At first the baby is itself a mixture of fluids, but when a month has passed it is a lump of blood (Laderman 1983: 85). It is rather vaguely assumed that these beliefs are drawn at least in part from Islamic notions, particularly in assigning to the father the roles of originator and contributor of rationality.

Thai beliefs are rooted in popular culture and in the teachings of Buddha. Conception is believed to occur when a soul flies into the womb of a woman during sexual intercourse. The teachings of Buddha state that, for rebirth to take place, not only must mother and father come together, but the one to be reborn must also be present. It is believed that the baby's body begins as a hair and is strengthened with semen by its father. Food eaten by the mother is transformed into blood that builds up the baby's body. For the first three months the baby is a clump of blood. Later it starts to move, this phenomenon being the result of its soul's flitting in and out of its heart.

I could not get much material on this area in the Philippines, but Filipinos seem to give equal importance to father's and mother's blood. Two kinds of fluid have to mingle for conception to occur.

There is no related explanation offered for the affiliation of a child with its father's name. The notion of male seed falling into female field is present; but the recognition of both parents accords with the bilateral kinship system.

In both South Asia and South-East Asia, pregnancy and childbirth are seen as involving danger. A woman's first pregnancy is proof of her fecundity and a matter for rejoicing. At the same time, she and the baby in her womb are vulnerable and need protection from the evil eye, malign spirits, and ghosts. Except in some regions (see Jeffrey et al. 1989 for the Bijnor area), generally care is bestowed on a pregnant woman. There are dos and don'ts concerning safe and unsafe places, appropriate foods and activities (Tan 1973, Strange 1981, Laderman 1983, Geertz 1961, Dhruvarajan 1989, Aziz 1979, Aziz and Maloney 1985, M. Islam 1980, 1985).

The cravings that pregnant women have receive special attention. It is believed that if they remain unfulfilled the baby may be born with defects. A treatise on the ancient Indian medical system *ayurveda* holds that if a desire of a sense organ of a pregnant woman is not fulfilled, that organ of the foetus will either suffer pain or become defective (L. Dube 1986).

In a Malay village described by Strange (1981), during the seventh month of a first pregnancy an important ceremony called "swaying the stomach" is held. It is believed to ward off misfortune, and some think that through a mystic influence it prepares the woman for an easy delivery. Although this ceremony is a part of *adat*, some Islamic elements have been added: pious and respected men are invited to recite verses from the Quran and to pray. Laderman (1983: 87) describes the special rites that must be performed during a first pregnancy to ensure ease of labour and safe birth.

Koentjaraningrat (1985: 103) mentions an important ceremony conducted by both rural and urban Javanese in the seventh month of a pregnancy. He asserts that the people have an ambivalent attitude towards it: "On the one hand, it is a happy anticipatory announcement of a birth, but on the other hand it includes elements which stress the dangers of childbirth." Many of the taboos and regulations he describes, most of them symbolic, have their counterparts in other societies of South and South-East Asia.

Thai women fear the invasion of the womb by the supernatural during pregnancy, which is seen as a time of danger. A number of customs, traditions, and rituals exist to protect a pregnant woman and her unborn child. For instance, she must not drive nails or sew up the ends of a pillow or a mattress, for these actions may cause the closure of the birth canal. The expectant mother's food cravings are thought to be those of the baby in her womb; and some foods are specially eaten to make the baby strong and to foster religious faith in it (Rajadhon 1961).

In South Asia, too, the first pregnancy of a woman is taken special note of. The most common elements are feeding the expectant mother with choice foods and those that she asks for, and giving her presents and blessings. This appears to be prevalent among all communities, including tribal groups and working-class people. Generally both the natal family and the affinal family, as also other relatives and friends, feed the expectant mother. Interestingly, although the safety of both mother and child is desired, spontaneous expressions may give away the real concern.

The content of the blessings and the songs that are sung is also interesting. "May you give birth to a healthy and beautiful son" is a common blessing. In songs the pregnancy cravings and labour pains of the mothers of Rama and Krishna, the two important incarnations of Vishnu, are narrated. The hope is expressed that the expectant mother will bear a son like these. In *shat*, a ceremony in Bangladesh at which the expectant mother is fed special foods, it is customary to invite a few children to share the food with the woman from the same plate. Only male children may eat from the same plate so that the birth of a son is assured. Girls may be present but are advised to eat separately (Mahmuda Islam, personal communication).

In modern medical ethics a mother's life is held to be more valuable than that of the child to be born. The views of natal and affinal families on this matter are difficult to assess. There is a firm notion rooted in the patrilineal ethos that an expectant mother is better cared for in her natal home. The baby, however, is held to belong to its father's family. It is interesting to note that, according to Catholic ideas, a child's life is more valuable than that of its mother, and this dictum should guide the actions of whoever is conducting its delivery (Rowena Robinson, personal communication).

Although in all these matters there are broad similarities among the cultures under consideration, a few differences may be discerned. The data from patrilineal South Asia give the impression that there is greater concern for the baby than for the mother-to-be. In several parts of India a woman is brought to her natal home for childbirth, particularly her first, because it is thought that she will not feel free in her affinal home, or be cared for so well. Elsewhere the baby is born in its father's home, for that is where it was conceived, and that will become its own home (Vatuk 1975, Jeffrey et al. 1989). This greater concern for the unborn child seems an intrinsic feature of the patrilineal system. A saying is prevalent in South Asia: if a son dies, that is the end of the line; but if a daughter-in-law dies there will be a wedding in the house (Dhruvarajan 1989). The daughter-in-law is replaceable, her role instrumental.

The childbirth practices described in various ethnographies of South-East Asia express great concern for the mother as well. This concern is not exactly lacking in South Asia, but in the affinal home the husband of the woman is not supposed to express it openly and the woman too is expected to contain herself. It is the people in her natal home who are most concerned about her well-being, but in those parts of north India where the pregnancy of a daughter is viewed as directly indicative of her sexuality (Vatuk 1975) it must not be made much of. She must be left largely to her fate. In the rest of India, among all communities concern is expressed for an expectant daughter, though often with caution: if the baby is to be born in the affinal home, care must be taken that concern shown for her does not imply that she is not being well cared for.

The total dependence of foetus and child on its mother is recognized in both regions. In patrilineal South Asia this bond has been turned into the strongest obligation for a mother: she must make great sacrifices – and indeed her role is given much cultural veneration – but her right to her offspring remains a purely moral one. In South-East Asia, on the other hand, the mother–child bond not only gives moral rights to mothers, it very often ignores even the religious or legal rights of fathers. Children always remain close to their mothers, and in the event of divorce or separation often cannot be separated from her.

A major point of contrast is the preference, or its absence, for children of a particular gender. In patrilineal South Asian societies the marked preference for sons is apparent in the ceremonies conducted during pregnancy and in the blessings that an expectant mother receives. In Pakistan a wife's ill health or her failure to produce sons are the two principal reasons for polygyny. The absence of male children results in the demand for more children. Female children are considered a bother and a problem for the honour of the family. A close watch must be kept on them and later they must be sent away with dowries. This negative evaluation results in tampering with bodily processes and approaching supernatural forces to achieve desired ends. In matrilineal societies a daughter is necessary for the continuation of the lineage, and in Thailand a son is valued because he brings merit to his parents through monkhood – but a daughter is also welcome, and certainly her birth is not treated as an unmitigated disaster.

7

Women and living spaces

Women's sense of security is crucially linked to their relationship with living space, which varies with residence rules, rights over material resources, and kinship ideology. On the Lakshadweep islands, where matriliny and visiting marriage are followed, domestic space is not only associated with women but belongs to them. Houses are constructed, expanded, and rebuilt with women in view, for they are seen as their permanent occupants. They receive their husbands and bring up their children there. Men are seen as having no permanent attachment to a house. When unmarried or out of marriage, they generally sleep on a verandah or in the coconut storehouse (L. Dube 1993).

In uxorilocal residence a man has to leave his wife's house on divorce. A wife might tell her visiting or uxorilocal husband that she does not want him any more. He has, in his own natal group, a place to go back to. Among the Khasi, a matrilineal tribe in north-eastern India, traditionally the youngest daughter inherited her mother's house, in which she gave shelter to male and female matrilineal kin, while the other daughters' husbands constructed houses for them. The norm that houses belonged to women was so strong that even British soldiers who lived with Khasi women left their houses for their wives and children. Among the Garo, too, the house and the land belong to the wife, even though the husband is the manager (Burling 1963). Prindiville (1981) has described the traditional house of the matrilineal Minangkabau of western Sumatra, which has specific and limited space for the men of the lineage. The husbands, who came from different places, slept in the mosque when they were not visiting their wives. Women were looked upon as the permanent residents and had no fear of displacement.

Among the matrilineal Nayar of south Malabar and middle Travancore, who had hypergamous and isogamous unions and a visiting pattern of marital relationships, the *taravad* house had a series of rooms for the women of the matrilineage, a common kitchen, a place for deities, and a long front room for the maternal uncle. When other males of the house were present, they were also accommodated there. In northern Kerala, Nayar women did live with their husbands and children on their husbands' *taravad* land; but they retained residential and property rights in their own *taravad*, to which they could return when they wished to or had to (Gough 1961).

Patrilineal South Asia poses a stark contrast. Marriage displaces the bride from her natal home to that of her husband. She does not acquire any right to the physical space of the conjugal house that she enters. She is ushered into it with rituals and fanfare, but she does not get the unconditional right to live there. If she displeases someone she can be asked to leave. Even in nuclear households the living space belongs to the husband; the wife has merely been brought into it.

Seema Sakhare, a colleague involved with the movement against rape and women's oppression in Maharashtra, narrated some experiences of her childhood. Her father was a teacher in a primary school, a man of principle who was opposed to the practice of rituals and who advocated devotion to a God who could be approached without the intervention of Brahmins. He belonged to one of the middle castes. He could be transferred from place to place, but the family kept some milch cattle in order that the children might have a good supply of milk and milk products. His wife was an efficient and hardworking person who looked after all the household work including the milking of the cattle and the processing of various products. She was undoubtedly overworked; but whenever her husband found her defaulting or slacking, he would scold her and tell her to leave the house if she could not work properly. This threat puzzled her little daughter. How could her mother, who ran the household, be asked to quit it? Did she have no right over it? Why not?

The threat that led Seema eventually to fight for the rights of women is still the everyday reality of women's lives. It is within this possibility that women must function, being available for their men's sexual satisfaction, making themselves indispensable by bringing up children and giving them security, earning merit and reputation in the network of kin and friends, and taking up careers, sometimes with distinction. There are innumerable instances each day of women being driven out of their marital homes for all manner of reasons. In upper castes and the higher classes it may be done in a more subtle manner, although even here fights and violence cannot be ruled out.

The point that needs to be made here is that a woman does seem to have a certain moral right to live in the affinal home. Expressions such as "You married me in the presence of gods and Brahmins" and "Fire was the witness when you took the vows and made me your wife" are in a way rooted in wedding rituals. It is commonly believed that a woman brought into a family after a proper marriage has a lifelong right to food and shelter, whether or not her husband likes her. Moreover, it is thought morally wrong to drive away a woman who has borne children for the family and has worshipped the family deities. Before bigamy was prohibited, a man would either let his first wife stay on, or else his family would see to it that she had a place to live. However, transgression of sexual or behavioural norms is always considered sufficient reason for throwing a woman out of the house.

A Muslim man in South Asia can divorce his wife and ask her to move out of his house. Others can drive away the wife without a divorce. The firm understanding is that the woman has no right over the house and that she may live there only as long as it pleases her husband and his kin to let her live there. In rural and tribal Chhattisgarh in central India a man claims the wages of his wife saying, "In whose house were you living and whose rice were you eating when you were earning these wages?" (L. Dube 1956). A Bangladeshi villager may claim his children thus: "When you came to this house you had no children. You got them in this house. Therefore you have no right to take them with you" (Aziz 1979, Aziz and Maloney 1985). In the context of South Asian patrilineal systems, neolocal residence actually means virilocal residence. The crucial test is, which of the partners can deny entry to the other, and which can be denied entry and be asked to leave.

It is only recently that a man's exclusive right to establish and control access to a marital home has been questioned in a few legal disputes in India. The general understanding is that, if a woman has a grievance against her husband, she may do what she can to make life hell for him – but she cannot deny him entry into his house.

There is nothing in the ceremonies and rituals of marriage, or in the legal content of marriage, in any patrilineal community in the region that gives a wife a firm right over physical space. Abandoned wives are not a rarity, and most of them become homeless, without shelter. Some may return to their parental homes, but many who are not self-supporting may have to seek shelter in institutions for destitute women. A woman who herself decides to leave her husband also has to adopt the same course. The support of parents is a possibility among the educated and well-to-do and for those women for whom divorce, separation, and remarriage are customarily acceptable. Even there, however, a daughter has no right over the physical space: she is allowed to occupy it as a courtesy and often as a temporary measure.

The relationship of women to physical space in bilateral South-East Asia poses a contrast. In Malaysia, *adat* law requires an equal division of property between male and female children. The tendency towards uxorilocal residence in the first few years of marriage helps to give women parity of status with men. The notion of conjugal property, over which both have a right, and the rights that each has over what s/he brought to the marriage give a certain flexibility to the question of control over the complex of material resources of the household. Tsubouchi (1977) mentions no special rules of marital residence in the three villages he studied. A choice is made between the compounds of the husband's and wife's sides and an entirely different one. Even a nuclear household established around a couple is set within a network of kin. In no case is a woman far from the support of her kin. In urban areas a woman may have to live away from her kin, but she keeps contact through reciprocal visits or by having a relative stay with her.

It is well known that in Indonesia parents look forward to being cared for by a daughter. There is a tendency on their part to give shares of various kinds of property to both male and female children and to give the house to the youngest child or to the one who is to look after them in their old age. Here again, both spouses bring individually owned property to the marriage and earn conjugal property within it. Women tend to remain in close contact with their parents and siblings. The flexibility of the residence pattern does not produce set ideas about rights to resources, and the establishment of a nuclear household with the notion of conjugal property militates against exclusive ownership by one spouse.

In the Philippines a young married couple set up their conjugal household, remaining a part of the support network of kin, mainly including members of their natal families, and "struggle to safeguard the survival of their new family unit" (Illo 1990). Until they have their own household the couple may live with either set of parents.

The choice is influenced by the tradition of the village as well as by practical considerations such as availability of space. Flexibility, choice, and the absence of compulsion in the name of set traditions make the issue of rights over physical space radically different from what it is in patrilineal South Asia.

In north-eastern Thailand, residence has a distinct matrilateral bias. Compounds often consist of the household of the parents and those of daughters, all cultivating together. Northern Thai kinship is characterized by matrilineality and bilateral inheritance. Property is inherited equally by all children but the house goes to the youngest daughter. Sons tend to sell their shares to their sisters. In central Thailand the pattern of residence is matrilocal for the first year of marriage.

Bilateral South-East Asia thus has much more flexibility and choice regarding conjugal arrangements. The nature and character of marriage here are radically different from in patrilineal South Asia. This difference is likely to explain some aspects of the differences in the quality of gender relations in the two regions.

I have discussed women's relationship with living space as a critical element in the quality of conjugal and familial relations with some trepidation. It is difficult to capture the essence of the differentiation between the genders even though one feels it within oneself. I hope that the material elsewhere will impart some clarity to what I have said in this chapter.

This special consideration given to women's relation with living space needs an explanation. It was not integrated with the chapter on residence because it needs to be seen in relation to various aspects of kinship, including patterns of inheritance, rights to resources and children, the nature and character of marriage, and conjugal rights. Its separate treatment preceding marriage and residence thus seems to be more effective.

8

Residence

Residence after marriage has profound implications for access to productive resources and control over them; for the organization of labour; for rights to the products of one's labour; for women's relation to living space; and for their bargaining power and relative autonomy. Residence has at least two connotations or referents: household or domestic groups, and locality or vicinage. The ideal-typical household in large parts of Bangladesh, India, and Nepal is the patrilineal, patri-virilocal joint family. Even in the absence of a joint household, close male agnates and their wives and children are viewed as belonging to one family, *kutumb*, or *khandan*. The other connotation – locality or vicinage – is strongly present in the countries named and in Pakistan, where the joint household too is not absent. Owing to the pattern of inheritance and the nature of rights to land, agnatically related conjugal families tend to live close to one another in the same village or locality. Even where it is customary for a son to establish a separate household upon marriage, it is into the house of his family of orientation that his bride is ceremonially ushered. For the bride this marks severance from her natal family and the beginning of the process of her incorporation into her husband's family.

In the patrilineal, patri-virilocal residence pattern of India and Nepal, marriage for a girl is associated with separation from her natal home and from her near and dear ones. It involves her being transferred to a strange and probably harsh environment. Hindu wedding rituals dramatize the transfer of a bride from one family to another; this is a poignant scene that stays in the hearts of little girls who witness it. *Rukhsat* (bidding goodbye to a bride and sending her away) is similarly a sad occasion among the patrilineal Muslims of South Asia. Feelings of separation, nostalgia, and apprehension are expressed in wedding songs. The message that separation from parents and siblings is inescapable is also put across through lullabies and nursery rhymes such as this one from Bengal:

> *A stranger's son has come to fetch me.*
> *Come, my playmates, come with our toys.*
> *Let us play, for I shall never play in the stranger's house.*

The natal home is constantly contrasted with the husband's home. In western India there is a special festival intended to ensure that little girls eventually get good husbands, where this song is sung:

> *The natal home is beautiful.*
> *There we can play to our hearts' content.*
> *The in-laws' place is cruel: it stifles and kills.*

This contrast is seen in women's songs all over India, as is the daughter's feeling of resentment. A song sung in the Hindi-speaking region when the bride is bid farewell expresses her feelings thus:

> *O father, you brought up my brother to be happy.*
> *You brought me up to shed tears.*
> *O father, you have brought up your son to give him your house,*
> *And you have left a cage for me.*

The finality of transfer is expressed in a famous Nepali folk-song (Kondos 1989: 181), which not only brings into relief the complexities involved but also accentuates the poignancy of it all. The daughter/wife sings:

> *There I cannot go back.*
> *Here I am not wanted.*
> *What's to become of me?*

All this goes into the socialization of a girl. Boys are brought up with the complementary notion that they are permanent members of the house, entitled to shares in the family's resources, while their sisters are only temporary members who will leave one day and who

89

have at best limited rights to resources. Even the prevalence of intra-kin marriages, as in much of southern India, has not done away with these feelings.

Much of the socialization of a girl is carried out in reference to an imaginary mother-in-law. I feel that a certain ambiguity characterizes the socialization of girls. While a girl is being trained for her present and future roles the fact that she will go into another family is never forgotten. Families differ, and what kind of home she will go to cannot be foretold. It is certain, though, that years will pass before she acquires the power of making decisions there. She is therefore conditioned to accept an unfamiliar setting in which her own status will be low. I believe this affects the development of self-confidence and initiative in girls.

At the same time, contradictory values and expectations essentially reflect the contradictions inherent in a patrilineal, patri-virilocal kinship system. For instance, although the transfer of a girl from one family to another is supposed to be total, the sister–brother tie is held to be life-long. There is also a chain of obligations that a girl's parents are expected to fulfil at various points. The advice to a bride is that she is entering a new family for life and that only her dead body must leave it. It is also dinned into a girl that her behaviour in her affinal home will be crucial to the reputation of her natal family. Interestingly, although a girl is told to be docile and to serve her affines, she is also given tips on how to keep her husband under her control and prevent her mother-in-law from dominating her. The lesson that a girl receives, indirectly, is that she must be able to manipulate and manage people (see Raheja and Gold 1996).

Parents view their daughters as liabilities who will have to be married off, very often with dowries, and who will thereafter not be available to render any kind of support. The custom of women making periodic long visits to their natal homes to give different kinds of assistance is reported by Palriwala (1990, 1991) for Rajasthan villages and by Doranne Jacobson (1977a) for central India; it should be prevalent elsewhere also, but as a matter of cultural understandng parents expect little of their daughters. This affects their willingness to make long-term investments in a daughter's future, as we see in the chapter on education. Daughters thus often enter new relationships with little or no bargaining power.

A daughter's immediate value is far more important than her deferred value. She is useful around the house and in productive activities. A son, on the other hand, is looked upon as the source of support in old age. He will also bring in extra hands to work, and he will continue the patriline.

Another consequence of such a vision of the future is that dowry is seen as a compensation for the denial to a daughter of a share in inheritance and of membership of the kin group. Daughters become keen that their parents give them dowries, often without regard to their ability to give. A girl is destined to go through the traumatic experience of alienation from her natal family. If she has no rights so far as that family is concerned, nor does she have obligations. Her main concern is to establish herself in her new family and acquire some standing there; and dowry contributes to this process. It has been argued that dowry and the harassment and violence related to it would be curtailed if daughters were to inherit equally with sons and were not so completely severed from their natal families upon marriage.

It is said that female children are of use to their natal families only in a negative way: they bring credit to them when they succeed in not going astray. In their affinal homes women have an essentially instrumental value. They are necessary for the perpetuation of the family through the production of sons; they look after the domestic work; their labour may go into the fields or into other forms of economic contribution; and they take care of the household deities and ensure the continuance of family traditions.

This brings us to a crucial point: the crisis of incorporating an outsider into the family. A bride is described as Lakshmi, goddess of wealth and prosperity, and is ceremonially ushered into the house; but she also represents uncertainty and danger. The ritual of consecration of the womb during a wedding is indicative of the danger posed by the bride's entry into the family, for she is to be the receptacle for its progeny (Saraswati 1977). Her entry should be auspicious for the family and particularly for the new husband. A number of rituals and practices seen across South Asia clearly indicate this. A Bengali bride, for instance, enters the affinal home carrying a live fish in a basket. The fish is auspicious, indicating *saubhagya* – the fortunate state of a married woman – for herself and prosperity for the family. Her husband's long life is in a way contingent on the bride's continuing to enjoy the fortunate married state. In Maharashtra a bride entering her affinal home for the first time is asked to kick a tumbler full of grain placed in the doorway. The grain's spilling into the house with the bride's entry is thought to augur well for the future. Everywhere such symbolic acts form part of the entry of a new bride.

Real incorporation is of course a long and slow process, but symbolic incorporation is accomplished through rituals and ceremonies. As Gray (1989: 147) says, "gaining admission to the household through marriage, the outsider wife is experienced as an inferior and dangerous being."

Gray (1982) and Bennett (1983) have dealt with the wife as a dangerous being among the Parbatiya of Nepal. They report that only in-marrying women – outsiders – are considered potential witches. They need to be contained and their sexuality controlled. States of impaired fertility such as miscarriage, failure to bear a male child, and childlessness, as well as widowhood, are particularly dangerous. A woman in one of these states is inauspicious and possesses the potential to become a *boksi* (a witch). This association of witchcraft with in-married women, particularly those who are childless or widowed, appears in fact to be a pan-Indian phenomenon.

Another danger is the control that a bride may gain over her husband through love and affection or through the intimacy of their sexual relationship. Closeness between husband and wife is thought to portend the break-up of a joint family (V. Das 1976b, S. C. Dube 1955, D. Jacobson 1982). Among the Kashmiri Pandits a daughter-in-law is called a "parrot of the pillow" (T. N. Madan, personal communication), indicating that in intimate moments she poisons her husband's mind against other members of his family.

I describe elsewhere the respect–avoidance practices that a bride in northern or central India must follow to maintain harmony within the family. A young couple are expected to show no signs of intimacy in the presence of others. These practices are present even among many Muslim groups. The new bride is constantly under the critical eye of several members of her husband's family. Folklore singles out the mother-in-law and the husband's sister as the natural enemies of the young bride. A Bengali folk song calls the husband's sister nothing but a poisonous thorn. A north Indian bridal song goes:

O my friend,
My in-laws' house is a wretched place.
My mother-in-law is a hard woman:
She always spurts about full of anger. (Kakar 1978: 219)

The incorporation of the in-marrying woman is indeed a difficult process. Incorporation is emphasized through rituals and is given a special value. Together with suspicion and subdued hostility towards the outsider is her overt acceptance as a full-fledged member of the family with obligations to other members and to deities and ancestors. The critical relationship is that between the more incorporated women and the less incorporated ones. Instructions and advice tend to flow in one direction. It appears that the lines of authority among women in a joint family household are very complex and are in a constant state of flux. Personal equation and the personalities of the women involved have a crucial significance. A woman's status in her affinal home is not constant: it changes with the attainment of motherhood, particularly when she bears a son; it depends on her hold over her husband, on his economic contribution to the joint household, on his prospects of moving out of the household for employment elsewhere. The state of health and the life-span of her father-in-law determines to a great degree the status of her mother-in-law. In time her mother-in-law may come to depend on her and even come under her authority and control.

Residence is a material as well as an ideological expression of principles of kinship. Even a nuclear household embedded in patrilineal kinship is considered part of the larger extended family. That there can be rivalry between brothers is recognized but, when a joint family breaks up, the blame for this usually falls upon women. The time considered appropriate for its fragmentation varies with class, caste, and region. Although the nature of the control that is exercised over women varies with household composition, the ideology of patrilineal, patri-virilocal residence governs a woman's life, whether she is a new daughter-in-law, a wife and mother running the household, or a mother-in-law who may be tyrannical to begin with but end old, widowed, and weak.

Demographic factors and life trajectories vary so much that it is difficult to make clear-cut generalizations. Personal equations also differ widely. Cordial and affectionate relationships can and often do develop between a woman and her affines over the years. This is the ideal whose value is imbibed during socialization and that is reiterated by others during day-to-day evaluative remarks.

What I wish to emphasize is that patri-virilocal residence makes a woman's existence precarious. For her natal kin she has little credibility and dependability; and in her affinal home she is suspect and potentially dangerous and must always be circumspect. In the patri-lineal system of kinship, residence is definitely conceived of as being virilocal. Even neolocal residence, which in most cases does bring a woman some autonomy, is really virilocal, the husband's kin having greater and more clearly defined rights than those of the wife. It is believed that a woman is often inclined more towards her natal kin and that a special effort is needed to achieve the ideal of the fully incorporated in-married woman. Women are often blamed for diverting family resources to "outsiders" such as their own parents and siblings and so on. Those who earn cash may try to keep some to dispose of in any manner they please. Understanding may be lacking on both sides. Women in such a patrilineal society are often forced to train themselves in double-talk and the use of strategies. Education and employment seem to help women to some extent in gaining respect and holding their own.

Rules of residence place hurdles in the way of women's access to resources. For instance, they can come in the way of a woman's being given immovable property such as land or a house by her parents. A woman living in her affinal village cannot easily manage land in her natal village. The asymmetrical status relation between bride-givers and bride-takers in much of non-peninsular India and the physical and social distance between natal and affinal homes also keep women from receiving much support from their natal kin. In regions such as Bengal, Maharashtra, and parts of Punjab, where women customarily return to their natal homes for childbirth, particularly the first child-birth, matters are not so difficult for them. This is a much-valued practice in southern India, a region of "reticent" patriliny.

It has been argued (see Karve 1965, Kolenda 1984, Ganesh 1988) that where there is a preference for intra-kin marriages (between cross-cousins or between mother's brother and sister's daughter, real or classificatory), largely in southern India, patriliny is softened: a young bride is not totally removed from her natal home to be thrown amongst complete strangers. Such marriages are not numerous in percentage terms, however; nor are marriages contracted within a village. As Dhruvarajan (1989) says, although there is no taboo on marrying within the village, for want of suitable partners there most girls marry into other villages. Only four women had married within the village she studied. However, there is always the likelihood that a bride will find kin in her affinal village; and, because at least some intra-kin marriages do take place, there is no sharp asymmetry between bride-givers and bride-takers. The ethos of intra-kin marriage pervades relationships even between unrelated affines, which are marked by considerable mutuality. Real or fictive kinship between the two sets of parents makes for the absence of the kind of avoidance that is normal in northern India. A woman's parents can have some say in the way she is treated in her affinal home. Her natal kin visit her freely there. No sharp contrast exists between daughters and daughters-in-law. In the absence of a rigid demarcation of kin and affines, women in southern India are far less constrained than women in the north; and they do not want for support. Further research is needed for assessing the nature and degree of mitigation of patriliny in southern India.[1]

Does the patrilineal, patri-virilocal system offer any choice to women? When their only child is a daughter or when all their children are daughters, parents try to get a son-in-law to live with them who can manage the property or business. A major consideration here is that one daughter can stay with them to care for them in their old age. All over India, though, a resident son-in-law is looked down upon. He is variously called a pariah dog, an ass to be loaded heavily, a lazy, good-for-nothing fellow. There are numerous sayings that demean such persons. In matrilineal communities, too, there are uncomplimentary epithets for a husband. Among the Khasi, for example, he is called a rooster, signifying that his sole function is to impregnate his wife; but he is also praised if he sweats for the sake of his children. He is one who keeps his bags packed, for he does not know when he might have to leave. The uncertain position of a man who lives in his wife's house is expressed in a number of ways in bilateral and matrilineal societies. One needs to remember, however, that a man in these societies always has his own natal home to go back to.

In patrilineal societies the epithets used for a resident son-in-law are clearly insulting. He is not seen to be in the ideal conjugal relationship where his status is clearly superior and where he may boss his wife and receive the respect of her kin. This is not simply a matter of a reversal of roles between kinship systems. In a patrilineal system a resident son-in-law is vilified. A woman in her affinal home may be treated harshly, but she is where she should be and has a clearly defined role there, even if it is instrumental and subordinate.

Depending, of course, on her personal equation with her husband, a woman who looks after the affairs of a nuclear household far from her husband's kin has considerable autonomy. But the boundaries of such a household are not particularly flexible: whereas the wife's kin may come there only as guests, the husband's kin expect to be treated as legitimate members. Thus even the less constrained women must function within certain limits. What actually happens may be different, but, in seeking explanations for the range of variations in actual situations and in the analyses of domestic politics, the points mentioned above must not be ignored.

Matters are much the same among the patrilineal Muslims of South Asia, although the religious sanction found among the Hindus is absent. Intra-kin marriages are often preferred, and they seem to soften the atmosphere. A support network usually exists, and women are not completely severed from their natal homes. In rural West Punjab, for instance, marriages between close kin are fairly common; and many women do not have to leave for another village upon marriage. Even when a woman does move elsewhere, she may remain surrounded by kin. Respect–avoidance is not practised between women. Ahmad and Ahmad (1990) say about a woman called Masi: "Masi, who has not moved from her birth place, has a sense of continuity.... There is a cohesion in her personality, an integration and integrity that has made it possible for her to face this social change with a degree of humour and grace." Masi has enjoyed her brother's support all through.

The relative rarity of intra-kin marriage in villages in Bangladesh is indicated clearly by both Aziz (1979) and Arefeen (1986) in their studies of kinship in Bangladesh. Kabeer (1985b) mentions the widespread preference of decision makers for forming marital connections elsewhere, which means that most married women do not live in their natal villages. Only 30 per cent of the women in the village she studied were born there, as against 88 per cent of the men. It is no wonder, therefore, that in Bangladeshi villages the ethos of patrilineal, patri-virilocal residence, in which a new bride enters her affinal home as a stranger, should be not very different from what is found among the Hindus of West Bengal.[2]

To turn to Pakistan again. Ahmad and Ahmad (1990) make it clear that in the changing situation it is recognized that the virtual compulsion towards intra-kin marriage leaves girls and boys little freedom in choosing partners. Their observation is that marriages between cousins do not necessarily ensure a good life and security. On the contrary, a betrothed girl is often expected to begin working in her uncle's (or future father-in-law's) house well before her marriage. It seems that a notion of transfer, the general subordination of women, and a firm belief in their inferiority and in the need to keep them under control do not permit any substantial softening of the patrilineal, patri-virilocal system. The same authors report that an emigrant son is expected to make remittances to his father, not to his wife.

Perhaps asymmetry in conjugality and gender relations can explain why intra-kin marriages may not always soften the patrilineal, patri-virilocal system even in Bangladesh or among the high-caste Brahmins of southern India. Gough (1956) indicates this in her comparison of Brahmin kinship with that among relatively low castes. Among the martial castes such as the Marathas, only matrilateral cross-cousin marriage is permitted. It does not reverse the asymmetrical relationship between bride-givers and bride-takers.

A few Muslim communities in India practise inter-generational, intra-*khandan* marriage. Here there are no clear boundaries between households as commensal and economic units. Members look after one another's comfort and needs and divide their time, perhaps eating in one house and sleeping in another. Patrilineal, patri-virilocal principles do not operate strictly. Vatuk (1989), who studied a Navayat *khandan* mainly concentrated in Madras and Hyderabad, mentions a cultural factor that is of great significance to household formation in the community: the open recognition of, and the legitimacy accorded to, close ties of affection and duty between parents and daughters, which are expected to remain just as strong after the daughters marry. Although a married woman must look after the needs and interests of her in-laws, there is no pressure on her to transfer her allegiance away from her natal family. A woman may even not share a household with her husband if she is needed to care for her aged parents. Her rights in the parental property are also honoured. Such instances in the patrilineal communities of South Asia are rare. Even in this Navayat *khandan*, marriages with outsiders are gradually increasing. It is possible that the situation will change with the end of *khandan* endogamy.

The implications of residence in patrilineal, patri-virilocal South Asia may now be compared with what prevails in bilateral South-East Asia and in matrilineal societies.

Among the Minangkabau, women have exclusive rights over the long-houses. Most remain there throughout their lives. Men out-migrate. On marriage a man moves into the house shared by his wife with her female kin and their husbands. A long-house contains a number of conjugal units, which function as individual "rice-pot" families. Such a family eats together and shares economic resources.

It is significant that membership of these rice-pot families is not fixed but is a matter of choice. Often an unmarried sister, mother, or other close relative may be included.

The core of the residential group is thus made up of matrilineally related women. Husbands who come to live there must learn to adapt. A man may out-migrate alone or with his wife and children, or he may build a new house for the family on the land of his wife's kin group. In the event of divorce the house becomes hers, and she also gets custody of her children.

Household composition is flexible but it does not extend beyond the wife's kin. The husband comes alone; and if he leaves, he leaves alone. He has rights in his own matrilineal group, of course. This form of residence gives unusual security to Minangkabau women. Rights to natal houses are combined with rights to cultivable land. Whether or not their husbands are present, they can provide for themselves and their children. Older women wield authority in the long-house. With the increase in the number of single-family houses this is diminishing. In a nuclear household, authority is more often than not shared by both spouses. A woman has the help of both husband and brothers, and mothers are always taken care of. Women thus live among supportive kin and are never estranged from home.

Things do not remain quite the same when Minangkabau couples or nuclear families migrate to towns. Nevertheless, women derive a sense of security from the knowledge of their rights at their natal homes and do not become entirely helpless.

Minangkabau patterns of inheritance and residence are not in keeping with Islamic injunctions. Here the distinction made by Keddie (1987) between *ibadat* (worship) and *muamlat* (worldly matters) is relevant. So far as *ibadat* is concerned, the Minangkabau are devout Muslims; but they tend to follow *adat* (custom, tradition, customary law) where property and residence are concerned.

Another form of matriliny is found on the Lakshadweep islands off the south-western coast of India. Whereas a Minangkabau husband not on *merantau* (out-migration) is usually to be found with his wife and children in uxorilocal residence, a Lakshadweep husband lives with his own matrilineal group and merely visits his wife. In some instances uxorilocal residence may be adopted, but usually only after the marriage has attained some stability. The periodic absence of males engaged in trade with the mainland and the small size of the islands have made this pattern of visiting marriage viable. In Lakshadweep both sexes have the right of use over part of their kin groups' productive resources, chiefly coconut trees. Houses belong to women, who are seen as their real, stable occupants and who have the responsibility of rearing children, permanent members of the *taravad*. Although women are mostly confined to their various islands while men are the principal actors in religious and political organizations and in many economic activities including trade, women have an undoubtedly privileged position (L. Dube 1969a, 1974, 1991a,b, 1993, Kutty 1972). This is also seen in the fact that the Islamic procedures of unilateral divorce and easy remarriage can be made to function in the interests of women as often as in the interests of men.

In two matrilineal tribal groups in north-eastern India – the Garo and the Khasi – residence has been essentially uxorilocal. Change has been taking place owing to factors such as conversion to Christianity, the spread of modern education, and new avenues of employment for both men and women, but it is worth our while to look at the traditional pattern of residence.

On the day of his marriage a Garo man leaves his parental home and joins his bride in her parents' home. The couple continue to live there until a child is born to them or until they decide that they are capable of maintaining an independent household. This new household is set up usually in the wife's village, where she is entitled to land for cultivation and for residence. A household is regarded as complete only when a daughter is born to a couple. In the absence of a daughter, a matrilineally related girl may be adopted to continue the household. Each household selects one of its daughters as the heiress who will continue to live in the parental home with her husband and children. In a Garo household the man is the manager of the land, which belongs to the woman. Larger issues concerning households and the lineage are dealt with by the male elders of the wife's lineage. A woman thus always lives in the midst of her own kin.

Among the Khasi, too, a man comes to live in his wife's home. The youngest daughter stays there for life with her husband and children, for she is considered the custodian of the household and its property and religion. Other daughters stay in the parental home only until they have one or two children or until the next sister in line is married. A new household is generally established in the wife's village, so residence may be regarded as uxorilocal. Houses are considered to belong to women, including those built by their husbands. There have been radical changes in the laws relating to property and to land tenure, but women still have a strong position. It has been argued that the very fact that women have superior rights over resources and children means that they have to bear the brunt of the responsibility; and indeed Khasi men are widely held to be irresponsible.

The pattern of post-marital residence is related to the mode of inheritance among both the Khasi and the Garo. Distribution of resources has been much more egalitarian among the Garo than among the Khasi, who accord a specially privileged position to the youngest daughter. It is also important to note that a man never loses his connection with his matrilineage, to which he can always return, although his rights to resources there are inferior to those of his sisters. Traditionally whatever a man earned belonged to his mother before he married and later to his wife and children. With the advent of the money economy, men now maintain their own bank accounts. A new act passed by the state of Meghalaya gives men the right to dispose of self-acquired property as they please (Nongbri 1990). Both Garo and Khasi men play important roles in local and provincial politics; but women retain a strong position because of the pattern of residence and because of their rights in inheritance and over children.

Bilateral kinship tends to encourage uxorilocal residence, or at least choice in the matter of residence. The Atjehnese, who live at the northern tip of Sumatra, follow bilateral kinship but residence is invariably matri-uxorilocal. Husbands move to the villages and households of their wives. Houses in a village are owned by women who are related to one another through women. The nuclear family household is the basic unit, but houses belonging to matrilineally related women are spatially contiguous. Structurally the Atjehnese kinship system falls between the Javanese and Minangkabau systems (Tanner 1974: 137).

The idiomatic expression for a wife is "she who owns the house." A girl grows up in her mother's house and does not move away upon marriage. The cluster of houses making up a village are owned by sisters and classificatory matrilateral female cousins. Women thus live in the midst of their own kin. Husbands may sometimes own arable land, but women cultivate it. Women produce rice and expect cash or goods from their husbands, who engage in trade or take jobs with cash incomes elsewhere and return to their wives and children for short periods. They come home most regularly for Ramadan, the month of fasting, and the subsequent festivities. Atjehnese women look down upon husbands who remain in the village and do not earn cash.

In this society men bring in the money, but they are peripheral in other respects. Women are the main workers in wet-rice cultivation.

100

Men make only sporadic contributions to the preparation of the fields and at harvest time. Women control the subsistence economy and bring up the children, caring for them and also instructing and disciplining them. In children's eyes mothers are responsible and important figures who work hard, who take care of most family affairs, and who are respected within the village. Children are also surrounded by their mothers' kin.

Husbands are treated as guests and do not wield any great authority: they are not involved even in family decisions. Among the Atjehnese several factors combine to place women in a very strong position: uxorilocal residence; their role as principal actors in most areas of life; and men's absence from the village for much of the time. Siegel (1969: 169) describes a fight between a woman and her husband, who overstayed after the money ran out and tried to interfere in her domain. The woman kicked him, slashed at him, and tried to stab him. She could not tolerate his hitting her. She moved his mattress out of the bedroom; and later, "whenever she recalled that he had hit her she would slap him or rip his shirt."

Atjehnese men have played economic and political roles in their own society as well as in Indonesia. As children and adolescents they are indulged by their mothers; but as husbands and fathers they become marginal in the kinship system, where women are the central figures. Motherhood is greatly valued, and women always remain secure in the villages of their birth.

Bilateral South-East Asia presents a contrast to patrilineal South Asia in respect of marital residence. Although among some groups such as the Atjehnese and in some areas such as northern and northeastern Thailand matri-uxorilocal residence is the standard practice, a fundamental principle governing residence in the region is that of choice. There is no cultural compulsion concerning the perpetuation of a descent line or the continuity of a family over generations. Hence neither a male child (as in patriliny) nor a female child (as in matriliny) has a special role in these matters. A couple may live with or near the wife's or the husband's parents. In central Thailand residence is generally uxorilocal in the first year of marriage and virilocal thereafter. It is not at all unusual for a couple to begin their married life in the house of one set of parents and later to move to the other set's house or into a new one of their own. When a couple establishes an independent household, this is likely to be in the compound of relatives or in the neighbourhood. There is a strong tendency to cluster around the mother's residence. As mentioned earlier, going to live with or near the husband's parents is a viable option, particularly in urban areas, and neolocal residence is also adopted. But what is important is the presence of choice in the matter.

As Laderman (1983) says of the eastern part of Peninsular Malaysia, although most young couples set up homes of their own, they tend to build these near their parents' houses. Rather than unrelated neighbours it is close female relatives who nurse their kin in sickness and assist in the care of children and in housework. Female kin tend to remain close to one another spatially, often in common compounds. It is said that there is the greatest solidarity among them and among persons related through women. Men often sell their rights in parental property to their sisters and move to their wife's house.

That parents look forward to being cared for in their old age by their offspring, particularly daughters, is true generally of the South-East Asian populations of which I am speaking. Koentjaraningrat (1985: 142, 143–144) writes of the Javanese:

One can often observe aged parents living with their children, usually with daughters as it is logical that they prefer to live with their own daughters instead of with a daughter-in-law. A mother who interferes in household matters is often the cause of conflict and she therefore busies herself with looking after the children or with the art of batik. A very skilful batik artist can produce a surplus, which can be very helpful to the household economy, as handmade batik is still a desirable and expensive product in Javanese society ....

The wife's mother especially is very close to the house after the birth of a first child. A reserved relationship is, however, more apparent between a woman and her mother-in-law. The wife's mother who comes to live with the family, seldom quarrels with her son-in-law, since the chief disagreements are household matters which are none of his concern. When the husband's mother comes to live with her son and daughter-in-law, however, there are greater possibilities of friction between the older woman and her daughter-in-law concerning household matters.

Geertz (1961), Jay (1969), and many other scholars of Javanese culture refer to the tendency towards uxorilocal residence, meaning residence with or around the parents of the wife. They speak also of a certain openness of the household to the kin of both spouses. The Javanese household is known to be a woman's domain, where her control over strategic resources is near complete. In household matters she takes decisions on her own.

It is significant that, in bilateral South-East Asia as a whole, kinship terminology shows a certain parity between similarly related kin, irrespective of their sex and regardless of whether they are patri-lateral or matrilateral. In the rural parts of eastern Malaysia a couple may move back and forth between the two parental houses until the birth of a child, after which they move to a house in an independent compound or construct one in either parental compound. Couples tend to locate themselves according to where income and housing are available. Expediency and convenience play an important part in their choice of residence. Certainly there is no social constraint deriving from the kinship system that obliges the couple to reside with the parents of either (Strange 1981). I have elaborated on this point in the chapter on kinship as well.

In the Philippines, too, there is a pronounced tendency towards uxorilocal residence. As Illo (1990) says, both partners to a marriage are hindered in giving support to their parents because they must establish a home and family and fend for themselves and their children; but women find it convenient to live close to the natal home. Often a couple may begin their married life in the house of one set of parents. The significant point is their perception of free choice in the matter of residence.

Among the Filipinos the principle of age is important in determining interpersonal behaviour in the family. Although Spanish influence institutionalized the legal and social dominance of the male, the Filipino family has not abandoned its predominantly Malay characteristic of equality between husband and wife in the allocation of authority within the household (Cordero and Panopio 1969). Many researchers suggest that the wife may be more influential in the household. The bilateral nature of kinship assures women the continued support of their kin. There is no discrimination between siblings on the basis of sex; it is age that brings respect and status. Sons and daughters inherit equally, and women have full control over property acquired before and after marriage. There is a long tradition of women engaging in income-earning activities either in the home or outside. Although husbands are formally the heads of households, women are in charge of money matters.

In these societies, then, girls do not grow up with a sense of insecurity, of inferior status relative to their brothers, of the inevitability of their transfer to a new kin group and change of residence at marriage, of a lack of control over their own lives; nor are they compelled to adjust and accommodate in entirely new surroundings in the midst of strangers. The implications of marriage are not what they are in South Asia. The painful process of being distanced from their own homes and being incorporated into another family does not pervade girls' and women's consciousness. A girl is not socialized under the shadow of an imaginary – and eventually to become real – mother-in-law. Nor is there a feeling that she cannot return to her natal home when she pleases. There is nothing remotely resembling a change of "ownership." Marriage does not put an end to a daughter's emotional and economic responsibility towards her natal kin; girls are in fact valued for their sustained help.

In the Philippines, religion views marriage as an unbreakable tie, but this tie formally encompasses only the conjugal relationship. One feels that in the rest of South-East Asia the initial stages of married life are looked upon as a kind of experimental phase. The two partners remain independent entities. A woman's personality is not obliterated as it is in most of South Asia. Nor does she lose the support of her kin. These points can be read in or inferred from most ethnographies of the region (Strange 1981, Laderman 1983, Firth 1966, Djmour 1959, Jay 1969, Geertz 1961, Koentjaraningrat 1985, Jocano 1969).

An important aspect of residence in South-East Asia is the flexibility of a household's composition and boundaries. A basically nuclear household may have as members old, young, or recently divorced relatives who contribute to it their labour or resources and find shelter and sustenance in it. As Laderman (1983) says of the eastern part of Peninsular Malaysia, the high incidence of divorce and remarriage makes it commonplace for the children of more than one marriage to live with a current conjugal pair. Koentjaraningrat (1985) observes that Javanese children are often divided equally between their parents, although they are free to decide which parent they wish to go with. Very small children who still need a mother's care are of course taken by their mothers.

In this context the practices of adoption and of fostering children are very important. What Laderman (1983) has said of the Trengganu Malays applies to most of South-East Asia. It is said that a household without children is rare indeed and is considered unbearably lonely. Grandparents and childless couples are often given children to raise by relatives who have an abundance of young. In the central Javanese principalities and in the Bagelen region it is customary for a young couple to leave their first child with its grandparents when they move away from the parental house. Childless couples commonly adopt a child, most usually a nephew or a niece from either side. It is interesting and significant that very often little girls are preferred, because they will be more useful about the house than boys and more caring. The children of other kin or even from outside the group may be adopted. Among the Javanese there is a small ceremonial act in which the foster parents make the biological parents a specific payment to avoid complications induced by supernatural agencies. There is no legality to such adoptions, and it should be noted that Islam forbids adoption. Although considered one's own, an adopted child is not entitled to inherit the *pusaka*, or ancestral family property (Koentjaraningrat 1985).

Even apart from adoption, in this region the movement of children from one relative's house to another's is common, as is the borrowing of children. Frequent divorce and the subsequent (dis)placement of children, the acceptance by their mothers' kin of babies born out of wedlock, the practice of leaving children with their parents by mothers who work in towns or away from home, and generally the sense of an obligation to help out one's close kin – these are some of the factors that contribute to the movement of children between households. It has been pointed out that a child who has a fight at home or who is seriously displeased with its parents can always escape to the houses of grandparents or other relatives. It is not unknown for harsh treatment to be meted out to children who are brought in by kin to assist them; but by and large children are valued in these cultures.

McKinley (1975) writes in the context of Peninsular Malaysia that despite anxiety that a transferred child may some day wish to return to its natal parents – which may make foster parents treat such children better than they treat their biological offspring – in general all Malay parent–child ties have the same basic qualities. They are built on the parents' commitment to nurture children regardless of their origin, and it is expected that the children will reciprocate. It is common to hear statements such as "My adoptive parents are my real parents: after all, it is they who fed me." In addition to the idiom of mutual nurturing, parent–child relations are characterized by a certain tentative quality that demands the expression of reciprocity. There is thus no fuss made over ties of blood. Here one is reminded of Phillips' (1965) controversial assertion that, in central Thailand, relations between parents and children are essentially contractual.

McKinley (1975) emphasizes the categorical nature of the Malay sibling relationship. Sibling ties are expressed in ordinary conversations, folk songs, kinship terminology, birth rituals, and the advice given to children. A Malay saying goes:

> *Water when slashed*
> *will not be severed.*
> *Part a chicken's feathers*
> *And they come right back together.*

It appears that the sibling relationship can absorb much conflict. Requests among siblings for the adoption of children are common. These may not all lead anywhere, but certainly there is a sense of mutual obligation. At the same time the network of kin in these bilateral societies is egocentric; and there is thus greater scope for activating and de-activating relationships. This impermanence of relationships is seen in unilineal systems as well – but less commonly, because there it goes against established ideology.

In South Asia the brother–sister relationship is institutionalized but the relationship between sisters is not. There are special days when a sister honours her brother and receives gifts from him. A brother is looked upon as a protector among both Hindus and Muslims. He "keeps the door of the natal home open." He represents the continuity of the natal family. In Nepal the festivals of *bhai tika* and *dasai* celebrate the relationship between cross-sex siblings. In India *rakshabandhan* and *bhaiyaduj* are meant to recognize and re-iterate the special tie between brother and sister. The relationship between brothers is characterized by both solidarity and rivalry.

Some of the features of residence that I have discussed may help explain South-East Asian women's strong position in the domestic sphere.

In uxorilocal residence a daughter's economic contribution is clearly recognized. She brings in adult male labour at marriage and creates more labour through her reproductive abilities. Put differently, she does what a son is expected to do in patrilineal, patri-virilocal systems. It should be no surprise, then, that traditions ascribe a special importance to females. One custom among the northern and central Thai concerns the duration of the post-partum ritual period. Should this be shorter than a month, it is thought likely that the child will leave its home. By making it last a month or more for a girl child, parents hope to ensure that she will stay on to care for them in their old age and to look after the domestic spirits. For a boy, conversely, the ritual period is made shorter, to encourage him to move to another house when he is of age and married (J. Hanks 1963: 48, Davis 1973: 55, Muecke 1976: 373–386).

Condominas (1975: 255) writes of the cult of protector territorial spirits common among the Thai people. There are different categories of spirits, and the care of those of the domestic sphere lies with women. Uxorilocal or neolocal residence within the territory is therefore preferred.

Most religions assign a distinctly inferior position to women; but men's headship may in fact be nominal. As housewife and mother, a woman wields direct control over the household economy. She is seen as a physically and mentally strong person who can do hard labour and endure the pain of childbirth. Her place in the business of living and in maintaining kin relationships is beyond dispute.

It has been argued that in South Asia a woman, particularly among the higher castes, enjoys economic and other security – control over her reproductive power as well as over her person and productive output notwithstanding – because of her incorporation into her husband's family (Tambiah 1989, V. Das 1975). She has definite roles to play in respect of family deities, ancestors, and rituals. The family's prestige hinges on her character and behaviour. The family is responsible for looking after her and her children even after she is widowed. Over the years, an incorporated woman absorbs the ways and traditions of her husband's family, comes to identify with it, and acquires a special identity because of her membership. She can then initiate younger incoming women into the ways of the family with a certain authority. Such expertise gives her self-confidence, a sense of pride, and a feeling of power. Within the accepted system she develops her own identity and self-worth, because command over the collection of rules and traditions constitutes an important avenue of self-expression and social recognition.

There is some truth in this argument, but its limitations have to be understood. Incorporation demands considerable self-denial and self-effacement. Acceptance of the husband's kin must be demonstrated through caring for them. The ways and traditions of the family must be painstakingly learnt. Further, a woman's relative status in her affinal family depends on her husband's attitude to her and on his own position in the group. Two sayings appear relevant in this connection. It is often said that a woman whose husband does not like her cannot get respect or status in the family; and that a weak man's wife is everyone's *bhabhi* (elder brother's wife), with whom even lewd joking is permissible. Thus domestic politics provides the context. It needs a strong personality to fight against such odds and make a place for oneself in the affinal home.

A woman's position in her affinal family also depends on the status and prestige that she carries with her from her natal family. This prestige must be sustained through a flow of gifts and is also influenced by the fortunes of her natal family. In this limited way incorporation into her affinal family does not obliterate a woman's earlier identity even though she may have no rights left in her natal family. In many rural areas a woman is consistently referred to in her affinal home as one coming from such-and-such family or village. She must be conscious that the name and prestige of her natal family are linked to her behaviour.

A woman is incorporated into her husband's *gotra* but not as someone born into it. She is merely an in-married person and does not relinquish her natal *gotra*. This is clear from the fact that in the event of remarriage she has to follow the rules regarding avoidance of natal and related *gotras*. Her rights in the family into which she has been incorporated are often not recognized. Unless she has the support of her natal kin a woman may find it difficult to assert her position and rights in her affinal family and often in respect of conjugal relations also. Although submission, subordination, hard work, and self-denial can be and often are used by women as means of self-assertion and to obtain the praise of others, no simple correlation exists between incorporation into the affinal family and security. Perhaps support from natal kin, individual earnings, and some bargaining power can provide a woman with greater security (Gough 1956, Kolenda 1987a,b).

The notion of incorporation operates also among upper-class Muslims and patrilineal Christians – indeed, in the whole of South Asia at the level of ideals and rituals – but whether it gives women security is arguable. In addition to the support of natal kin, clear legal provisions go towards ensuring security. Women tend to recognize the structural and cultural limitations in their attempts to carve out living space for themselves.[3]

9

Marriage

Marriage is Destiny for nearly all women in Bangladesh, India, Nepal, and Pakistan. Its near universality is evident in the statistics. Women who never marry are few and are confined to the urban areas, where they are considered an oddity; however, those who are in high positions and have demonstrated their competence receive respect. A larger number of men may remain unmarried; for they are not cause for concern to parents in the way in which girls are. Both men and women are deemed to achieve the social status of adults only upon marriage.

Among Hindus marriage sacralizes and sanctifies female sexuality, while Islam wholly disapproves of sex outside marriage. Since sex is viewed as a natural craving of human beings, marriage is visualized as an event that is a necessary part of life, particularly for women. However, those few Muslim women who remain unmarried are not considered incomplete as believers. They have every right to follow Islam. Jains and Buddhists in India provide for nunhood, but few opt for it. In Thailand and the Philippines there does not seem to be such a preoccupation with marriage. Both Buddhism and Christianity allow for the theoretical possibility of people remaining single. Other careers and avenues besides establishing a household and bearing children seem to be acceptable in these countries.

In South Asia arranged marriages are the norm. Among Hindus the value placed on virginity at first marriage, segregation by sex, prescriptive and proscriptive rules and norms of caste endogamy and exogamy (of the *gotra*, clan, lineage, or village), and considerations of class put a premium on negotiated marriage. Since the management of female sexuality is one of the predominant concerns of society and ostensible virginity is a must for girls, a first marriage is thought to be the responsibility of elders. To many the very idea of young people choosing their partners for themselves is scandalizing. It smacks of loose behaviour, particularly on the part of the girl. For subsequent marriages – which are in any case not so common as they are in South-East Asia, traditionally being permitted only at the middle and lower caste levels, rare among the higher castes even though permitted by law, and almost unthinkable after a certain age – the rules are not so strict. Even among the urban educated population first marriages are generally arranged with the help of elders. In cases where a young man and woman decide to marry, they try to obtain the approval of their parents. Very often parents step in and arrange the details, making the affair resemble an arranged marriage.

Among South Asian patrilineal Muslims, too, marriages are generally arranged by elders. Ruzicka and Chowdhury (1978) report that only 5 per cent of all marriages registered in a rural area of Bangladesh in 1975 were arranged by the partners themselves (cited in Shaikh 1982).

In Peninsular Malaysia and bilateral Java self-choice is acceptable; but in the rural and semi-urban areas a first marriage is usually arranged on the initiative of the parents and with their consent. Very often it is considered their responsibility. Strange (1981) reports that women are the principal actors in arranging first marriages. In Indonesia the young couple seem to have somewhat more freedom of choice. The effect of Islam on expectations about unmarried girls' behaviour and on age at marriage is clearly discernible here, particularly in Malaysia. Young girls in the rural areas are placed under some restrictions. Shyness is an expected part of their demeanour. Girls who go out of the village to study or to work tend to become free and bold, but this change is not demonstrated within the village. It nevertheless seems that young people have at least some opportunities to meet and to make marital choices (Strange 1981). However, talking about western Malaysia, Kuchiba et al. (1979) report that efforts are made to keep young people segregated by sex so that they do not have many opportunities to meet or to talk to one another. They can, of course, eye one another; and each sex is well informed about the other. Those who work or study away from home have considerable freedom.

It is pertinent here to refer to Karim's (1987) statement that in Peninsular Malaysia unmarried men and women are both subject to the same moral codes. A young man is not expected to make serious advances towards a young woman unless he is prepared to marry her. Although there is a greater emphasis on female virginity, sexual promiscuity among young men is condemned. Quiet, demure men are preferred for marriage.

Subsequent marriages are in the hands of the partners. There is social pressure on unattached men and women not to remain single. Those who have been widowed or divorced are expected to remarry, and they may choose whom they like. Friends and relatives are also expected to help in finding suitable partners.

In Thailand, courtship is in some sense institutionalized (Woodtikarn n.d.). It cannot be compared to the dating of the West, for the locations are limited, often to the girl's house. Marriage conforms to the pragmatic character of rural Thai social structure and is by choice, although parents may give their opinion. In the face of opposition the couple may elope. Theoretically no girl is married against her wishes. In the event of an elopement, a household may be set up without any further formalities.

In central Thailand the wedding ceremony is generally elaborate. In northern Thailand, by contrast, the main requirement is that before coming to live with a woman a man should placate the spirits of her matriline; after this he is accepted as a member of her household. Among the Thai, by and large, the fact of living together is the seal of marriage in the eyes of the community. Only the socially mobile are inclined to celebrate the initiation of a union with a formal ceremony. When Buddhist ritual is used it is just a blessing of the union, little different from that invoked at a house-warming or at the opening of a new shop. The combination of Buddhism and bilateral kinship seems to have made marriage in Thailand very uncomplicated and informal. However, in children's rights to their father's property a distinction is made between the children of the first or main wife and those of minor wives, who are not wives in the strict sense.

The idea of courtship forms a part of Filipino culture. The parents of girls, however, are concerned lest their daughters land in trouble. Double standards of morality are to some extent tolerated by the community as a part of the male subculture. Brothers and neighbourhood youth try to protect girls from gossip and loose talk and from sexual experimentation in "stay-in" parties that often continue late into the night. Parents are not so concerned over a son's sexual activities as they are over a daughter's: "A man is a man, and nothing is lost in case things happen; but a woman – that is another story." These attitudes are gradually changing. Group dating rather than single dating appears to be more common at the acquaintance stage (Pinard 1975, Raymundo and Ruiz 1985). Peer groups play an important part in dating.

As regards the choice of a spouse, parents may indicate their preference for one suitor over another, but they rarely force their choice on their daughter. The principles of romantic love and freedom of choice are operative in the Philippines. There are no rigid rules regarding eligible partners. People tend to be endogamous in as much as social class, regional and linguistic background, and religious affiliation are generally taken into consideration. But there are many marriages across these lines, particularly in metropolitan areas. This appears to be a new development. Further, although the law forbids intermarriage between collateral blood relatives up to the fourth civil degree, marriages occur between both types of cross-cousins. There is no thought of keeping property within the patrilineal group as there is among the Catholics of Goa, because the kinship system is bilateral and both sons and daughters are included in inheritance.

Once a couple are engaged with their parents' blessings, they can date and the community does not gossip any more, although an early wedding is expected. An engagement may break if it stretches longer than two or three years. Neither is supposed to entertain another visitor of the opposite sex. The wedding takes the Catholic form. Socially, marriage confers maturity on the couple. As the residence pattern is not fixed, where the couple will stay is a matter for serious consideration, especially if they have not begun to earn enough to set up an independent household.

In Hindu patrilineal South Asia, marriage is looked upon as the necessary and the only honourable means of managing female sexuality. Both the future roles of a woman – those of wife and mother – are tied to this. The first or primary marriage of a girl involves giving away an unsullied virgin daughter. This is looked upon as a means of acquiring merit, and failure to do so is thought a great sin. Belief in the inviolability or indissolubility of Hindu marriage is very strong and is related to the prohibition of widow remarriage among the higher castes. Even today, and despite a law that has done away with the prohibition, widow remarriage is not common among the higher and some middle castes. It is particularly difficult if the widow has children.

Among the Parbatiya Brahmin and Chhetri of Nepal, only a few women whose first, "proper," marriage breaks up take other husbands; but this is through an informal union (Bennett 1983). Thus the principle that a woman may be married only once with full rites is a part of Parbatiya culture also. These informal unions are in a way secondary marriages. In Hindu India, divorce and remarriage have traditionally been permitted among the lower and many middle castes, but a clear distinction is made between the primary marriage and secondary marriages: a secondary marriage is performed with a very simple ceremony or with no ceremony at all. Even elopement and living together, once it is accepted, is considered a legitimate union. In some parts "sitting," or going to live in a man's house and starting to work and eat there, represents a socially noted sexual union that is accorded acceptance either immediately or in course of time, sometimes after compensation to the previous husband and a fine have been paid and a feast given. The terms used for secondary unions, including those arranged by the kin of the women involved, are different from those used for primary marriages: *pat* in Marathi, *churi pahanana* (giving glass bangles) in Rajasthan and other Hindi-speaking regions, *baithna* (sitting) in Uttar Pradesh, *paithu* (sitting) in Chhattisgarhi, *karewa* in Haryanvi, *kari* (to make a woman into a wife) in parts of the Hindi-speaking belt, and *chadar dalna* or *chadar andazi* (throwing over the woman's head a sheet with red corners) in Punjab and Haryana are some examples (see, among others, L. Dube 1956, Kolenda 1983, Chowdhry 1994). These are in sharp contrast to *vivah, byah, shadi, lagna*, and so on, which are the terms for a first marriage performed with full rites. Secondary unions are not thought so sacrosanct as a first marriage (Dumont 1970, L. Dube 1996).

One may mention *ihi* or *yihi*, a pre-puberty mock marriage of a girl with a *bel* fruit performed among the Newaris of Nepal (Allen 1982a) to ensure that the girl is married with full rites even before her sexuality is awakened. This seems to be related to the degree of freedom enjoyed by women. Among the Newaris there is no real stigma attached to divorce and remarriage; many women marry three or four times. Similar pre-pubertal mock marriage with an object and its association with relative freedom of movement and ease of divorce and remarriage was reported from north-eastern Madhya Pradesh (S. C. Dube 1953). The ritual has become rare now. But divorce and secondary marriage are practised on a fairly large scale.

In Hindu South Asia, a woman may be married with full rites only once, and the status of subsequent marriages is not equal to that of the first marriage. A man, on the other hand, can marry with full rites any number of times, provided that the bride has not been married before and is technically a virgin.

The desirability of marriage for girls is expressed in many ways by Hindus. Blessings for a male commonly ask for a long life, those for a female ask that she get a good husband. A number of *vratas* – the observance of fasting and of prayer rituals – are recommended to girls to ensure that they obtain good husbands resembling the deities Shiva and Vishnu. Some collective festivals for little girls in Gujarat, Maharashtra, and Rajasthan have the same object. Marriage signifies good fortune and a state of bliss. These ideas are expressed all over India through the terms used for a married woman with a living husband: "the fortunate one" or "the auspicious one" (L. Dube 1988a,b).

This state of good fortune is to be carefully nurtured through *vratas* and through festivals commemorating the good deeds of mythological females who married the men they desired or enhanced their lives or saved them from danger. Feeding a "fortunate" married woman on special occasions increases one's good fortune, as does the exchange of various accessories symbolizing that state – *kumkum* (vermilion), glass bangles, mirror, comb. Some of these beliefs and practices are more characteristic of the upper castes, but they are widely found also on the middle and lower rungs of the caste hierarchy.

Widowhood is greatly dreaded. Married women avoid all that is associated with widowhood, including certain kinds of attire and certain kinds of food (L. Dube 1988a,b, Dhruvarajan 1989). Among upper castes, widows are ceremonially divested of the significata of the married state and are turned into unattractive creatures. Some of the cruel customs that rendered a widow unattractive and denied her any of the pleasures of life are disappearing; but the idea persists that sins committed in a previous life brought about her widowhood. Inauspiciousness is still associated with a widow. There remains an ideological compulsion for a widow to lead a life of deprivation. Interestingly, even among high-caste Catholics of Goa a widow is considered inauspicious. Widows do not play a prominent part in weddings and other festivities connected with life-crises. When the bride comes to the bridegroom's house for the first time the two are not received by the groom's mother if she is a widow. A widowed woman changes to a black or dark sari or dress for life (Rowena Robinson, personal communication).

Whatever may have been the economic motivations behind *sati* (a woman's immolation on her dead husband's funeral pyre),[1] ideologically it signified that a woman who had lost her husband had forfeited her right to live. This act of supreme sacrifice would also assure her of her lord's company in the after-life. Recent incidents show that the admiration and valorization of *sati* are still alive (Sangari and Vaid 1989, Mani 1989). In various parts of India it is customary for a newly married couple to visit the shrine of a woman who has committed *sati*. This is done to pay obeisance and to pray for the long life of the bridegroom and the consequent state of good fortune for the bride.

Among the lower and middle castes *sati* may be venerated but life is not so bleak for widows. They are not associated so much with inauspiciousness. Widowhood results mainly in economic deprivation and the giving up of active participation in various ceremonies. A widow has the significata of marriage removed, but they are restored to her when she remarries. The notion is not so strong that widowhood is brought about by the sins of a previous birth.

Theoretically a widow has the right to maintenance in her husband's family. She can look after her children and manage her deceased husband's share of land. But, the law notwithstanding, in rural areas she is thought to have only a life interest in her husband's share of property. It cannot belong to her exclusively and in no case can she get it if she should remarry. If she has no children, or often if she has only daughters, her husband's agnatic kin will assert *their* rights over his share. What is the widow, after all? An outsider to the patrilineage. Customary rules regarding a widow's access to her husband's property and her daughters' rights are variable. As a broad generalization one may say that where there is strong patrilineal ideology and a kind of corporate character to the property-holding group, as among the Jats of Rajasthan for example (Palriwala 1990), the collaterals' claims are more forceful, often resulting in the denial of rights to the conjugal family of a dead man who has left no male child.

In contrast, a widower does not have to make any change in his style of living. He is not even remotely associated with inauspiciousness. He can marry any number of times. If he has children by his deceased wife, that is all the more reason for him to remarry; for it is argued that he will find it difficult to bring them up without another wife.

Wedding rituals accompanied by *mantras* (Vedic incantations or Puranic verses) express the value of the patriline, the continuance of which is the purpose of marriage. They involve the feeding of ancestors and the paying back of dues to Brahmins, preceptors, and ancestors. A man marries in order to become a householder and fulfil these obligations. A woman marries to enter a blessed state and to produce sons (Saraswati 1977). A bride is asked to be steadfast for the sake of her progeny. She is blessed in order that she may produce sons. She is referred to as the *kshetra*, or field, in which will fall the man's seed. Her instrumental value for the husband's patriline is thus clearly expressed: she is a receptacle, a vehicle for the perpetuation of the group (Dube 1986). The offspring derive their social identity from the father and belong to him.

I should mention here the practice among the matrilineal Nayar. Traditionally the sexuality of Nayar women was sacralized through the pre-pubertal ritual of tying on the *tali* (an auspicious necklace, a sign of marriage for women) (Gough 1955), which gave a girl the status of woman. Subsequent unions were not ritualized with the usual Hindu rites but got sanction through a simple ceremony in which the man gave the woman the traditional attire of two pieces of cloth. Divorce was very easy and widowhood was not considered inauspicious. A Nayar woman did not wear the various significata of the married state and did not have to remove her *tali* until her death. Within Hinduism, thus, a difference in the system of descent led to a very great difference in the nature and character of marriage.

The woman was the originator and perpetuator of the matriline, not an instrument for the continuation of her husband's patriline. The husband was necessary for her impregnation but he was not her provider and her social status did not depend on him. These unions were known as *sambandham* (a socially accepted sexual relationship) and did not have a sacramental character. A *sambandham* could be ended by either partner. The children of the union belonged to the woman and her matrilineage. Although the Nayar system has changed radically through legal "reforms," exposure to the Western world, and contact with the mainstream culture, the matrilineal ethos persists to some extent (Gough 1961, Saradamoni 1983, 1992a, L. Dube 1988c).

In Hindu patrilineal communities the gap in status between husband and wife is clearly expressed. A husband is like God, to be worshipped. This ideal is expressed in a number of mythological stories describing the devotion of wives and the advice of important figures from the epics (Leslie 1989, P. Mukherjee 1978). In everyday life service is the ideal for a wife – to keep her husband under her control through what might be called submissive self-assertion and by making herself indispensable. Complementarity does not mean equality. As Bennett (1981, 1983) and Gray (1982) point out, Brahmin and Chhetri women in Nepal follow the high-caste Hindu woman's norms and values. Deference to the husband can be seen in their drinking every day water in which his toe has been dipped, called *charanamrit* (nectar of the feet). In many parts of India a wife customarily touches the feet of her husband on certain occasions and takes *charanamrit* in certain *vratas*. Touching the groom's feet is part of the wedding rituals in some subcultures, Bengal being an example.

We should look at how the nature of conjugal relations varies across castes and caste levels and try to understand the bases of these differences. A Newar woman of Bulu, for instance, does not fit into the accepted norms, values, and behaviour patterns of the ideal Hindu woman, who should stay indoors, not mix with men or participate in public life, be modest and soft-spoken, and refrain from smoking or drinking in public. The women of Bulu are assertive and expressive. They are outside the house for much of the time, working in the fields or in the village square or in their back yards. They are independent, self-confident, and outspoken. Pradhan (1981) has tried to analyse the factors behind Newar women's behaviour. Two of these are: divorce or separation and remarriage are socially acceptable; and a woman's children by a previous husband are socially and ritually acceptable in the new family group, which is most unusual for a patrilineal community. It may be recalled here that *ihi* (ritual marriage before puberty) sacralizes female sexuality and sets a woman relatively free. Among those caste groups for whom remarriage is permitted, women are economically productive and have some freedom of movement. In spite of physical violence against the wife, her relationship with her husband is less unequal and is not burdened with much religious ideology.

Over the past several decades, particularly since India attained independence, laws relating to marriage, divorce, custody of children, and alimony have changed radically. Polygyny is prohibited. Divorce and remarriage are legally approved for all Hindus and are taking place, although not commonly, even in those castes to whose women they were not allowed earlier. Among the upper castes there is still a stigma attached to divorce, separation, and remarriage. The issues of alimony, of the custody of children, and of women's right to get back their possessions on divorce have proved to be difficult to handle. Moreover, the remarriage of a divorcee who has children poses problems: men do not wish to accept social fatherhood of someone else's child. In single-parent families, mothers find it difficult to bring up children. Even other children make the position of a fatherless child of a divorcee uncomfortable. A divorcee does not easily get the emotional and economic support of her natal home. The notion is very strong that marriage means a transfer for good. In divorces, very often it is the woman who is held to have been at fault; and the stigma attaches also to her natal kin.

In communities where divorce and remarriage have been traditionally accepted, difficulties may be settled either by a council of elders or, expensively, in the law courts. Where customary law is applied it may be difficult for a woman to get custody of her children – unless their father does not want them – and to get alimony. Basic notions concerning marriage and its break-up are different from those that obtain in modern law. The husband is believed to be giving up his rights over his wife; and, unless there is clear proof of cruelty on his part, he is not thought to have any obligation towards her after she has left him. On the contrary, in many communities it is the subsequent husband of the woman who should compensate the earlier one for having "broken his cooking pot" and for the expenses incurred in the earlier marriage. Customarily children belong to the father and his patrilineage, for they are his "seed." A woman's leaving her children behind is viewed as antithetical to the very essence of motherhood. Women often shy away from divorce even in unbearable conditions because of their children, to whom they feel they have a moral duty but over whom they have no rights.

Polygyny is not a cognizable offence, and the law does not take note of it unless there is a legitimate aggrieved party who complains. Very often the person likely to be aggrieved – the first wife – has no other financial support and does not want to leave her children behind or spoil their prospects by depriving them of their father's support. She therefore quietly accepts developments. Norms and customs do not exactly disapprove of polygyny. The massive "People of India" project of the Anthropological Survey of India reveals that, besides many tribal groups to whom Hindu law does not apply, there are many caste groups that do not forbid polygyny. The custom that prescribes or prefers the remarriage of a widow to her deceased husband's brother – real or classificatory – may often lead to polygyny. In instances of sexual entanglements between married men and unattached women, should the woman become pregnant the elders may first try to ascertain whose "seed" is involved and then ask the man responsible to marry the woman. A polygynous union would thus be encouraged in preference to having a child born out of wedlock.

Irregular polygynous unions are prevalent among the urban poor. A husband may discard his wife and children and start living with another woman, whom he may marry informally. This is a common feature in Calcutta, where there have been migrations from Bangladesh. Innumerable domestic servants and women working in the informal sector are in this position. Unlike in villages, there is no council of elders or caste *panchayat* to take note of such situations.

Among educated people there is some concern that a second wife is not recognized by the law as being wedded. The first wife may then be compelled to accept a legal divorce to clear the way. In rare cases a spirited, financially self-sufficient woman may refuse to grant a divorce, so her husband cannot marry another woman with whom he may already be living. But by and large, in polygyny as in divorce, women are placed at a disadvantage because they may have limited resources, because their kin may offer no support, and because children may complicate the issue.

At times, however, it is difficult for a lawfully wedded wife to complain if her husband is living with a second woman. She may be educated and even employed, but she may be able to produce no proof of marriage. Hindu marriages have not had to be compulsorily registered and even today not all marriages are registered. A marriage is essentially a social occasion. Proof of a wedding can come from the priest who officiates at it or from people who attend it. To locate the same priest after many years and persuade him to give evidence is no easy task for a woman, particularly if her husband is rich and powerful. A man could then claim that he had never married the first woman, which would render her children illegitimate and ineligible for support. Some feminist lawyers are trying to remedy the situation.

Another form of sexual union that needs brief mention is polyandry, which has been prevalent in some castes and communities of South Asia. The pastoralist Toda of southern India are the most studied group. They practised non-fraternal polyandry combined with female infanticide. It is said that neither a ban on infanticide nor Christianity could wean them away from polyandry. Polyandry was also reported among a few castes in Kerala and Sri Lanka, but in today's context we need to look at the fraternal polyandry of northern India.

The Jats, a large caste of agriculturalists settled mainly in Haryana,

Punjab, and Rajasthan, have been known for sharing a wife among brothers. Ostensibly a proper marriage was performed with one brother but the others, both younger and older, also had access to the woman so acquired. Women's labour was extremely important and on no account would a family like to lose a woman. An adverse sex ratio, due perhaps to female infanticide and the requirement of payment of bride-price, made it difficult to obtain a wife for each brother. Jat polyandry was practised surreptitiously, so even with a legal ban on multiple marriages it could not be eradicated. Another device to keep a woman in the family has been to remarry her to a younger brother of her deceased husband irrespective of disparity in age. There are a number of folk songs and stories related to these practices (for an excellent description and analysis, see Chowdhry 1994).

The largest population practising polyandry is found in the northwestern Himalayas. In India it covers Ladakh, the northern fringe of Himachal Pradesh, and tracts of Garhwal comprising Jaunsar Bawar, Rawain, and Jaunpur, where brothers share a wife or wives in common. There are considerable variations across the area. The people of Jaunsar Bawar belong to various Hindu castes but have been accorded the status of Scheduled Tribes for the sake of maintaining the legality of polyandry. They have developed a vested interest in the custom and, in spite of changes such as a decrease in its practice and a strengthening of the norms of monogamy, like to emphasize its presence. The inhabitants of Rawain and Jaunpur are struggling to obtain Scheduled Tribe status.

In these communities a woman does not remain in the same kind of marital union all along. She may be shared in her first marriage or in the next one, and still later may live in a monogamous marriage. Bride-price is prevalent. If a woman dissolves her marriage she has to compensate her husband for the bride-price paid and for the expenses of the wedding. These details are negotiated and executed by males. It is common for fathers to dissolve their daughters' marriages and have them remarried with bride-price.

Without going into the intricacies of the various forms of polyandry, the point that needs to be made is that, justified by bride-price, a woman is customarily obliged to be shared by a set of brothers. Nowadays many girls decline to marry where they are likely to be shared, or even elope to avoid the predicament. In Rawain–Jaunpur there is a clear distinction between *dan vivah* (marriage by gifting a daughter) and *dam vivah* (marriage by accepting a bride-price). It is in the latter kind of marriage that a woman is shared (Bhatt 1991).

Polyandry has been analysed as a mechanism to keep the men of a family together, ensure economic cooperation, and avoid the fragmentation of landholdings. It has been seen also as offering continuous protection to women and children in difficult hilly terrain and as keeping the population – heirs to land – under control. However, in a patrilineal, patri-virilocal setting, polyandry does not give any freedom of choice to a woman and makes her a tool in the hands of men.

The case of the Nayar of central Kerala should also be mentioned here. Matrilineally related women lived in the *taravad* house and received their husbands as visitors. A woman could entertain more than one husband during a certain spell of time (Gough 1961). How much freedom of choice they had is arguable. It is said that they were under pressure from maternal uncles – the *karnavar* (head, elders with an authoritative voice) of their *taravads* – whose calculations about the benefits that their *taravads* – as tenants – would derive from a *sambandham* with a particular Namboodiri landlord formed an important basis for women's marital relationships (Panikkar 1977). However, this economic explanation does not appear convincing. Personal interviews indicate that women must have had some choice. Moreover, unlike the women in patrilineal Jaunsar Bawar, Rawain, and Jaunpur, they did not supply labour and progeny to their husbands. Within the limits of caste norms they were secure in their own matrilineal homes.

It will be pertinent to compare the content and character of marriage in Muslim communities rooted in different kinship systems in South Asia and South-East Asia. Although marriage is everywhere based on the *sharia* and fulfils the basic requirements of scriptures and law, its nature in many communities is radically different from that visualized and emphasized in Islam. The contrast between patrilineal South Asia and bilateral and matrilineal South-East Asia comes out clearly.

Islam assumes patriliny to be the natural form of social organization and emphasizes a code of conduct and a system of law conforming to this assumption. In Bangladesh and northern India, although marriage with parallel and cross-cousins is deemed to preserve the purity of lineage and to keep property within the family, in reality such marriages are not very common. In one study in Bangladesh, of 1,719 first marriages among Muslims, 146 were between cousins (Aziz 1979). Studies by Ellickson (1975) and others indicate that there is a shift away from marriages between cousins. Korson (1968, 1971) has also made this point on the basis of his fieldwork in Pakistan. Besides the higher dowry that can be had from unrelated people, widening one's circle creates opportunities for increasing economic cooperation and for raising social status as well as ensuring different kinds of support through the network of kin and affines.

I have already mentioned the universality of marriage in Bangladesh. Monogamous marriage is the dominant form, there being very few polygynous marriages. *Mahr* is an agreed payment to be made to the bride. A certain portion has to be paid before consummation. In many cases the right to the remainder is forfeited by the wife either voluntarily or under pressure from her husband. In the event of divorce the husband must make over to the wife the amount of the *mahr*. With the increase in the importance of dowry, that of *mahr* is decreasing.

Muslim marriage is a contract, and its terms are usually formally documented. The relationship between the spouses is one of superiority and inferiority. The husband is looked upon as the provider and supporter. Deference, obedience, and service on the part of the wife constitute an important part of marriage. The Quran says that because a man pays for his wife he has a right over her. In the event of disobedience or misbehaviour he is entitled to inflict physical punishment. His wife may not refuse him sexual access. Both his wife and her children belong to the man. At marriage there is a clear transference of authority over the woman from her father to her husband. Patrilineal South Asian Muslims seem to be guided by these notions. There are books in Urdu containing detailed advice to wives and husbands on how to behave with their spouses and about their duties. *Hidayatnama Khavind* and *Hidayatnama Bibi* are well known. In rural Bangladesh a forceful indication of the transfer of authority and of the overall effacement of the wife's identity is the loss of her maiden name: she is called either after her natal village, or as the wife of so and so, or as the mother of so and so. There is thus a definite rupture in the continuity of a young woman's identity. As we have seen, this phenomenon is found in many parts of India among both Muslims and Hindus.

A Muslim woman's right to divorce is limited. A man, however, may divorce his wife very simply, and without assigning any reason. In most cases the *mahr* has already been forfeited. What the wife can expect is maintenance during the period of *iddat* (compulsory waiting for a divorced woman before remarriage), which is a little over three months. She can no longer live in her husband's house and usually seeks the support of her parents. She can remarry, but this may be difficult if she has children.

By all accounts divorce carries with it considerable social stigma for Muslim women in Bangladesh, Pakistan, and India at the upper and middle socio-economic levels. Another important point is the sense of insecurity with which Muslim women in South Asia live, for the pronouncement of *talaq* (repudiation or disavowal) is a matter of minutes and may result merely from impulse, caprice, or a minor provocation. Under the strict Islamic provisions a woman is not entitled to any support from her husband once the contract has thus been nullified; and legal reforms for providing her with maintenance have not been particularly effective.[2] A divorced woman thus faces deprivation and hardship, as does a widow.

Among the patrilineal Muslims of South Asia a widow is considered merely unfortunate: she does not carry any stigma as she would among Hindus. Although she does become vulnerable and lacks support, she is not considered inauspicious. Many widows look for and get support from their parents and brothers. In the case of intra-kin marriages or where the *khandan* of the widow and her husband is common, she may go to live with her natal family. Often, however, she continues to live among her husband's people, looking after her children. If she remarries, her children can only be accommodated in their father's family. Thus, although widows are permitted to remarry, in practice this can prove to be very difficult; and without a husband a woman may well be without any support at all. The statistics for Bangladesh show considerably more widows than widowers who have not subsequently remarried – although the difference is not as great as it is among Indians, especially Hindus.

In patrilineal South Asia one of the manifestations of inequality in conjugal relations is the beating and battering that women receive at the hands of their husbands. This is an expression of a man's right over his wife's person. "Do I need somebody's permission to beat my own wife?" is an expression signifying independence that is heard in Tamil Nadu. The Marathi saying "To whom does one complain when battered by rain or beaten by one's husband?" points towards the helplessness and resignation of wives faced with this form of abuse. A wife may retaliate by thrashing her drunken husband, but this reversal of the relationship can infuriate the husband further.

In the event of infidelity a woman is likely to receive ruthless treatment. The husband's exclusive right over the wife's sexuality is unquestioned. The phenomenon of noseless women that one comes

123

across in central India is unmistakable proof of this right, for one of the commonest reactions of a husband to his wife's infidelity is to disgrace her by cutting off her nose. The nose is considered the repository of an individual's shame or honour. Another possible reaction is to kill the paramour of the wife. In the words of Srinivas (1976: 155), "a man could play around but not so a woman. A man's sense of private property in his wife's genital organs was as profound as in his ancestral land. And just as, traditionally, a wife lacked any right to land she lacked an exclusive right to her husband's sexual prowess."

Islam demands obedience from a wife towards her husband in unequivocal terms and gives him the right to impart physical punishment. With patrilineal kinship and virilocal residence, Muslim women in Bangladesh, India, and Pakistan, particularly at the lower and middle socio-economic levels, routinely face the threat of physical violence from their husbands and occasionally from their husbands' kin (Akanda and Shamim 1985). In South-East Asia, by contrast, physical violence towards a wife is unthinkable in some populations. Where it does occur, for example when the husband is the sole earner and the couple live away from supportive kin, the woman is unlikely to tolerate it for long. And physical violence may be specifically put into a marriage contract as a cause of automatic divorce.

Marriage, divorce, and remarriage are radically different among bilateral and matrilineal Muslims in South and South-East Asia. They are governed basically by the *sharia*, specifically the Shafi'i school of jurisprudence. In South-East Asia there are special Islamic courts; but, as we have seen, people are often guided by *adat* (custom, tradition), which has also influenced the law together with modern demands.

In rural areas marriages take place at an early age. A girl may be married before puberty, with the consent of her father or her father's father, with consummation awaiting her coming of age. Marriage is universal for women. Since virginity is valued, the safest course is to marry off girls while they are still very young. Marriage removes some of the restrictions on a girl's movements. It is viewed as conferring adulthood on both sexes. Whereas parents are responsible for first marriages, in subsequent marriages the partners can make their own choices. On the whole there is no stigma attached to divorce, and remarriage is common; indeed, remaining single for long is not appreciated.

Mahr is usually small; and its payment may be deferred. It does not act as a deterrent to divorce and does not establish the husband's authority over the wife in keeping with the Quranic injunction. In matrilineal communities *nikah* does not establish a man's rights over his children; and among bilateral Javanese and Malays, despite what the law says, children either follow the mother or, if they are old enough, decide for themselves where they wish to go. Although the essentials of the religious injunctions are formally observed, the nature of conjugal relations is entirely different. Here I shall briefly deal with marriage and divorce among the Minangkabau and the Kalpeni islanders, who are matrilineal, the bilateral and matrilocal Atjehnese, and the bilateral Malaysians and Javanese. All but the Kalpeni islanders are from South-East Asia.

Among the Minangkabau of western Sumatra women receive life-long rights of use to specific parcels of their kin group's land. Men wander to distant places to earn, returning periodically to their wives. A man is expected to contribute in cash and in kind to his wife's house, but this does not either make him the provider or establish his superiority over his wife.

Since a high value is placed on male mobility and on institutionalized temporary migration out of the home area, husbands and kinsmen are often absent. Schwede (1989) argues that the assumption commonly made by anthropologists that men have authority and control over women does not hold true for the Minangkabau. Even when the husband makes remittances or is present, he may not be looked upon as the head of the family. That a man's existence in his wife's house is precarious has been reported by many: he always remains partially packed, and his wife has many ways of showing her displeasure with him and indicating that she does not want him any longer. Again, children belong to the matrilineage and *mahr* can scarcely be a deterrent to divorce. Conjugal relations are not built upon gender asymmetry and the wife's subservience. It is possible that things are different when families live away from their region and the husband is the principal or sole earning member; but even there the matrilineal ethos is present and a woman does not lose her rights in her matrilineage.

In Minangkabau marriage we have also to look at the mother–son relationship and at man's roles as son-in-law, son, and mother's brother. The most enduring and valued relationship is between mother and son. A man is required to support his mother financially and in other ways; this is almost a sacred duty. The composite image of woman as mother includes wisdom, strength, nurturing, refinement, dependability, and stability (Prindiville 1981). She initiates and implements important decisions.

The Atjehnese stand between the Minangkabau and the Javanese, with bilateral kinship but firmly matri-uxorilocal residence. A man's value depends on his contribution to his wife's household: he makes this by working away from home and returning there from time to time. But men are not seen as providers or as decision makers. Being sporadic members of the conjugal household and lacking authority, men are essentially peripheral. Descriptions of conjugal relations and behaviour bring out the incongruity of reality with the injunctions of Islam.

On Kalpeni island of the Lakshadweep group, *mahr* was only a formal compliance with the religious prescription. In the 1960s it was of negligible value; and the Kazi's register showed that it was sometimes not paid at all or was paid only in part. (The Kazi is the highest ritual functionary and adjudicator within Islamic personal law.) This matter had to be settled in the event of a divorce, but it was more important to deal with the dues of the rice, coconuts, and some other necessities that a husband had to contribute to his wife's household each year so long as the marriage lasted. In fact neither *mahr* nor such dues acted to prevent divorce. There has not been much change in subsequent decades.

Mahr in this matrilineal society does not establish the authority of a man over his wife. She is not expected to render personal services to him or to be subservient. Even when a woman flouts her husband's exclusive right to sexual access, he has no means of punishing her. There is discussion of the husband's customary annual dues to support his wife and children; but there is no clear notion of his being responsible for their maintenance in the real sense of the term. Because they live in separate units of production and consumption, neither spouse has a right to the other's productive labour. *Nikah* establishes the paternity of children but gives their father no rights over them.

Enduring polygyny is rare – women react sharply if their husbands have extra-marital affairs or contract other marriages. In 1962 only 6 of the 670 married men had more than one wife. Children are no deterrent to divorce: although they remain with their mothers, their affective bonds with their fathers may not be disrupted, and the fathers continue to have socio-religious obligations towards them.

Talaq, or repudiation, is the most common form of divorce on the island. The other two forms – *khula*, the purchase by the wife of her freedom, and *fasaq*, pronounced by the Kazi on grounds such as lunacy, impotence, or disease – are rare. Although the initiative in *talaq* formally lies with the husband, a woman may indicate to her husband that she does not want him to visit her any more and thus create a situation in which he has no option but to pronounce *talaq*.

Divorce is fairly frequent. More than half of the men and women on the island had married more than once, and many had been married several times. Because marriage does not entail living together, cooperation, or interdependence in economic or social spheres, or even a common overall responsibility towards children, its dissolution has no great disruptive effect.

In looking at matrilineal kinship systems from the point of view of women's situation and contrasting them with South Asian patrilineal kinship systems, it seems that the kind of concentration of control over property and over women's sexuality that husbands and other affinal males can achieve in a patrilineal, patri-virilocal system, often deriving justification from religion, is simply not available to a matrilineally related kinsman. For a discussion of the inherent instability of matrilineal systems, the inbuilt conflicts in them, and the well-known "matrilineal puzzle" (Richards 1950), see Poewe (1979), Schwede (1986), Tanner (1974), Weiner (1979, 1980), and Thomas (1980). See also Nongbri (1990) and L. Dube (1993).

Among the bilateral Javanese a conjugal pair forms the nucleus of the family unit; but this does not prevent other people from joining the household. There is a certain flexibility in the constitution of households. Adopted and foster children are readily accepted. The fact that children may move from one household to another, being brought up by persons other than their biological parents, has important implications for conjugal relations and divorce.

A Javanese woman is in full command over the domestic domain. She is the main figure of authority for children and is also in charge of the religious ceremonies performed periodically. She generally has an income from independent economic activity. She is expected to show respect for her husband, who should be older than her and whom she addresses as "elder brother." At the normative level there is a certain recognition of the equality of men and women, husbands and wives. Women are not as active as men in public affairs – husbands or sons are usually the representatives at village meetings. But, as Stoler (1977) has pointed out, the status of a woman is determined not so much by the rights that the legal system confers on her, or by her participation in social and political affairs, as by the extent to which she controls strategic resources.

The Javanese do not believe in continuing a marriage in the face of constant conflict. Divorce is rather rare in urban areas among the high and upper middle classes, although polygyny may be present; but among the rest of the population, and more so in rural areas, divorce is common. Its frequency is higher in the early years of marriage. In order to avoid conflict between close relations, marriages between third cousins or between persons further apart are preferred. As we see elsewhere in this book, individuals' rights to property are respected.

Javanese marriage is characterized by an overall absence of asymmetry, at least normatively. Women seem to exercise considerable choice in their entry into and exit from marriage and domestic groups. Their independent incomes, the presence of supportive kin, the ease of remarriage, and conditions that favour their asserting their rights over their children all contribute to their exercise of choice in forming or breaking marital links. Even *talaq*, the unilateral divorce pronounced by the husband, may well be initiated by the wife's packing her things and returning to her parents.

The nature of conjugality and the simple procedures of divorce among the Malays have been discussed by a number of scholars (Laderman 1983, Strange 1981, Tsubouchi 1977, Kassim 1984, Karim 1987). The state evinces much concern over the fragility of marriage. In some areas the rate of divorce has fallen, but it remains high. In the period 1951–1955 the rate per 100 marriages was 76.0 in Kelantan and 61.4 in Kedah. In Kelantan in 1966–1970 it was 56.0; and in Kedah in 1964 it was 50.7. Laderman (1983) reports that in Trengganu, where the divorce rate is the highest in the country, divorces were 71.25 per cent of all Muslim marriages over a 10-year period.

The marital bond is weak, particularly in the first few years of marriage. Marriage very often begins with uxorilocal residence. Even when the family household consists of the conjugal pair, there is a network of supportive kindred, and women maintain close links with their kin. This feature of Malay kinship and its influence on conjugal relations and divorce have been widely discussed (Djmour 1959, Firth 1966, Tsubouchi 1977, Strange 1981, Laderman 1983). Another important factor in women's relative independence is their engagement in remunerative work and the existence of conjugal property.

A Malay woman may be proud of her *ahli rumah* (housewife) status, but she usually does something or other towards an independent income. Providing for the family is an important role of a man, but this does not give his wife the feeling of being a dependant. She has her work, at least as wife and mother, and he has his work – the two are complementary. Lip-service may be accorded to the religious dictate that the husband is the head of a family. For instance, theoretically a wife needs her husband's permission to absent herself from home; but in practice she goes about her business without asking permission. And what she earns, she keeps, using it for the household's needs when the occasion arises or for her own expenses.

Talaq is the most common form of divorce. Formally pronounced by the husband, it is not really viewed as unilateral; for a woman may begin the process by making her husband's life a misery. Malay cultural values severely discredit a man who holds his wife against her will (Karim 1987).

It is a common practice to put conditions into a marriage contract the contravention of which automatically frees the woman. The most common of these are abandonment, insufficient maintenance, physical violence, and keeping or taking a wife away from her close kin. Maintenance is thus essential without giving a husband much authority or power over his wife. The condition that a wife be free to remain in close contact with her own kin makes Islamic marriage in bilateral societies entirely different in quality from that in patrilineal, patri-virilocal South Asia.

Thai society is hierarchically structured but the positions of individuals within it are not fixed. Ascriptive loyalties and ties of all kinds are minimized (Kirsch 1982). This has important implications for marriage. Marriage is not governed by specific prescriptions or proscriptions. There is a tendency to marry within the circle of people whom one knows. Young men's far greater mobility offers them much greater opportunities of finding spouses away from home; but young women are not circumscribed by rules governing their choice of partners.

Individuals generally decide whom they want to marry, and elopement is an established method of circumventing parental objections. An eloping couple may set up a household without going through any formalities. Marriage may involve no ceremonies at all, barring perhaps a private one to placate the spirits. Matrilocal residence is common, particularly at the beginning of a marriage, but ties are generally maintained with the husband's relatives as well. The typical and ideal unit of residence is the independent nuclear family household. As this is often close to the wife's kin, the majority of married men live away from the places of their birth.

The traditional view of conjugal relations is guided by notions of differences between the sexes. The husband should be the head, the taker of decisions, the earner of income; while the wife should be the subservient, modest follower whose duties relate to children and the household. In the traditional view man is strong, woman is weak. Woman is more easily defiled than is man. Virginity is important only for women. These ideas, together with depictions of women as deceitful and full of guile, with numerous faults and weaknesses, appear to have their roots in Buddhism and in early Hinduism.

There is, however, a tremendous difference between the ideal and the actual; and one may wonder about the degree to which the ideal is promoted. A wife does not really have to defer to her husband. Although there is a broad assignment of responsibilities, the division of work is flexible. Women are active in production, even doing such work as ploughing. In Buddhism men are superior, for only they can be ordained; but this does not permeate profane domestic life. Buddhism has little to say about worldly relationships, including the tie of marriage. Thai kinship relations are not group based, and kinship terminology is symmetrical for gender. For these reasons the conjugal relationship is not characterized by any considerable asymmetry. In the political and religious spheres, however, Buddhist notions of male superiority have their influence.

A mother's position is very strong. In the event of divorce she need not lose her children or, in most cases, shelter. She need not give up her children even when she remarries. She has some economic independence because the man in a family is seldom its sole earner. The marked preference for kin ties between women or for those related through women assures her of support in all circumstances. Although a woman's right to maintenance from a divorced husband will end on her remarriage, at the time of divorce she will have taken possession of what she brought to the marriage and also of a part of the property accumulated during the marriage. It is clear that the perceptions of relationships, rights, and responsibilities that stem from the kinship system place women in a tolerably fair situation.[3]

Double standards are applied, however, to extramarital sexual activity: adultery by the wife can be a ground for divorce, but not adultery by the husband. For both, divorce is relatively easy to obtain. The unfortunate situation of a family that disintegrates because of lack of means is distinguished from divorce brought about by other factors. The most common cause of conjugal discord is the squandering of money by men on women, liquor, or opium. According to Kirsch (1967), separations appear to be most frequent during matrilocal residence.

Marriage means different things to men and women. Men have other alternatives such as monkhood. In any marriage, the wife has to be more committed to it than does the husband. If nothing else, theirs is the responsibility of caring for the children. They are not, however, as firmly bound to a marriage as are women in South Asia. They are almost always involved in income-earning activities, they have charge of household income and expenses, and they can always count on the support of kin. Marriage is seen less as a union of hearts than as a coming together of complementary functions. Love is not considered a necessary component of a marital union (Rajadhon 1961). The instability of marriages is accepted by villagers with equanimity.

Pongsapich (1986) has traced the changes in the law relating to marriage. The traditional marriage law allowed polygyny and permitted adultery to men. After repeated protests, monogamy was made obligatory in 1935; but this did not bring about the disappearance of polygyny. In general the law appears to have many intricacies that permit it to be flouted relatively easily.

Although the Spanish influence in the Philippines accorded a low status to women in society and in law, the bilateral ethos was retained. Women remained active in the economy, particularly in rural areas and among the poor. In urban areas too, women are engaged in the informal sector and those who acquire education and training also work. The regime of the United States extended educational facilities to all regardless of sex, and today Filipino women are better educated than most others and have a presence in predominantly male spheres of activity.

The influence of Roman Catholicism is strong where marriage and divorce are concerned, and it combines with local peculiarities to work against women. Divorce is not permitted, although a marriage may be annulled in certain circumstances. Legal separation, which does not amount to severance of the marital tie, is provided for. In this the fault principle operates rather than that of mutual consent. Adultery by the wife is sufficient ground, but adultery by the husband must be shown to amount to concubinage.

As Illo (1990) observes, girls and boys are socialized into gender-based work roles, but these are seldom inflexible. Thus girls may be asked to help with fishing and with the harvesting of rice, while boys may be trained to cook and to care for younger siblings. This flexibility is apparent in the work roles assumed by married couples, which depend largely on the time available to each.

A wife plays a major role in the financial affairs of her household, whether rich or poor, rural or urban. Women who must contribute to the domestic economy in the phase of reproduction and child-raising often do this through home-based or neighbourhood-based enterprise. Although women are proud of their "house-owner" and home-maker status, they try also to earn some income. Apart from controlling family budgets, women also take extra-domestic economic decisions on such matters as the lending and borrowing of money, the buying and selling of property, and the running of family businesses.

A significant feature of marriage in patrilineal South Asia, which stands in sharp contrast to South-East Asia, is the prevalence of dowry and its growth during the past few decades. In the world outside, news of dowry deaths and of the harassment of women for dowry in South Asia, particularly in non-peninsular India, is received with bewilderment. The phenomenon of dowry has been analysed extensively (see, for example, Government of India 1974, L. Dube 1983b, U. Sharma 1984, Akanda and Shamim 1985, L. Caplan 1984, Visvanathan 1989, Ghadially and Kumar 1988, Srinivas 1984). In order to explain dowry it is necessary to examine some social structural and cultural features of Indian society that have provided the bases and the context for the new influences that have brought about this bizarre commercialization of marriage.

It cannot be denied that marriage has an economic dimension everywhere; but dowry as it is found in South Asia is rooted in patrilineal, patri-virilocal kinship. Among Hindus, particularly the middle and upper castes, dowry has a strong religious sanction. As we have seen, in South-East Asia parents are concerned to help their children settle down as a conjugal unit – either separately or as part of a larger domestic unit – upon marriage. In bilateral societies there is some choice in respect of where the new couple may live. They may get some land, a garden plot, a house, or some capital, but this is not necessarily related to marriage. There do not seem to be any institutionalized transactions of goods and cash as an inevitable part of marriage. Importantly, the notion of purchase of rights over a woman's labour and reproductive capacities implicit in bride-price and that of grateful offerings by a girl's family to her groom and his kin for taking her into the "auspicious" married state – which is what is embodied in dowry – are absent. There may be a semblance of bride-price or bride-service in some groups, and of course *mahr* is prevalent in all Islamic populations; but these do not assume enormous proportions either as indicators of status or as preventive measures against divorce. Very often they are merely of a token nature. The ideas of conjugal property and of spouses' individual property are quite clearly established.

South Asia presents a different picture. Dowry has assumed enormous proportions and has spread even to groups such as peasants, artisans, and lower castes who earlier practised bride-price. Bride-price has been common among tribal groups. Undoubtedly it symbolizes compensation for the loss of a productive member who is acquired by her husband and his kin group. The expressions used by people do signify purchase. This is clear from the fact that, if a woman leaves her husband to live with another man, that man has to pay compensation to the first husband. The custom of bride-price does not turn a daughter into a liability – she remains a source of some earning. Even in such marriages some household goods, clothes, and ornaments may be given to a daughter as a kind of support. According to Srinivas (1984), the custom of bride-price was prevalent even among the Brahmins of Karnataka and other parts of southern India. This can be explained by the concern over obtaining a suitable bride from within the endogamous group.

However, gradually dowry has been replacing bride-price. The influence of the upper castes and their Sanskritic ways has been an important factor in this change, but the causes run deeper. It results in the devaluation of daughters, who become a distinct liability.

In southern India, perhaps owing to the preference for intra-kin marriages, there has been some reciprocity in prestations between bride-givers and bride-takers, although typically the bride's family must spend more. This relative reciprocity is found also in many parts of central India, Maharashtra, and Bengal, but the two sides are distinctly unequal not only in status but in the considerably greater expenses that bride-givers are expected to incur.

Dowry, or *dahej* as it is called in north India, includes gifts for the bride such as clothes, jewellery, and household goods, ideally treated as her personal possessions forming the nucleus of the conjugal estate; gifts for the son-in-law, including cash; gifts for the groom's parents and other kin; and money as a contribution towards the expenses of the groom's party. There is also lavish expenditure on hospitality. Depending on socio-economic level, kitchen equipment, furniture, electronic equipment, and vehicles have also come to form part of dowry (Vatuk 1975, U. Sharma 1984, Uberoi 1993, Tambiah 1989).

Large dowries have traditionally been common among castes that are internally ranked and that practise intra-caste hypergamy (marriage in which the female has a lower familial status than the male). The compulsions of marrying within well-defined limits combined with internal gradations render the position of young women and their families precarious. It is not surprising that some groups have practised female infanticide. A decrease in marriages among kin (applicable to southern India and to Muslim populations), economic or social differentiation within an endogamous *jati* (caste group), and an expansion of marriage circles to cover cognate *jatis* have all contributed to the escalation of dowry.

There is competition among the fathers of marriageable girls with something akin to bidding involved. The parents of young men expect large dowries and demand them. With differentiation in occupations within families and the possibility of earning sons establishing their own households, young men's parents are keen to recover what they have spent on their education and training. Investment in education has increased many times over and dowry seems to be the only way of recovering it. Consumerism has added to the list of commodities that are included in dowries. Because marriages are contracted within limited connubial circles and negotiations are the accepted method of making matches, girls' parents have no option but to spend beyond their means.

Although on the sentimental plane dowry is a compensation for a girl's loss of membership in her natal family (for is it not an accident that she was born female?), to call it pre-mortem inheritance is far-fetched. More often than not a girl's parents have to spend on her marriage well before the time for the distribution of property, and their expenses may be quite disproportionately high. Broadly speaking, the amount and nature of dowry depends on the socio-economic status of the bridegroom and his family and the accomplishments and appearance of the bride.

Daughters themselves are often keen to marry with dowry, for they are aware that, although they are legally entitled to shares in the property of their natal families, they are unlikely to get them. Perhaps more important, their status in their affinal families depends on what they take with them. This does not mean that a girl has a firm right over what she takes to her affinal home. Much of it may be regarded as being for the use of the whole family. Usually no records are kept of the bride's possessions, and any insistence on an exclusive right to them would strike at the roots of the solidarity of the family.

Harassment for dowry after marriage has been reported mainly from north India. Dowry is no longer a one-time payment: often a series of demands are made, and if these are not met the bride is sent back or is ill-treated even to the point of being killed. Marriage establishes an unequal relationship between the two sides. Bride-givers become permanent gift-givers and there is no obligation on bride-takers to give anything in return. Moreover, although their obligations towards their daughter continue, as does the flow of gifts to her affinal family, her parents' rights over her are snapped at marriage. Women's organizations have the bitter experience that after a dowry death the dead woman's parents usually say that their daughter had expressed the wish to return but that they themselves had advised her to stay on and try to adjust. Orissa, for example, an eastern state, reports that "accidental deaths" of women, generally through burning, have assumed enormous proportions in recent years. Because of the tradition of communication between natal and affinal families in south India and parts of central India a woman is not left entirely at the mercy of her affinal kin. However, escalation of dowry has been a general phenomenon in all regions. This has resulted in many girls not marrying at all, and gruesome reports of suicides by girls who see no hope of marriage are published in the press.

Laws against dowry in Bangladesh, India, and Pakistan have proved ineffective. Although dowry does not have religious sanction among Muslims, violence and torture are reported to accompany demands for dowry. According to Akanda and Shamim (1985), since the war of liberation in Bangladesh the desire to get rich overnight has spread among the population. "Black" (unaccounted) money increased, which gave an impetus to dowry. They report that torture and death associated with dowry are more common in the villages than in the towns. Even a poor farmer or day labourer does not hesitate to demand money or land not only at a wedding but also years later. Wives commit suicide, and violence such as acid-throwing and murder, more or less absent in the past, has arisen.

Dowries of clothes, jewellery, and household goods for the bride and cash for the son-in-law and his father are prevalent among the essentially patrilineal Christians of various denominations in southern and south-western India (L. Caplan 1984, Visvanathan 1989, R. Robinson 1994). Many young women earn their own dowries, migrating all over the world for jobs; and many marry relatively late. There have been efforts to conduct marriages without dowries and at little expense. There is not the kind of dowry-related violence that is seen among Hindus and Muslims.

Visvanathan argues that, among Orthodox Syrian Christians, it is virtually impossible to marry without *streedhanam*, which entitles a woman to become an integrated labouring member of her husband's group. It is through *streedhanam* at marriage that a woman receives the right to work and to reproduce. For a few days after marriage a bride is treated as a guest and does no housework. Gradually she becomes a part of the household. Although the father of the groom, who controls the property and interests of his son, also controls the cash dowry that comes with the bride, when the son establishes a separate home or when his wife gives birth, it is the received dowry that forms the basis of the new household.

It is clear that dowry and its various manifestations in South Asia are a function of patrilineal, patri-virilocal kinship, women's dependence, caste endogamy, and marriage by negotiation. Deep structural changes are needed if the menace of dowry is to be eradicated. It has further devalued women; and son preference, female foeticide, and the neglect of female infants are not unrelated to it.

10

Nutrition and discrimination

Nutrition is one of the significant axes of gender differentiation in South Asia. Many of the factors responsible for differences in the quantity and quality of food that a household gives to male and female children are interlinked and can be traced to the values and ideas generated in the kinship system, family structure, and ideology linked to them. The different rates of mortality and morbidity for girls and boys are explained in part by discrimination in nutrition and health care. Female infanticide and foeticide are extreme manifestations of the devaluation of daughters.

A number of empirical studies have presented this bitter truth about Bangladesh, India, and Pakistan. In well-to-do homes girls are not really deprived of food; but there is a tendency carefully to cater to the tastes, wishes, and whims of male adults and male children. The choicest items are reserved for them.

A young woman narrated her experience, which is revealing. Her grandmother would have any number of extra pieces of sweets for her grandson when he asked for them. But when the narrator asked for one, the old lady would refuse it. She would say, "You are a girl; you should learn to eat less and to swallow suffering" (*kam khao, gham khao*).

Customarily a girl is not given milk to drink. This is a common pattern among Marathas and Brahmins in western Maharashtra, and is in fact a general feature of Indian culture except among educated upper-middle-class and well-to-do sections. Milk is a boys' privilege, for they must grow tall and strong. Girls, on the contrary, should not grow much or fast; their growth needs to be controlled. A large share of proteins, particularly milk products, meat, fats, and delicacies specially prepared at the cost of much labour, goes to the more valuable offspring. In Masi Jheelo's house in a western Pakistani village, described by Ahmad and Ahmad (1990), the boys were given milk and eggs. The girls looked upon this and occasionally remarked in a slightly protesting tone that nothing seemed good enough for boys. The mother would point out that boys would, after all, be the support of the family, whereas girls could not be relied upon, as they might leave for another house any day.

In large parts of Maharashtra there is a tradition of drinking milk fresh from the udders of cows and buffaloes. This is the privilege of men and boys. In most parts of non-peninsular India, among those who can afford it, milk forms part of men's diet, not of women's. Women are entitled to milk only in special circumstances such as lactation or illness, and sometimes pregnancy. This pattern is an institutionalized one and is not even thought about. Whereas boys may be given breakfast, girls (and daughters-in-law) are not. Women and girls are not only the last to receive food, they also get less of it and of a lower quality. Expectations of self-denial are also given expression here. If a girl cries or shouts for food she is considered fussy and is teased and taunted about her lack of self-restraint.

When resources are scarce this discrimination can be acute, and girls may remain underfed and undernourished. Boys too may not have enough to eat, but girls are much worse off. An incident in a girls' school in a small town in Maharashtra is worth narrating here. The school's principal insisted that each child bring some tiffin for the afternoon recess. One day she identified a girl who did not bring any tiffin for herself. She scolded the girl, who brought a small tiffin box the next day but did not eat from it. When questioned, the girl was trapped; she opened the box, which was empty. With tears in her eyes she explained: "In the morning there is only enough food left for my brother to carry to school. My mother cannot find the time to cook in the morning, so I have to come without any tiffin" (Vidya Panday, personal communication).

Leftovers are expected to be eaten by the women and girls of the house; they are not meant for males. Girls must learn this when they are still little. Any expression of resentment on their part may bring concessions, but usually with the remark that the capacity to adjust is of prime importance for girls, as is consideration for others.

A consciously cultivated feminine role is that of food-giver. The cooking and serving of food are the constituents of this valued role, which is emphasized in the ritual by which a bride is incorporated into her husband's kin group. The ideal of Annapurna, the unfailing supplier of food, is accepted throughout India. Among South Asian Muslims, too, this role of food-giver is central to the definition of many female kinship roles.

Linked to this is the expectation that females should think of the comfort of others, without being bothered about what is left for them. It is well known that in South Asian cultures women eat last of all, after they have served everyone else. Paul (1992) has graphically described how in a Maru Charan family women use ingenious ways of using preserves of various kinds to make some kind of a curry to go with the food left over for them. Girls are specifically trained to this behaviour. An inevitable consequence is the lack of proper nutrition for females. This is related to the division of work, role allocations, the notion of *seva* (service), the instrumental role of women in the kinship system, as well as to a clear distinction between male and female children in terms of their value.

The practice of *dastarkhwan* among Muslims symbolizes a meal shared. Food is spread out on a sheet for all to eat, which may suggest equality in its allocation, but that is not the reality. I have referred already to discrimination by the mother between sons and daughters in matters of choice items such as milk and eggs in a Pakistani village. In villages, of course, *dastarkhwan* cannot always be followed. Some of my friends and colleagues have described a definite hierarchy in middle-class households. The whole family sits down together to eat, but a definite order is followed. Although the mother comes next to the head of the household she is careful to leave the better and larger portions for her sons, who precede daughters and daughters-in-law (Mohini Anjum, personal communication).

What Papanek has called "compulsory emotions" (1991) can also be called culturally constructed gender-linked notions of "proper" behaviour. What Maher (1984: 128–129) has written of Morocco seems also to apply to the Muslims of Bangladesh, India, and Pakistan who follow the patrilineal kinship system. According to her, hierarchy is expressed in the sharing of food within a household. Men consider prized foods such as meat their prerogative whereas women and girls learn to refuse these foods, to offer their shares to guests, and to save the best portions for brothers, sons, and husbands.

When discussing patterns of food consumption in Bangladesh, Kabeer (1985b: 85) mentions that adult males have the first claim on consumption resources. Women's claims vary with their position in the life cycle, and children's claims vary with age and sex. According to the Bangladesh Nutrition Survey of 1976/77 to which she refers, the average intake of food is higher for males than it is for women. In the 1–15 age group, nutritional deficiency is greater at the younger ages. Young girls demonstrate acute undernourishment far more often than do young boys. Adult males' claims spring from their supposed roles of bread-winner, protector, and guardian. As in India and in Pakistan, so in Bangladesh women function as the makers and distributors of food, practising discrimination against themselves and their female children. Ideology rooted in the materiality of kinship is one of the major factors at work here.

In South Asia women are in charge of the kitchen and take most day-to-day decisions. There may be hierarchy among the women themselves, and as time passes roles may be reversed. But it is important to examine decisions concerning cooking to see whom they are taken in reference to. Most of the menu is decided in reference to the needs and preferences of the men of the family and those of the children, possibly of both sexes. In a family of five in which both husband and wife are university teachers, if the man is out of town his widowed mother would say, "Let us make something very simple for dinner. Who is in the house tonight?" Her son was absent and the remaining people did not amount to much.

At socio-economic levels and in ethnic groups where women do considerable productive work or are effective wage-earners, and where the ideology of the husband as a distinctly superior god-like being is not operative, women and girls may not suffer from deprivation in the matter of food much more than the males of the family. Many tribal communities and lower-status groups in Hindu society demonstrate this.

In South-East Asia, too, women are recognized as home-makers. Although there is considerable flexibility in the sharing of work, the kitchen is considered the domain of women. Descriptions of feasts in Malaysia and Indonesia bring out the qualities of initiative and leadership that women show in the preparation and distribution of food (Stoler 1977, Suratman 1986). Although it is said of Thailand and the Philippines that mothers tend to pamper sons, who then become irresponsible about sharing food with others, there does not seem to be any conscious discrimination between male and female children.

Certain not immediately obvious factors may be involved where nutrition is concerned: the state of knowledge about nutrition, the supposedly different nutritional requirements of males and females, beliefs about foods prescribed and proscribed during pregnancy, and so on (Laderman 1983, Strange 1981, Tan 1973, n.d.). But the kind of deliberate discrimination that we find in South Asia is not to be seen in South-East Asia. Where there is no great difference in the value accorded to children of the two sexes, any notion of discrimination in food must seem incredible.

It may be useful to take a brief look at some practices related to the distribution and eating of food. In Indonesia it is customary to place cooked food on a table in bowls, together with plates, spoons, and so on. There is a distinct preference for lukewarm food, and rice is not eaten hot. Members of the household come to the table and serve themselves when they wish to eat. They remove used dishes and leave the table tidy once again. This procedure leaves no scope for discrimination among the children (Papanek, personal communication).

In much of South Asia, on the other hand, there is a marked preference for steaming-hot food. Most preparations of grain are thought best when taken straight from the fire. As a consequence, women generally have to simultaneously prepare and serve at least part of the food. They can neither prepare everything in advance nor eat together with the males. Even where everything is prepared beforehand, women are expected to serve men and children first. It is significant that they are thus required to wait upon the males of the family, even when the food does not have to be served straight from the fire. That women should think of others before thinking of themselves is part of the training of girls in South Asia (L. Dube 1988a,b). Women's role as nourishers is greatly extolled; and they must make do with what is left over, with something hastily improvised, or with nothing.

In South Asia in ordinary homes food is almost entirely home-cooked and the housewife is its sole provider. In South-East Asia food may be purchased and eaten outside the home, and people are quite accustomed to eating from roadside stalls. Clearly the notions of motherhood and womanhood do not include the provision of food as virtually the only medium of communication. Nor is food used by mothers as an instrument of power over their children, as is typical of South Asia.

If we compare the north and south of India (leaving aside Kerala, which is in a class by itself), perhaps at certain ages and bodily states girls in south India are better cared for. For example, at puberty and childbirth women receive special attention.

Studies of Nepal, including those focusing on women, do not mention discrimination by gender in the distribution of food. Even the special reports produced under the Status of Women Project do not note this phenomenon. This may be an instance of a common tendency in the social sciences not to ask questions that use gender as a variable (L. Dube 1980). My discussions with researchers on Nepal brought the statement that, except in milk and its products, there was no discrimination between male and female children. Perhaps this needs further investigation. If it is true, the only explanation that strikes me is the special place of the daughter in Nepali culture. She is sacred, always to be respected, and to be honoured through special festivals (Gray 1982, Bennett 1983). However, in-marrying women must function under the same constraints and ideology as in India. As for the importance given to daughters and the sacredness attributed to them, Kondos (1991) differs from Bennett and Gray. The comparative tables for South and South-East Asia do not show Nepal in a particularly good light.

There is more protein deficiency in females than there is among males in South Asia. If we go by the inferences that may be drawn from the statistics on disease and health, mortality and morbidity, there is hardly any room for doubt that girls are far more deficient in nutrition than boys. That hospitals record far fewer admissions of female children points to another field of discrimination – that of health care. If girls are taken to hospital at all, it is at a relatively late stage of illness. Time, energy, and money seem unaffordable when there is a tacit compliance with the notion that a girl is expendable anyway. Where son preference is strong, neglect of female children is not surprising. There is a tremendous difference between the cost of saving the life of a low-priority female child and the cost of saving and improving the life of a male child (Miller 1989a).

Fact-finding is going only half-way: the *why* of a phenomenon must be sought. Thinking over the evidence, one is forced to conclude that the kinship system and family organization are to a very great degree responsible for the undernourishment of girls and the neglect of their health. At any socio-economic level in patrilineal societies, girls are deprived relative to boys.

For sexual discrimination in nutrition and health care, see Batliwala (1982, 1985), M. Chatterjee (1983, 1989), Ganesh (1988), Krishna Raj (1987), Miller (1981, 1989a), Sen and Sen Gupta (1988), Kynch and Sen (1983), Shatrughna (1988, n.d.), Visaria (1985).

The neglect of female children in South Asia, particularly in

Bangladesh, India, and Pakistan, is clearly demonstrated in the differences between the sex ratios in the region and those in South-East Asia. A cursory look at the male–female ratios in north and south India indicates less discrimination in the south. Kerala stands in a category of its own. Here, besides women's active participation in productive activities, the continuance of the matrilineal ethos cannot be ruled out as a contributory factor. Low fertility, high literacy, and an even sex ratio are all combined in Kerala. Studies in greater depth involving various Christian and Muslim communities along with matrilineal caste groups are required before we start debating whether the Kerala model can be replicated elsewhere.

The north–south difference can be explained by a very strong preference for sons in the north and only a relatively mild preference for sons in the south. The results of various surveys of attitudes and behaviour have brought this out (see Basu 1993a,b for references to these). However, figures from the 1991 census show that, although birth rates have definitely begun falling, declining fertility is indicative of further devaluation of the female sex. The practice of female infanticide persists, but whether it has increased during the past decade cannot be ascertained.

The new technology that makes it possible to determine the sex of the unborn child may be responsible for part of the decrease in the proportion of females in the country. From 934 females per 1,000 males in 1981, the sex ratio had come down to 921 females in 1991 (*Ravivarta* 1994). Vibhuti Patel (1988) expresses the protest against and anxiety about the abuse of technology when she discusses the consequences of sex determination or pre-selection tests. Amniocentesis has become quite inexpensive and is within the reach even of working-class people. However, it has been used by or upon women of all socio-economic classes, even up to the highest educational levels. The test cannot be carried out before a pregnancy is 16 weeks old, and abortion at this stage poses quite some risks to a woman's health. But this test as well as ultrasound examination, which is as simple as an X-ray and need not even be recorded, are being used to determine the sex of foetuses so that the birth of unwanted female children may be forestalled.

The *Times of India* reported that between 1978 and 1983 around 78,000 female foetuses were aborted in India after sex determination tests. In 1986/87 the number of such abortions was between 30,000 and 50,000. In Bombay city alone about 7,000 female foetuses were aborted during 1989/90. Acts prohibiting sex determination tests have

143

been passed in Maharashtra, Punjab, and Rajasthan and a similar act is proposed to cover the whole country. However, since the use of the technology has to be permitted for diagnosing abnormalities, its use for identifying female foetuses is not likely to stop. As some people have argued, female foeticide is not so bad as female infanticide, which in turn is better than slow death through neglect and discrimination.

It is a peculiarity of South Asia that the female sex is denied the right to be born, to survive after birth, and to live a healthy life avoiding the risks of pregnancy and childbirth. Poverty alone cannot explain this.

The denial of survival can be imposed immediately after birth. Female infanticide forcefully reflects the patrifocal, hierarchical, and oppressive character of Indian patrilineality. It used to be practised in large parts of India among specific caste groups at the middle and upper levels (Vishwanath 1973, 1976, Parry 1979). Even today old Khatri women describe how the midwife had specific instructions to kill a newborn female by suffocation and report a stillbirth. The British took note of the problem and tried to end it by legal and punitive measures, but it persists in some places and among caste groups to this day. In the villages of Jaisalmer district, for example, about 300 newborn females are put to death every year (*Ravivarta* 1993).

Several methods have been used for killing newborn females: suffocating the baby by pressing the afterbirth over its face, putting opium on the mother's nipples, feeding the baby an extract of poisonous oleander berries or with the poisonous milk of a wild plant. The last method is reported to be in use among the Kallar of Tamil Nadu, who have been in the news for the widespread practice of female infanticide. Two other methods are to step on the throat of the infant and to put a few grains of paddy (unhusked rice) into its mouth (Venkatramani 1986). The Kallar are a caste of warriors whose women are not very active in productive activities (Krishnaswamy 1988). The main argument in favour of female infanticide, which is seen as a cultural practice, is the increase in dowries and the never-ending expense on daughters' childbirth and prestations even after they are married.

In northern India the Rajput and Jat were known for practising female infanticide. The division of the former into clans with different statuses and the practice of hypergamy, according to which girls of the highest sub-castes had very little choice in the marriage market, made daughters a burden. Having a daughter also meant loss of status for the father as a bride-giver. It is difficult to assess the prevalence of female infanticide across the country. As for female foeticide, it is being practised even by those who had never practised female infanticide. The menace of dowry appears to be the main factor in the discrimination against daughters.

Cultural perceptions regarding daughters and sons may be contrasted across the two regions. In South Asia, sons are considered future providers and easy to bring up. Their reputations are not easily tarnished. Daughters, on the other hand, are viewed as potential creators of problems for their families. They are also expensive and of no use after they are married. They may be useful around the house but demand watchfulness and protection. Although both sexes should marry, there is much greater compulsion about the marriage of daughters. If a son gets married it becomes necessary to provide for a newcomer, whereas if a daughter remains unmarried she needs to be supported and looked after unless she is herself earning. Moreover, an unmarried male's share of patrimonial property has no inheritor and is likely to go to his brothers' children. His sexuality is not so explosive as a sister's. Talking about a village in Rajasthan, Palriwala (1990) brings out these differences between men's and women's marriages.

In South-East Asia, in contrast, girls are valued for their support. They are considered easy to raise compared with boys. It is said that they are more amenable to discipline and more attached to and concerned about parents and siblings. They help around the house more and create fewer problems than boys do. A daughter's marriage often means acquiring an extra helping hand. If necessary a daughter can support her parents even after she is married. As I have noted, parents look forward to being cared for by daughters in old age.

11

Gender and education

Here I shall deal briefly with a few important issues related to differences between South Asia and South-East Asia in the operation of gender in the field of education. It is only suggestive and in no way definitive.

Jayaweera (1988) clearly brings out the gender-linked disparities in education in countries such as Bangladesh, India, Nepal, and Pakistan and contrasts them with the situation in Indonesia, Malaysia, the Philippines, Sri Lanka, and Thailand, where the expansion of education has resulted in a diminishing of gender disparities. There is a general tendency to condemn this state and urge its rectification without looking into the bases of the discrimination, which might indicate the need for structural changes.

In Bangladesh, India, and Pakistan, parents prefer to give higher education to sons rather than to daughters, mainly because boys are considered positive economic assets to the family. Because daughters leave upon marriage, sons are looked upon as a form of insurance in the uncertain world of peasants and the urban lower middle class. It has been suggested that this preference should be discouraged by emphasizing the need for girls' education in the overall economic development of the country and through a reduction in fertility (Chaudhury and Ahmed 1980: 156). But will such emphases alone change something that is rooted in the ideology and the structural principles of kinship?

A certain delinking of women's education and employment seems to occur in the upper and middle classes. Girls are educated to become efficient housewives and mothers who can properly socialize

146

their children. They also become more attractive in the marriage market by offering better companionship and supportive social roles to their prospective husbands. Where education and employment are linked, this is usually for eventualities such as widowhood and in order to supplement the husband's income. The motive in permitting a daughter to work is often that she can earn some of her own dowry by that means. Some parents may visualize careers for their daughters, but they seldom count on being supported by them. Where circumstances require the making of such plans, it is not done to speak of them openly. Also, studies have shown that, when women work and support their parents or younger siblings, this usually traps them in a situation where marriage does not remain an option at all.

The roles here are all derived from the kinship system and family structure. Marriage transfers a woman from her natal home, and her primary or sole duty is towards her husband's family. Anything she earns should contribute to the upkeep of her new home; she has no recognized moral right to use it to support her parents or siblings. There are of course cultural arrangements under which a married woman periodically visits her natal home and even does household and productive work there at times when her labour is specially welcome (D. Jacobson 1977a, Palriwala 1991, Minturn and Hitchcock 1963).

Among the semi-tribal Gond, among peasant communities, and among some urban populations there are references to the manipulative skills of young wives who send supplies to their natal homes and sometimes even have assets transferred to them. Folk songs in Chhattisgarh, for instance, detail the charges and counter-charges that are made by daughter-in-law and mother-in-law. The younger woman is accused of stealing grain and valuable foodstuffs such as ghee, sugar, and jaggery (unrefined sugar) to send to her parents. The older woman is accused of stealthily sending the same things to her daughter, who is now at her own husband's home (L. Dube 1956).

Such firm notions about the legitimacy of the transfer of a woman and the illegitimacy of her trying to support her natal kin are rooted in the conception of the family structure and the kinship network. Because of them, employed young women in urban areas who support their natal families must often remain unmarried. From their parents' point of view, accepting their support is a matter for some embarrassment; but at least they have not been given away in marriage. They may be pampered as bread-winners, but a vigilant watch is nevertheless kept over them lest they disgrace themselves through friendships with men and to keep them from finding matches for themselves. Once married, they would become *parai* ("belonging to others"), from whom the natal families could expect no support.

The patrilineal, patri-virilocal kinship and family system thus makes a daughter a liability. Among the Muslims of Bangladesh, even though there are at least some intra-kin marriages, a daughter is referred to as "a temporary guest." In Andhra Pradesh and Karnataka, where intra-kin marriages are preferred, there are sayings such as "Bringing up a girl is like planting a sapling in another's courtyard" and "Bringing up a daughter is like pouring water into sand." Similar sayings are prevalent throughout the Indian subcontinent (Aziz and Maloney 1985).

The notions of the immediate and the future (or deferred) value of sons and daughters may be examined against this background. Because girls do not have any future value in ensuring family continuity, in providing support to siblings and parents, or in bringing in the labour of their spouses, it is their immediate value that assumes greater importance.

All over South and South-East Asia girls are seen as being useful around the house, assisting in domestic chores, looking after younger siblings, and helping in the productive activities that are undertaken by women. Data from Indonesia, where the sexual division of labour is not so rigid as it is in South Asia, show that young girls work longer hours than young boys do (White 1976). Similar information is available for other South-East Asian countries. The devaluation of daughters in South Asia is clearly associated with the conception of their future value to the family and is, to repeat, rooted in kinship and family organization, which regards them as only temporary members over whom their parents lose their rights when they are married off.

There are clear differences between South Asia and South-East Asia. In South Asia the logic of the deferred value of a child, leading to an investment in its future in the form of education and training, is based on contrasting evaluations of sons and daughters. What use is it to send a girl to school and deprive the family of her labour? What is the family going to get in return for forgoing her immediate usefulness? In South-East Asian countries, daughters' immediate value and notions of the division of work between the sexes – emphasizing the domestic and reproductive roles of women – may have some effect on the level of education of girls and on the occupations and professions for which they opt; but a differential evaluation of the young of the two sexes is not at the root as it is in patrilineal, patri-virilocal South Asia.

Many studies of South-East Asian societies indicate that parents often look forward to being cared for in their old age by their daughters. Flexibility in kinship in regard to residence and responsibility is of obvious relevance here.

A related consideration is the necessity in South Asia of isolating girls from males before marriage. A consequence has been the emphasis on single-sex schools and colleges. The absence of separate institutions for girls is often described as a major handicap for girls' education. The large percentage of drop-outs among girls around the age of puberty is attributable to a concern with the management of female sexuality at its most vulnerable stage (L. Dube 1988a,b).

The rates of adult literacy among women in 1992 (table 1 in the Appendix) show a contrast between South Asia and South-East Asia. In some South Asian countries they were: Nepal, 14 per cent; Pakistan, 22 per cent; Bangladesh, 23 per cent; and India, 35 per cent. In some countries in South-East Asia they were: Indonesia, 77 per cent; Malaysia, 72 per cent; the Philippines, 90 per cent; and Thailand, 92 per cent. In Indonesia and Malaysia, illiteracy was considerably higher among the older age groups (Jayaweera 1988). Gender disparities in literacy are high in South Asia, but not in South-East Asia. In 1992 the difference was 25 per cent in Nepal, 26 per cent in Bangladesh, 27 per cent in Pakistan, and 29 per cent in India. By contrast, the difference was 14 per cent in Indonesia and 17 per cent in Malaysia, while in the Philippines there was no difference at all and in Thailand it was only 4 per cent (table 1). Sri Lanka, with 85 per cent literacy among adult women and a narrow disparity between genders, is in a class by itself in South Asia.

The content of the education of females reflects norms of domesticity, with emphases on domestic skills and feminine social accomplishments. Curriculum differentiation is often gender based. The stress on sex-role stereotypes during socialization tends to push girls towards courses of study that are associated with their gender. Technology and other areas supposedly of male excellence have very few women except in the Philippines and Thailand, where access to education and the choosing of particular forms of it are determined less by gender than by socio-economic standing.

In some Islamic countries such as Indonesia and Malaysia, state education policies seem to be influenced by considerations of gender that may be thought to be in keeping with religious values. However, a somewhat similar situation can be seen even in countries such as India, where religion is not supposed to guide secular matters. It appears that, although notions of gender roles may not always restrict educational opportunities for women, they do affect the content of education.

Statistics provided by Jayaweera (1988) indicate that men and women have had equal access to education for some time now in the Philippines and Thailand and that gender-based disparities are diminishing in Malaysia and Indonesia, although they persist in tertiary education in Malaysia and in secondary and tertiary education in Indonesia.

In Malaysia and Indonesia there is some resistance to sending unmarried females away from home for education or employment, but it is nowhere near what is seen in patrilineal South Asia. Moreover, daughters are not looked upon as liabilities who will have no value in the future.

12

Conclusion

This study was planned with the conviction that kinship can provide an appropriate context for understanding gender in a society and that the adoption of a comparative approach in looking at gender across two regions with different kinship systems is likely to yield significant results. Since I began looking at material from diverse sources, the realization has gained ground that the study of kinship can in fact be made the study of gender. A number of micro-studies have attempted to investigate specific issues relating to gender with a consciousness of the relevance of kinship. However, those engaged in women's studies as such have not yet fully realized the crucial importance of kinship in grasping the situation of women.

It is necessary for those in the women's movement to keep this dimension in mind while devising strategies to bring about changes – legal, social and cultural, political and economic – in the interests of women and for understanding the limits within which women function and why certain measures have not succeeded. This is not to deny that in recent years the women's movement has demonstrated much awareness of the relevance of kinship and family structures in deliberating amendments to the laws regarding the prohibition of dowry, adoption, abortion, inheritance, divorce, maintenance and alimony, and the custody of children. But a much better understanding of the basic principles of kinship and their implications has to go into these efforts.

Further, the academic teaching of kinship and family has still not altered its ways or incorporated new researches that strike at the mythologies that have been created in various disciplines in relation to gender relations and the situation of women.

Kinship systems are neither innocuous nor immutable; and they are not self-sustaining. Given that they operate through material relations but tend to express themselves more effectively through values and ideology, and that they very often seem to be supported by religion and reinforced through ritual and social ceremony, we need to assess the assumptions that underlie the behaviour and speech of the people. I would argue that not only in traditional legal systems and in customary law but also in the content and character of the new laws that have been framed ostensibly to favour women, there is an unmistakable stamp of kinship ideology and kinship organization, whose principles are effective even when not articulated.

I have taken up a few dimensions of kinship partly in an attempt to add to our understanding of the nature and character of the changes taking place in the societies covered. Instead of looking at the changes themselves, except where this was unavoidable, I have tried to provide a background against which they might be understood. Generalizations and comparisons are both risky, the latter being at times odious as well; but I have indulged in both, while trying not to lose sight of important specificities.

In his list of measures to be used for studying gender relations and differences between women and men in different societies in terms of the degree of control they exercise and the autonomy they enjoy in various domains, Tambiah (1989) includes the following: the rights of men and women relating to inheritance, ownership, and transmission and disposal of property; the rights of spouses with regard to property acquired in the course of marriage and accruing after the death of one spouse; economic roles and occupational activities; the freedom to initiate divorce, the possible grounds for divorce, and the allocation of children; the degree of freedom of physical movement and social interaction allowed at different stages of the life cycle; and the special features of the speech codes and linguistic forms that signal gender and sexual differences, evaluations, and specializations.

In this study I have dealt with most of the above matters and many more, not as with a laundry list but offering explanations in terms of their bases in kinship and their support in often intertwined specific principles of religion, caste, class, and law. The implications of gender differences for group membership and rights to space, of contrasts between male and female sexuality with specific controls over the latter, of the nature and character of marriage – with choices in entry and exit and the quality of conjugal relations – and of residence patterns can all be seen to be rooted in principles of kinship, often mediated by religion. They have been spelt out in their multiple dimensions. Undoubtedly they provide the logic for many of the issues raised by Tambiah. Rights over children seem to derive their justification from conceptions of bodily processes but in essence they are a function of kinship systems, which are seen as both biological and cultural.

Gender discrimination or its absence in respect of nutrition, health, and education bring out the contrast between patrilineal South Asia and bilateral and matrilineal South-East Asia. Gender differences and relative gender parity have both been described and analysed at appropriate points in this book.

The larger political arena and the economy as such were beyond the scope of this work. In many countries women have held the highest political and other positions. But these individuals do not represent the majority of women. However, although women in South Asia have become a high-profile presence in the tertiary sector, it is in South-East Asia that women are known for their active participation in the economy. High rates of literacy, education, and training for various occupations and professions are strikingly characteristic of this region.

Spanish and Catholic influence tried to turn Filipino women into shy, diffident, and puritanical creatures. The notion of machismo and its female counterpart belonged to this culture but their influence can be seen only among the well-to-do in urban areas. Rural women and women of the labouring classes were able to escape this influence to a great extent. During the American regime, education was extended to both men and women and Filipino woman entered predominantly male spheres of activity in a big way much earlier than did the women of other countries.

It is not possible to deal with the law and its ramifications in all these societies but a few significant points may be made. The legal status of Filipino women, which had gone down during the Spanish period, has improved tremendously. In the Philippines and in Thailand there is no inequality in the treatment of women as far as inheritance and rights over resources are concerned. But in respect of marriage the Catholic influence has put severe constraints on Filipino women. There is no divorce but only separation. Adultery is a legal ground for the man alone to apply for separation; a woman may file a petition for separation only in instances of concubinage. In Thailand, on the other hand, a marriage can be dissolved by mutual consent or by judicial decree.

In Thailand and the Philippines the law is relatively equitable in respect of the division of conjugal property; and as regards the custody of children, the mother's position is quite strong. However, this may result in the mother's becoming wholly responsible for her children.

Although Islam is the accepted faith in Malaysia, among the people of Negri Sembilan and Malacca – who follow *adat perpateh* (which essentially applies to matrilineal communities) rather than *adat temanggong* (which essentially applies to bilateral communities) – local custom rather than Muslim law is effective in inheritance and in the custody of children and the division of property following divorce. In other regions Islam has considerable influence, but *adat* moderates its strict interpretation. For instance, a woman who has worked land is entitled to half of it whereas one who has not worked it is entitled only to a third.

Finally, we may look at some of the ways in which kinship systems affect gender.

There are undoubted critical differences between South Asia and South-East Asia and within each region. Close scrutiny makes us realize that in both types of unilineal descent system it is necessary to underplay the role of one parent – that of the father in matriliny and that of the mother in patriliny. In both there seems to be less flexibility in the formation of groupings and in the exercise of inter-personal relations than there is in bilateral kinship. Notions of male and female oppositions are more pronounced (Postel-Coster 1987, Prindiville 1981). Natural differences between males and females are believed to affect social organization and rights and obligations.

In patrilineal systems mothers tend to be both devalued and eulogized, controlled as well as compensated. A mother is needed as a receptacle and a nurturer. Patrilineal and patrilocal kinship and family organization in South Asia result in patriarchal controls and work to the cost of women. Sharp contrasts are drawn in the nature, propensities, capabilities, and duties of the two sexes from ancient literature to folk literature.

In matrilineal societies, too, differences are emphasized; but, to refer to the Minangkabau, *ibu*, the mother, is the epitome of wisdom. There are relatively so few matrilineal societies that they are often considered oddities. Androcentric analyses of matrilineal societies

have been based on certain biases and assumptions rooted in Western cultures. It is argued that in all societies males exercise authority,
and whereas in the patrilineal system the lines of authority and
descent converge, in matrilineal societies they do not: the line of
descent passes through females but the line of authority passes to
males through females. Men wield authority – whether over their
sisters and other matrilineal kin or over wives and children – but
descent is traced through women. A man's authority passes to his
sister's son and not to his own son. This creates conflict (see
Schneider and Gough 1961). Thus, according to an anthropological
formulation whose influence has been widespread, matrilineal systems are unstable owing to their in-built conflict. The "matrilineal
puzzle" of Richards (1950) refers to the situation in which there is a
conflict between a man's roles of father and of mother's brother.
Women and children have to submit to two kinds of authority: that of
the husband–father in the domestic group and that of matrilineal kin
in the descent group. It becomes necessary to arrive at some kind of
balance, which is always precarious. As a consequence, the argument
goes, matrilineal systems are unstable and are affected by any kind of
change.

But authority need not be concentrated in one person. Even in a
household or a kin group it can be diffused. As pointed out earlier, it
has been argued that matriliny is a type of political economy in which
the type of concentration of control over property and over women's
sexuality and reproductive power that a husband or other affinal
males can achieve in a patrilineal system, often deriving justification
from religion, is simply not available to a matrilineally related kinsman. Studies of the Minangkabau (e.g. Schwede 1986, 1989, Tanner
1974) have questioned the assumption that authority is always a male
function. Authority is very often diffused.

On the Lakshadweep island of Kalpeni (L. Dube 1991a,b, 1993,
1994) we do not find evidence of the concentration of authority in
a single individual or only in males. Elderly women, particularly
those with respected kinship statuses, have considerable influence.
Women's centrality in the perpetuation of the group and their role in
production and management have their effect in the sphere of
authority. Typically a matrilineal male finds it difficult to establish
control over his sisters' children. He cannot have them under his
thumb as does a father in a strongly patrilineal system. The relationship between mother's brother and sister's son is not direct but is

mediated by a woman. And a woman's sexuality is generally not under the oppressive control of either her matrikin or her husband and his kin.

Poewe (1979) and Weiner (1979, 1980) have also questioned the assumptions of anthropologists on matriliny in central Africa and the Trobriand islands respectively. Colson (1980) has spoken of the resilience and adaptability of a matrilineal system in the face of recent changes. One of the arguments put forward by feminists is that in many matrilineal societies stability is associated with women because it is they who live on and use the land, attend to rituals, and nurture children.

Thomas (1980) contests the assumption that authority within the matrilineal descent group is predominantly vested in males and that there is the constant problem of striking a balance between a man's authority over his wife and children in the domestic group and male matrilineal kin's authority over them in the descent group. He demonstrates the solution to the "matrilineal puzzle" on the island of Nemonuito (near Truk), where women have the primary authority over land, "for it is they who stay and safeguard our children," and it is women who are most knowledgeable about the boundaries and histories of different plots of land.

Stivens (1985b) has shown that it is wrong to conclude on the basis of stereotypical notions that women in Negri Sembilan are losing ownership of rice lands because of the increased cultivation of rubber.

A patrilineal system, too, is beset with conflict and contradiction in as much as the biologically unrepudiable parent is ignored in respect of the group placement of her children. Patrilineal systems function and survive at the cost of women. Women's peripheral membership of their natal group, their transfer to their husband's group, and their purely instrumental value as bearers of children for their affinal groups all have definite implications. The absence of rights over property, over the means of living, and over their children makes women vulnerable to oppression of different kinds.

The opposition between outsider and insider, control over women's sexuality, the asymmetry between brother and sister and between husband and wife, the internalization of roles and of an ideology that circumscribes and devalues women – these are pointers to some of the conflicts and contradictions in a strongly patrilineal, patri-virilocal system. Rivalry between brothers and patrilineal kin over property is a ubiquitous feature. In-marrying females are needed for the perpetuation of the group but they also carry within them the break-up of joint families and the disruption of earlier relationships. Patrilineal systems certainly do not function as they are made out to when contrasted with matrilineal systems.

There is, however, one difference that needs attention. Rivalries and disputes over strategic resources among patrikin do not ordinarily disrupt the essence of the patrilineal principle. The descending generations fighting over resources do, after all, belong to a common descent group. Even mothers who undertake politicking for their sons do not subvert the patrilineal principle. In a matrilineal system, on the other hand, a man's interest in his children in place of his sisters' children can subvert the principles of descent and inheritance, for his children belong to their mother's group and have their rights there. But does this always happen? As Colson (1980) has said, matrilineality need not be associated with a disregard for paternal claims, and the situation on the Lakshadweep island discussed earlier corroborates this.

Bilaterality in South-East Asia seems to enshrine the principle of flexibility. Anthropological literature classifies a number of societies all over the world as following bilateral or cognatic kinship, but bilaterality in South-East Asia is unique in some ways. It accepts hierarchies of age, seniority, and class rather than of gender. In spite of the patrilineally inclined religions that have come to the region, bilaterality has been able to hold its own and maintain relative parity in gender relations. It differs not only from South and West Asia but also from the West.

In the West, bilaterality has emerged through political history – lately the suffragette movement, the women's liberation movement, and increasing social awareness of the need for social autonomy and representation (courtesy Wazir Jahan Karim). Changes in laws relating to property, conjugality, divorce, custody of children, etc., have contributed significantly towards bringing in bilaterality. Patronymy is an age-old tradition and even the loosely used concept of patriarchy conveys meaning. The separation between home and workplace, the contrast between femininity and masculinity, the distinction between private and public space, ideas about the division of work, the father's instrumental role contrasted with the mother's expressive one, and attraction as the main basis of the man–woman relationship – all these put bilaterality in the West in a different category.

A pervasive feeling of envy of men, who seem to have far greater freedom and opportunities, and of rivalry with them is characteristic of the West. In many ways women's solidarity is a war against patriarchy and male oppression. This war drives some women to ignore men altogether.

The gender ideology of South-East Asia derives from an entirely different tradition of bilaterality. Ego-centred family and kinship structures have rendered social organization flexible. Women have been enabled to maintain a fair share of control over family and community resources. Women can work independently of men, manage their own and their spouse's incomes, participate in trade and business, and be efficient producers in agriculture and agro-based industries.

Bilaterality has been an established characteristic of South-East Asia. Despite various kinds of religious, cultural, and political influences, it has been able to hold its own to a great extent. Even in situations of change and mobility the system has offered ways of making choices in limiting or expanding the kinship circle (Nagata 1976, Kemp 1983).

When authority is diffused, responsibility tends to be concentrated. The very flexibility that offers so much to women can place harsh responsibilities on them. Women must struggle to maintain their position in relation to men, for the balance of power and responsibility seems always to be at risk.

Women may, for one reason or another, be relegated to inconsequential positions and exposed to different forms of exploitation. As Karim (1987) has pointed out, in Malaysia both religious fundamentalism and industrialization have lowered women's status by bringing in controls and limitations believed to have the sanction of religion and by concentrating them in assembly-line jobs. Thai bilaterality has had to hold its own against Buddhist notions of male superiority. Neo-colonial developments have led to drastic political and economic changes and to women's migration to towns. While women have lost much of the protection and support they had earlier, their own sense of familial responsibility has forced many to enter ignoble or lowly occupations (Szanton 1990, Phongpaichit 1982). A largely similar process can be seen in the Philippines. Nevertheless, it is bilateral kinship that seems to serve and protect women's interests best.

If kinship acts as a buffer in this uncertain and competitive world, the flexibility and existence of choices in bilaterality seem the most promising.[1]

158

Notes

Chapter 1

1. It is true that some work relating gender with kinship has been done by anthropologists in recent years: see, for example, Hirschon (1984), Young et al. (1984), Papanek and Minault (1982), Weiner (1976), and Collier and Yanagisako (1987). But my contention is that by and large, while looking at the situation of women either at the macro level or at the micro level, feminists have not shown a clear realization of the significance of varying patterns of kinship for understanding gender relations and explaining disparities, inabilities, and exploitation. Even in the discussion of the family as the seat of oppression, the wider context of kinship has not been considered. The term *patriarchy*, which has been used rather indiscriminately, does not generally indicate any relationship to specific kinds of kinship organization.

   Women did appear in the field of kinship, which has traditionally been one of the identifying features of anthropology, but much faulty understanding and interpretation of gender has acquired the status of accepted concepts and theories. Barring a few exceptions such as Karve (1965), even insightful anthropological studies of kinship are bereft of what I would call concern for women. In South Asia it is only during the past two decades that a few micro-studies of women have appeared that take note of kinship.

Chapter 2

1. Earlier, Nayar men were not permitted to take individual shares of their ancestral property; they could only use their independent earnings to build houses for their wives and children in joint ownership. These then constituted *tavazhi-taravad* or branch property groups. With the legal provision to claim individual shares of their *taravad* property, partitions of *taravad* property increased but the *taravad* remained operative. Gough's data on a village for 1949 show a variety of patterns for Nayar households, ranging from the traditional to the nuclear family household. But when a nuclear family grew into a joint family it contained one or more married daughters and their children. Many men still lived with their matrilineal kinswomen and visited their wife's natal household. The composition of the household was gradually changing. Gough's comparison of the households of 1949 with those of 1964 in the same village indicates further changes in Nayar kinship and family organization, with a clear movement from matriliny to bilaterality (Gough 1975).

In terms of emotional ties and sense of responsibility a kind of matrilineal ethos seems to have persisted, but changes are occurring rapidly. Dowry is becoming institutionalized and Hindu rituals of marriage are being adopted.

2. The traditional family is to be seen much more in northern and north-eastern Thailand than in central Thailand. In central Thailand there is a strong preference for living with those parents who have more strategic resources. The options are to live with the wife's or the husband's parents or with relatives of one of the spouses. Flexibility in place and duration of joint living is characteristic of the Thai pattern of residence. A couple is expected to create a neolocal residence. Among the urban Thai people, patrilocal and matrilocal residence may be seen in equal proportions, and a large number of couples establish their own residence immediately after marriage.

Loss or unavailability of land, diversification of occupations, and the engaging of both spouses in earning activities of very different kinds can also lead to their living separately for much of the time. Marital discord, too, may result in separate living (Pongsapich 1992). It is estimated that modernization will lead to a decline in extended families.

Chapter 3

1. If a daughter is given ancestral land, a resident son-in-law may be given the authority to look after it.

Among orthodox Syrian Christians, where there were no sons the practice of what might be called affinal adoption was prevalent. The youngest daughter would stay back to look after her parents and a man would be found who would be willing to reside with her. Sometimes he would even adopt his wife's family name. The material advantages of this arrangement were balanced out by the slight discomfiture that was involved for the man (Visvanathan 1989).

Chapter 6

1. The belief that two kinds of fluids – from the male and from the female – have to mix together for conception to occur seems to be present in both regions. It appears in the treatises of *ayurveda*, the Indian medical system. The notion also forms part of popular culture, being regarded as an empirical fact amenable to empirical understanding.

Chapter 8

1. In contrasting north and south the evidence has generally been drawn from the belt of the Indo-Gangetic plain, which is characterized by village or territorial exogamy, a hypergamous ethos, unidirectional flow of gifts, a strongly asymmetrical relationship between bride-givers and bride-takers, and limited contact between a woman's natal and affinal kin (see, for example, Hitchcock 1956, Lewis 1965, Gould 1960, 1961, Marriott 1955, Luschinsky 1962, Parry 1979, Jeffrey et al. 1989). However, in many parts of non-peninsular India (such as Kashmir, Orissa, Bengal, Madhya Pradesh, Maharashtra) strict rules of village exogamy do not operate although there is a preference for marriages at some distance so that affines are kept at a structural remove and the bride is better incorporated in the absence of their interference. Even where marriages between close kin such as mother's brother's daughter and father's sister's son are preferred, the positions of bride-givers and bride-takers are not reversed.

However, as Palriwala (1994) says, the contrast can be overstressed. Mutual visits may not be infrequent and married women may visit their kin regularly. Marital alliances may be repeated, taking care only that the superiority of bride-takers is not disturbed except in small endogamous groups who do not mind such reversals.

Undoubtedly the sex ratio has been far more favourable for females in southern India. Oppression and violence in affinal homes, especially owing to dowry demands, are more common in non-peninsular India, particularly northern India. But the escalation of dowry is to be seen in southern India as well. In recent years the number of intra-kin marriages in the south has been decreasing owing to awareness of possible genetic risks, greater concern with choosing suitable partners, and the desire to widen the circle from within which spouses are obtained. The earlier ethos of intra-kin marriages may still be present but the nature of affinal relations seems to be changing. An increasing sex imbalance and reports of female infanticide both indicate that even in south India women are being devalued further. At the same time, traditional restrictions relating to contacts with married daughters in their affinal homes are loosening in the north.

These changes notwithstanding, and irrespective of the presence or absence of intra-kin marriages, it appears that there is something in common between the Dravidian south, the Indo-Aryan north, and the regions in between. Trautmann (1981) says that the Indo-Aryan rite of *kanyadan* (the gift of a maiden) is a country-wide phenomenon found also in the southern region where the Dravidian pattern is followed in which a reversal of bride-takers and bride-givers may take place. In many areas the ideal of *kanyadan* is found together with exchange marriages for the sake of expediency and survival (Madan 1965).

2. Research among Pakistani and Indian Muslims reports a decline in kin marriage brought about by a disruption of the *biradari* (brotherhood, endogenous group), caused by Partition and migration and the resultant scarcity of eligible cousins (Korson 1971, Roy 1979, Rizvi, personal communication). Hindi and Urdu literature of the post-Partition period contains sensitively written short stories and novels about this problem. Essentially it is daughters who have had to suffer for want of eligible partners, as a result of their parents' insistence on not marrying below their status even when they cannot amass a dowry large enough for an appropriate groom outside the *biradari*.

   It has now been established that in Bangladesh the general practice of non-kin marriage and the rarity of intra-kin marriage are not age-old phenomena. Evidence indicates that intra-kin marriages were an established feature in East Bengal and that the decline in such marriages began only early this century (Palriwala 1994, citing Blei 1990).

3. Here it is pertinent to remember Fatima Mernissi's grandmother's advice to her daughter. According to her, there were many ways of creating a strong personality. One of them was to develop the capacity to feel responsible for others. If a girl was taught to feel responsible for the younger ones around her, it gave her room to build strength. Thus, by learning how to protect others, she also learnt to use that skill for herself (Mernissi 1994: 10). This is relevant for South Asia. Caring for others, self-denial, and service can generate in women a sense of self-worth, confidence, and power and can impart skills that they can use to their own advantage.

Chapter 9

1. Becoming a *sati* has wrongly been called "widow immolation." A woman who immolates herself on her dead husband's pyre never becomes a widow. The very purpose of immolation is to avoid widowhood. Such a woman attains the eternal status of the "fortunate and the auspicious one" when, decked in finery and wearing the significata of the married state, she is consumed by the fire along with her husband's body.

2. In Pakistan there have been changes in the law forbidding unilateral divorce at will by men and providing some scope for women to seek divorce. Their effect has to be assessed. There

have been changes in the marriage contract that give women greater security and rights. A man has to get the permission of his first wife before contracting a polygynous marriage.

As regards the right of *haq-mahr* (marriage payment due to the wife), it has been annulled in two different ways. In the tribal areas it has been converted into bride-price. Among sedentary people and in urban areas it has been reduced to a formality on paper. The institution of dowry has gained in importance. Moreover, it has come to be equated with women's share of inheritance in parental property. This leaves a woman with no more rights, and without resources she cannot enter business or trade.

The nature of the marriage contract has become distorted. In the north-west and in Baluchistan, once the bride-price has been paid a woman is considered the property of her in-laws and has no recourse to the protection of her natal family (Shaheed 1985).

In India, the Shah Bano case, which involved regular maintenance to a woman from her former husband under a section of the penal code, provoked a violent reaction from many Muslims. It has been argued that to consider a divorced woman a wife and accede to her demands for maintenance is against Islam and the personal law based on it. It should have been possible to follow a provision of the Quran and make Shah Bano's husband pay her a fair and reasonable amount in accordance with his status and the actual needs of the divorcee, in addition to the obligatory *mahr* and maintenance during *iddat*. Instead, the Law on Muslim Women (Protection of Rights on Divorce) has been passed. It appears to maintain Muslim identity but goes against the interests of women (see Pathak and Sunder Rajan 1989, Ansari 1991).

3. A word about violence here. Where the woman is located among or close to her kin it is difficult for a man to use violence against her. In neolocal households, away from kin, a man may sometimes beat up his wife under the influence of alcohol. The wife may retaliate by beating up the husband. It is worth mentioning, however, that a man who beats up his wife would be considered brutal. It is said that since a woman has less physical strength the man must not use violence against her. To take such advantage of one's brute strength is looked down upon.

Chapter 12

1. Today there is a worldwide concern with the future of the family. The material presented in this book should help us take a fresh look at the family. Certain misconceptions regarding institutions, practices, and actualities of life can be effectively questioned. Dominant norms regarding the family can be challenged. Is it possible to work towards according legitimate status to a wide array of viable domestic units, sexual arrangements, and strategies of adoption and nurture? Must we stick to the model of man's role as provider and woman's role as nurturer, given its partial approximation to reality and its denial of the possibility of meaningful and tender fatherhood?

This comparative study poses some fundamental questions. Is stable marriage absolutely essential for continuity of the family? At whose cost is this stability maintained? Is divorce always a calamity and a disaster for the children? Is a high rate of divorce necessarily harmful to the personalities and development of children? Does a family necessarily need an exclusive head in order to run smoothly? Can we not think in terms of shared responsibility in the making of decisions? Is authority a prerequisite for a man to be imbued with a sense of responsibility towards his wife and children?

Appendix

These brief notes on the countries whose populations or communities I have discussed in the contexts of kinship and gender should prove helpful.

According to the provisional figures of the 1991 census, India's total population was 843,930,861 distributed in 32 administrative units. The break-down of the population by religion according to the 1981 census was:

Hindus	82.35%
Muslims	11.74
Christians	2.44
Sikhs	1.97
Others	1.57

Of the 98 million population of Bangladesh estimated in 1984, 87 per cent were Muslims; most others were Hindus and there was a sprinkling of Christians and Buddhists. There were also a few tribal groups. In Bangladesh 85 per cent of the people live in rural areas. Most engage in rice and jute farming and there are some fisherfolk. Only 400,000 are employed in large and medium industry.

Peninsular Malaysia and Sabah and Sarawak consist of a number of islands and are divided into 14 states. Malaysia is a multi-racial country. The principal ethnic groups are the Malays, followed by the Chinese and various communities from the Indian subcontinent and Sri Lanka. Other numerically significant groups are the indigenous peoples of Sarawak and Sabah. According to 1985 figures, Malaysia's population was divided as follows:

Malays	7,343,500
Chinese	4,245,100
Indians	1,307,000
Others	82,000

In this work I have dealt only with the Malays of Peninsular Malaysia. Islam is the official religion. The languages spoken in the country are Malay, English, Chinese, and Tamil, besides the few tongues indigenous to Sabah and Sarawak. Besides Islam, Confucianism, Buddhism, Taoism, Hinduism, and Christianity are also practised. The economy is dependent on the export of primary commodities and manufactured goods.

Sri Lanka, with a population of 14.8 million, has the following main ethnic groups:

Sinhalese	73.98%
Ceylon Tamil	12.60
Indian Tamil	5.66
Ceylon Moors	7.12
Malays	0.29
Burghers	0.26
Others	0.20

It is estimated that 69.31 per cent of the population is Buddhist, with 15.46 per cent Hindus, 7.49 per cent Roman Catholics and other Christians, and 7.64 per cent Muslims. Sri Lanka is divided into nine provinces. Major commodities exported include tea, rubber, coconuts and their products, precious stones, and other mineral products.

Nepal is a small state that was reported to have a population of 11,555,983 in 1971. The break-down by religion is as follows:

Hindus	89.3
Buddhists	7.6
Muslims	0.06
Others	3.04

About 15 per cent of the land mass in the north is perpetually snow-clad and devoid of vegetation and habitation. Nepal was never colonized. The country has a number of tiny tribal groups. The official religion is Hinduism. The mainstream culture is Hindu, with a mixture of Hindu and Buddhist faiths in some groups.

Thailand, with a population of over 40 million, is located on the mainland of South-East Asia. Its economy has been based on agriculture and has recently begun to diversify. Thailand has never been a colony but with an open economy it has come under the influence of neo-colonialism. In the past hundred years modernization has occurred gradually, with much greater change taking place in urban areas. Compared with other countries of South-East Asia, Thailand is a relatively homogeneous society with only some diversity in ethnic backgrounds and local dialects.

Thais constitute over 80 per cent of the population. There are, however, a number of regional subgroups among them. The religion professed by the Thais is Buddhism but it is permeated with animism. The worship and propitiation of spirits are prominent. Among the ethnic minorities are the hill tribes, Muslims, and Sino-Thais. There are also some Chinese and Indians in the urban economy.

Indonesia has nine main islands including the arid little Madura. According to the 1971 census, the total population was 119,232,499, with great ethnic and cultural diversity. Islam predominates but Christianity and Hinduism are also present. Bilaterality, matriliny, as well as some patriliny are found. The Javanese are characteristically bilateral, while the Minangkabau of West Sumatra are known for matriliny under the rubric of Islam. Java, a crowded island, accommodates 60 per cent of the Indonesian population, which resides on 7 per cent of the total land area. The Javanese occupy only the central and eastern parts of Indonesia.

The population of Pakistan was 83.8 million according to the 1981 census. The population density was 106/km^2. The population was unevenly distributed among the various provinces. Punjab was the most populous, with 56 per cent of the total population. Sind had 22.6 per cent, NWFP 13.1 per cent, and Baluchistan 5.1 per cent. About 97 per cent of the people are Muslim. Pakistan is predominantly an agricultural country with wheat, rice, cotton, sugarcane, and tobacco as its principal crops. It is a leading exporter of rice and cotton.

Table 1 **Adult literacy rates and years of schooling, 1992**

Country	Literacy as % at age 15+			Mean years of schooling at age 25+		
	Total	Female	Male	Total	Female	Male
South Asia						
Bangladesh	37	23	49	2.0	0.9	3.1
India	50	35	64	2.4	1.2	3.5
Nepal	27	14	39	2.1	1.0	3.2
Pakistan	36	22	49	1.9	0.7	2.9
Sri Lanka	89	85	94	7.2	6.3	8.0
South-East Asia						
Indonesia	84	77	91	4.1	3.1	5.3
Malaysia	80	72	89	5.6	5.2	5.9
Philippines	90	90	90	7.6	7.2	8.0
Thailand	94	92	96	3.9	3.4	4.4

Source: *Human Development Report 1994*, UNDP and Oxford University Press, 1994.

Table 2 **Indicators of the status of women**

Country	Life expectancy at birth, 1992	Average age at first marriage, 1980–1990	% literacy in age group 15–24, 1980–1990	% of tertiary sector women in science and development, 1990–1991	% of tertiary sector women as managers and administrators, 1980–1989	% of seats occupied by women in parliament, 1992
South Asia						
Bangladesh	51.9	16.7	27	24	2	10
India	59.9	18.7	40	25	2	7
Nepal	52.2	17.9	15	n.a.	n.a.	3
Pakistan	58.3	19.8	25	41	n.a.	1
Sri Lanka	73.4	24.4	90	26	7	5
South-East Asia						
Indonesia	63.8	21.1	82	21	7	12
Malaysia	72.6	23.5	83	16	8	8
Philippines	66.5	22.4	92	n.a.	25	11
Thailand	71.3	22.7	96	n.a.	21	4

Source: *Human Development Report 1994*, UNDP and Oxford University Press, 1994.

Table 3 **Females as percentage of males**

Country	Life expectancy, 1992	Population, 1992	Literacy, 1970	Literacy, 1992	Years of schooling 1992	Labour force, 1990–1992
South Asia						
Bangladesh	99	94	33	47	29	69
India	101	93	43	55	34	41
Nepal	107	103	n.a.	n.a.	23	56
Pakistan	100	92	37	45	23	n.a.
Sri Lanka	106	99	81	90	79	49
South-East Asia						
Indonesia	106	101	64	85	58	67
Malaysia	106	98	68	80	89	56
Philippines	106	99	96	100	90	59
Thailand	108	99	84	96	77	89

Source: *Human Development Report 1994*, UNDP and Oxford University Press, 1994.

Table 4 **Rural population as percentage of total, 1992**

Country	%
South Asia	
Bangladesh	82
India	74
Nepal	88
Pakistan	67
Sri Lanka	78
South-East Asia	
Indonesia	70
Malaysia	55
Philippines	56
Thailand	77

Source: *Human Development Report 1994*, UNDP and Oxford University Press, 1994.

Table 5 **Child and maternal mortality**

Country	Maternal mortality rate (per 100,000 live births), 1988	Infant mortality rate (per 1,000 live births), 1992	Under-5 mortality rate (per 1,000 live births), 1992
South Asia			
Bangladesh	650	109	150
India	550	89	130
Nepal	850	100	155
Pakistan	600	99	130
Sri Lanka	180	24	30
South-East Asia			
Indonesia	300	66	95
Malaysia	120	14	18
Philippines	250	40	55
Thailand	180	26	34

Source: *Human Development Report 1994*, UNDP and Oxford University Press, 1994.

Bibliography

Abdulla, Farouq, 1980. "Time Use of Rural Women: A Six Village Survey in Bangladesh," Bureau of Economic Research.

Abdullah, Tahrunnesa, 1976. "Village Women as I Saw Them," Bangladesh Academy for Rural Development.

———, 1986. "Home-based Agricultural Production in Rural Bangladesh," *Adab News*, 13, 5.

———, n.d. "Report on Homebased Agricultural Production in Rural Bangladesh," The Ford Foundation.

Abdullah, T. A. and Sondra A. Zeildenstein, 1982. *Village Women of Bangladesh: Prospects for Change*, Pergamon Press.

Abeyasekere, Susan, 1983. "Women as Cultural Intermediaries in Nineteenth-century Batavia," in Lenore Manderson, ed., *Women's Work and Women's Roles: Economics and Everyday Life in Indonesia, Malaysia and Singapore*, Australian National University.

Abraham, Ammu, 1987. "Personal Laws in India," paper for Asian Conference on Women, Religion and Family Laws, Bombay.

Acharya, Meena and Lynn Bennett, 1981. *The Rural Women of Nepal: An Aggregate Analysis and Summary of Eight Village Studies*, Volume 2, Part 9 of *The Status of Women in Nepal*, Centre for Economic Development and Administration, Kathmandu.

Afshar, Haleh, ed., 1985. *Women, Work and Ideology in the Third World*, Tavistock Publications.

Agarwal, Bina, 1988a. "Who Sows? Who Reaps? Women and Land Rights in India," *Journal of Peasant Studies*, 15, 4.

———, ed., 1988b. *Structures of Patriarchy: State, Community and Household in Modernizing Asia*, Sage.

Agnes, Flavia, 1992. "Review of a Decade of Legislation, 1980–1989: Protecting Women Against Violence?" *Economic and Political Weekly*, 27, 17.

Ahmad, Imtiaz, ed., 1976. *Family, Kinship and Marriage among Muslims in India*, Manohar Book Service.

———, ed., 1981. *Ritual and Religion among Muslims in India*, Manohar.

Ahmad, Nigar and Shahnaz Ahmad, 1990. "A Day in the Life of Masi Jhulo," in Leela Dube and Rajni Palriwala, eds., *Structures and Strategies: Women, Work and Family*, Sage.

Ahmed, Rahnuma, 1985. "Women's Movement in Bangladesh and the Left's Understanding of the Women Question," *Journal of Social Studies*, 30.

Ahmed, Shaheen, 1984. "Marriage and the Status of Rural Women in Bangladesh," University of Cambridge M.Phil. thesis.

Akanda, Latifa and Ishrat Shamim, 1985. *Women and Violence: A Comparative Study of Rural and Urban Violence against Women in Bangladesh*, Women for Women.

Alam, S. M. Nurul, 1987. "An Analysis of Cost, Productivity and Returns of Rice Production in Bangladesh: A Case Study of Two Villages," *Journal of Social Studies*, 36.

Alavi, H., 1971. "The Politics of Dependence: A Village in West Punjab," *South Asian Review*, 4, 2.

———, 1972. "Kinship in West Punjab Villages," *Contributions to Indian Sociology*, 6, 1.

Ali, S. Husin, 1979. *Malay Peasant Society and Leadership*, Oxford University Press.

———, 1981. *The Malays: Their Problems and Future*, Heinemann Asia.

Allen, Michael R., 1975. *The Cult of Kumari: Virgin Worship in Nepal*, Tribhuvan University Press.

———, 1976. "Kumari or 'Virgin' Worship in Kathmandu Valley," *Contributions to Indian Sociology*, 10, 2.

———, 1982a. "Girls' Prepuberty Rites amongst the Newars of Kathmandu Valley," in Michael Allen and S. N. Mukherjee, eds., *Women in India and Nepal*, Australian National University Monographs on South Asia No. 8.

———, 1982b. "The Hindu View of Women," in Michael Allen and S. N. Mukherjee, eds., *Women in India and Nepal*, Australian National University Monographs on South Asia No. 8.

Altekar, A. S., 1938. *The Position of Women in Hindu Civilization*, Culture Publication House.

AmaraSingham, L. R., 1978. "The Misery of the Embodied: Representation of Women in Sinhalese Myth," in J. Hock-Smith and A. Spring, eds., *Women in Ritual and Symbolic Roles*, [New York].

Amyot, Jacques, 1976. *Village Ayuttha*, Chulalongkorn University Social Research Institute.

Anderson, Wanni W., 1985. "World View in Thai Children's Play and Games," in *Traditional and Changing Thai World View*, Chulalongkorn University Social Research Institute.

Anjum, Mohini, 1992. "Behind Burqa," in Mohini Anjum, ed., *Muslim Women in India*, Radiant Publishers.

Ansari, Iqbal A., 1991. "Muslim Women's Rights: Goals and Strategies of Reform," *Economic and Political Weekly*, 26, 17.

Apichart, C., 1984. *Perspectives on the Thai Marriage*, Mahidol University.

Appadurai, A., 1981. "Gastro-politics in Hindu South Asia," *American Ethnologist*, 8, 3.

Arce, Wilfredo F., 1979. "The Structural Bases of Compadre Characteristics in a Bikol Town," in Mary Racelis Hollnsteiner, ed., *Society, Culture and the Filipino*, Institute of Philippine Culture.

Arefeen, H. K., 1982. "Muslim Stratification Patterns in Bangladesh: An Attempt to Build a Theory," *Journal of Social Studies*, 16.

——, 1985. "Some Aspects of Marriage Practices among the Muslims of Bangladesh," *Journal of Social Studies*, 29.

——, 1986. *Changing Agrarian Structure in Bangladesh: Shimulia, a Study of a Periurban Village*, Centre for Social Studies, Dhaka University.

Ariffin, Jamilah, 1982. "Industrialization, Female Labour Migration, and the Changing Pattern of Malay Women's Labour Force Participation," *Southeast Asian Studies*, 19, 4.

——, 1983. "Impact of Modern Electronics Technology on Women Workers in Malaysia: Some Selected Findings from the HAWA Survey," unpublished.

——, 1984a. "Migration of Women Workers in Peninsular Malaysia: Impact and Implications," in *Women in the Cities of Asia: Migration and Urban Adaptation*, Westview Press.

——, 1984b. "Women in Malaysia: Priority Research Issues," *Ilmu Masyarakat*, 7.

——, 1986. "Women in Malaysia: Priority Research Issues," *Asian Exchange*, 4, 4 and 5, 1.

Ariffin, Noor Farida, 1986. "Legal Protection for Women Workers Within and Outside the Home," in Hing Ai Yun and Rokiah Talib, eds., *Women and Employment in Malaysia*, University of Malaya.

Aziz, K. M. A., 1978. "Marriage Practices in a Rural Area of Bangladesh," *Journal of the Indian Anthropological Society*, 13.

——, 1979. *Kinship in Bangladesh*, International Centre for Diarrhoeal Disease Research.

——, and Clarence Maloney, 1985. *Life Stages, Gender and Fertility in Bangladesh*, International Centre for Diarrhoeal Disease Research Monograph No. 3.

Babb, L. A., 1970a. "Marriage and Malevolence: The Use of Sexual Opposition in a Hindu Pantheon," *Ethnology*, 9.

——, 1970b. "The Food of the Gods in Chhattisgarh: Some Structural Features of Hindu Ritual," *Southwestern Journal of Anthropology*, 26.

——, 1975. *The Divine Hierarchy: Popular Hinduism in Central India*, Columbia University Press.

Bandarage, Asoka, 1983. *Colonialism in Sri Lanka: The Political Economy of the Kandeyan Highlands, 1833–1886*, Mouton.

——, 1984. "Toward International Feminism," *Economic Review*, 10, 6/7, Colombo People's Bank Research Department.

Bandhumedha, Navavan, 1985. "Thai Views of Man as a Social Being," in *Traditional and Changing Thai World View*, Chulalongkorn University Social Research Institute.

Bangladesh, 1985. *Situation of Women in Bangladesh*, Ministry of Social Welfare and Women's Affairs.

Bangladesh Rural Advancement Committee, 1984. *Peasant Perceptions: Credit Needs*, BRAC.

——, 1986a. *Who Gets What and Why: Resource Allocation in a Bangladesh Village*, BRAC Prokashana Rural Study Series No. 1.

——, 1986b. *The Net: Power Structure in Ten Villages*, BRAC Prokashana Rural Study Series No. 2.

Banks , David J., 1969. "Malay Kinship," University of Chicago Ph.D. thesis.

———, 1972. "Changing Kinship in North Malaya," *American Anthropologist*, 74.

———, ed., 1976. *Changing Identities in Modern Southeast Asia*, Mouton.

Banzon-Bautista, C. R. and N. G. Dungo, 1987. "The Differential Impact of Changes in Farm Technology on Men and Women in Two Philippine Villages," in Noeleen Heyzer, ed., *Women Farmers and Rural Change in Asia: Towards Equal Access and Participation*, Asian and Pacific Development Centre.

Bardhan, Pranab, 1982. "Little Girls and Death in India," *Economic and Political Weekly*, 17.

Barkat-e-Khuda, 1979. "Women and Work in a Bangladesh Village," *Political Economy*, 4, 1.

Barlow, Colin, 1985. "Indonesian and Malayan Agricultural Development, 1870–1940," *Bulletin of Indonesian Economic Studies*, 21, 1.

Barnard, Rosemary, 1983. "Housewives and Farmers: Malay Women in the Muda Irrigation Scheme," in Lenore Manderson, ed., *Women's Work and Women's Roles*, Australian National University.

Barnes, R. H., 1985a. "The Leiden Version of the Comparative Method in Southeast Asia," *Journal of the Anthropological Society of Oxford*, 16, 2.

———, 1985b. "Tanebar-Evav and Ema: Variations within the Eastern Indonesian Field of Study," *Journal of the Anthropological Society of Oxford*, 16, 3.

Barnett, Steve, 1976. "Coconuts and Gold: Relational Identity in a South Indian Caste," *Contributions to Indian Sociology*, 10, 1.

Basham, Richard, 1981. "Merit and Power in Thailand: A Reappraisal," unpublished.

Basu, Alaka Malwade, 1993a. "Cultural Influences on the Timing of First Births in India: Large Differences That Add up to Little Differences," *Population Studies*, 47.

———, 1993b. "Fertility Decline and Increasing Gender Imbalance in India including the South Indian Turnaround," unpublished.

Basu, S. K. and S. Roy, 1972. "Change in the Frequency of Consanguineous Marriages among the Delhi Muslims after Partition," *Eastern Anthropologist*, 25.

Batliwala, S., 1982. "Rural Energy Scarcity and Nutrition: A New Perspective," *Economic and Political Weekly*, 17, 9.

———, 1983. "Women in Poverty: The Energy, Health and Nutrition Syndrome," Foundation for Research in Community Health.

———, 1985. "Women's Access to Food within the Family," unpublished.

Bautista, V. A. 1985. "An Evaluation of the Philippine Pre-marriage Counselling Programme," *Philippine Population Journal*, 1 and 3.

Beck, Brenda E. F., 1974. "The Kin Nucleus in Tamil Folklore," in Thomas R. Trautmann, ed., *Kinship and History in South Asia*, Michigan Papers on South and Southeast Asia No. 7.

Becker, Stan and Mridul K. Chowdhury, 1981. "The 1978 Sex Ratio at Birth," International Centre for Diarrhoeal Disease Research Working Paper No. 24.

Becker, Stan and Helen Hiltabidle, 1981. "Comparison of Measures of Childbearing: Patterns by Age and Parity in Matlab, Bangladesh," International Centre for Diarrhoeal Disease Research Working Paper No. 15.

Beech, Mary Higdon, 1982. "The Domestic Realm in the Lives of Hindu Women in Calcutta," in Hanna Papanek and Gail Minault, eds., *Separate Worlds: Studies of Purdah in South Asia*, Chanakya Publications.

Behura, N. R., 1963. "Rajaparba: The Festival of Fertility Cult in Orissa," *Eastern Anthropologist*, 16.

Bencha, Yoddumnern, 1981. "Premarital Use of Family Planning: Effects on Age at Marriage," Mahidol University.

Benda-Beckmann, Keebet von, 1984. *The Broken Stairways to Consensus: Village Justice and State Courts in Minangkabau*, Foris Publications.

———, 1986. "Evidence and Legal Reasoning in Minangkabau," in Keebet von Benda-Beckmann and Fons Strijbosch, eds., *Anthropology of Law in the Netherlands*, Foris Publications.

Beneria, Lourdes, 1979. "Reproduction and the Sexual Division of Labour," *Cambridge Journal of Economics*, 3.

Bennett, Lynn, 1976. "Sex and Motherhood among the Brahmins and Chhetris of East Central Nepal," *Contributions to Nepalese Studies*, 3.

———, 1978. "Maiti-ghar: The Dual Role of Women in Northern Hindu Kinship from the Perspective of the Chhetris and Brahmans of Nepal," in James Fisher, ed., *Himalayan Anthropology*, Mouton.

———, 1979. *Tradition and Change in the Legal Status of Nepalese Women*, Volume 1, Part 2 of *The Status of Women in Nepal*, Centre for Economic Development and Administration, Kathmandu.

———, 1981. *The Parbatiya Women of Bakundol*, Volume 2, Part 7 of *The Status of Women in Nepal*, Centre for Economic Development and Administration, Kathmandu.

———, 1983. *Dangerous Wives and Sacred Sisters: Social and Symbolic Roles of High-caste Women in Nepal*, Columbia University Press.

Bernstein, Henry, 1987. "Capitalism and Petty Commodity Production," *Journal of Social Studies*, 36.

Bertocci, Peter J., 1970. "Elusive Villages: Social Structure and Community Organization in Rural East Pakistan," Michigan State University Ph.D. thesis.

———, 1974. "Rural Communities in Bangladesh: Hajipur and Tinpara," in Clarence Maloney, ed., *South Asia: Seven Community Profiles*, Holt, Rinehart & Winston.

Bhagwat, Vidyut, ed., 1984. *Mee Bai Ahe Mhanun*, Bharatiya Arthavigyan Vardhin (in Marathi).

Bhatia, Shushum, J. Chakraborty, and A. S. G. Faruque, 1979. "Indigenous Birth Practices in Rural Bangladesh and their Implications for a Maternal and Child Health Programme," International Centre for Diarrhoeal Disease Research Scientific Report No. 26.

Bhatt, G. S., 1991. *Women and Polyandry in Rawain-Jaunpur*, Rawat Publications.

Bhatty, Zarina, 1975. "Women in Uttar Pradesh: Social Mobility and Directions of Change," in A. de Souza, ed., *Women in Contemporary India*, Manohar.

———, 1976. "Status of Muslim Woman and Social Change," in B. R. Nanda, ed., *Indian Woman: From Purdah to Modernity*, Vikas Publishing House.

———, 1988. "Socialisation of the Female Muslim Child in Uttar Pradesh," in Karuna Chanana, ed., *Socialisation, Education and Women: Explorations in Gender Identity*, Nehru Memorial Museum and Library and Orient Longman.

Blanchet, Therese, 1984. *Meanings and Rituals of Birth in Rural Bangladesh: Women, Pollution and Marginality*, Dhaka University Press.

Blei, T., 1990. "Dowry and Bridewealth Presentations in Bangladesh: Commodities, Gifts or Hybrid Forms?" Christian Michelson Institute Working Paper.

Bose, Ashish, 1993. *India and the Asian Population Perspective*, B. R. Publishing Corporation.

Boserup, Ester, 1970. *Women's Role in Economic Development*, St. Martin's Press.

Bossen, Laurel, 1975. "Women in Modernizing Societies," *American Ethnologist*, 2.

Boyd, James W., 1971. "Symbols of Evil in Buddhism," *Journal of Asian Studies*, 31.

Bradford, Nicholas J., 1985. "From Bridewealth to Groom-fee: Transformed Marriage Customs and Socio-economic Polarisation amongst Lingayats," *Contributions to Indian Sociology*, 19.

Breman, Jan, 1974. *Patronage and Exploitation: Changing Agrarian Relations in South Gujarat*, University of California Press.

———, 1983. *Control of Land and Labour in Colonial Java: A Case Study of Agrarian Crisis and Reform in the Region of Cirebon during the First Decades of the Twentieth Century*, Foris Publications.

Brijbhushan, Jamila, 1980. *Muslim Women in Purdah and out of It*, Vikas.

Broch, Harald Beyer, 1983. "The Matrifocal Warp of Bonerate Culture," in Bo Utas, ed., *Women in Islamic Societies*, Curzon Press.

Brummelhuis, Han ten and Jeremy H. Kemp, eds., 1984. *Strategies and Structures in Thai Society*, Anthropological-Sociological Centre, University of Amsterdam.

Bulatao, R. A., 1975a. "The Double Standard in Sex Roles," *Philippine Sociological Review*, 26, 3&4.

———, 1975b. *The Value of Children: A Cross-National Study*, Volume 2, East–West Population Institute.

Burling, Robbins, 1963. *Rengsanggri: Family and Kinship in a Garo Village*, University of Pennsylvania Press.

Cain, Mead, 1978. "The Household Life Cycle and Economic Mobility in Rural Bangladesh," *Population and Development Review*, 4, 3.

——— et al., 1979. "Class Patriarchy and Women's Work in Bangladesh," *Population and Development Review*, 5, 3.

Caldwell, J. C., P. H. Reddy, and P. Caldwell, 1988. *The Causes of Demographic Change: Experimental Research in South India*, University of Wisconsin Press.

Caplan, L., 1984. "Bridegroom Price in Urban India: Class, Caste and 'Dowry Evil' among Christians in Madras," *Man*, 19, 2.

Caplan, Patricia, 1985. *Class and Gender in India: Women and their Organizations in a South Indian City*, Tavistock Publications.

——— and Janet Bujra, eds., 1978. *Women United, Women Divided*, Tavistock Publications.

Carey, P. B. R., 1986. *Maritime Southeast Asian Studies in the United Kingdom: A Survey of their Post-War Development and Current Resources*, JASO Occasional Paper No. 6.

Carey, Peter and Vincent Houben, 1987. "Spirited Srikandhis and Sly Sumbadras: The Social, Political and Economic Role of Women at the Central Javanese Courts in the 18th and Early 19th Centuries," in Elsbeth Locher-Scholten and Anke Niehof, eds., *Indonesian Women in Focus*, Foris Publications.

Carrol, Lucy, 1982. "Talaq-i-tafurid and the Stipulations in a Muslim Marriage Contract," *Modern Asian Studies*, 16.

Carter, Anthony T., 1983. "Hierarchy and the Concept of the Person in Western India," in Akos Ostor, Lina Fruzzetti, and Steve Barnett, eds., *Concepts of Person: Kinship, Caste and Marriage in India*, Oxford University Press.

Castillo, Gelia T., 1969. "The Filipino Woman: A Study of Multiple Roles," *Journal of Asian and African Studies*, 4, 1.

———, 1976. *The Filipino Woman as Manpower: The Image and the Empirical Reality*, University of the Philippines.

——— and J. F. Pua, 1963. "Research Notes on the Contemporary Filipino Family: Findings in a Tagalog Area," *Philippine Journal of Economics*, 14, 3.

———, A. M. Weisblat, and F. R. Villareal, 1968. "The Concept of Nuclear and Extended Family: An Exploration of Empirical Referents," *International Journal of Comparative Sociology*, 9, 1.

Chanana, Karuna, 1989. "Introduction," Section II, in Maithreyi Krishna Raj and Karuna Chanana, eds., *Gender and the Household Domain: Social and Cultural Dimensions*, Sage.

———, 1990. "The Dialectics of Tradition and Modernity and Women's Education in India," *Sociological Bulletin*, 39, 1&2.

———, ed., 1988. *Socialisation, Education and Women: Explorations in Gender Identity*, Nehru Memorial Museum and Library and Orient Longman.

Chantornvong, Sombat, 1985. "The Political World of Sunthonphu," in *Traditional and Changing Thai World View*, Chulalongkorn University Social Research Institute.

Chapon, Diana, n.d. *Divorce and Fertility: A Study in Rural Java*, Gadjah Mada University Population Institute.

Chatterjee, M., 1977. "Conjugal Roles and Social Networks in an Indian Urban Sweeper Locality," *Journal of Marriage and the Family*, 39, 1.

Chatterjee, Meera, 1983. "Women's Access to Health Care: A Critical Issue for Child Health," paper for ICMR conference, Bangalore.

———, 1989. "Competence and Care for Women: Health Policy Perspectives in the Household Context," in Maithreyi Krishna Raj and Karuna Chanana, eds., *Gender and the Household Domain: Social and Cultural Dimensions*, Sage.

Chaudhury, R., 1961. *Hindu Woman's Rights to Property, Past and Present*, Firma K. L. Mukhopadhyay.

Chaudhury, R. H. and N. R. Ahmed, 1980. *Female Status in Bangladesh*, Institute of Development Studies.

Chee, Tham Seong, 1979. "Social Change and the Malay Family," in C. Y. Kuo Eddie and Aline K. Wong, eds., *The Contemporary Family in Singapore*, Singapore University Press.

Chen, L., E. Huo, and S. D'Souza, 1981. "Sex Bias in the Family Allocation of Food and Health Care in Rural Bangladesh," *Population and Development Review*, 7, 1.

Chen, Marty, 1986. "Poverty, Gender and Work in Bangladesh," *Economic and Political Weekly*, 21, 5.

———, 1990. "Poverty, Gender and Work in Bangladesh," in Leela Dube and Rajni Palriwala, eds., *Structures and Strategies: Women, Work and Family*, Sage.

Chng, Nancy, ed., 1977. *Questioning Development in Southeast Asia*, Select Books.

Choudhury, Alimuzzaman, 1987. *The Family Courts Ordinance, 1985, and Other Personal Laws*, Desh Publications.

Chowdhry, Prem, 1989. "Customs in a Peasant Economy: Women in Colonial Haryana," in Kumkum Sangari and Sudesh Vaid, eds., *Recasting Women: Essays in Colonial History*, Kali for Women.

———, 1990. "An Alternative to the *Sati* Model: Perceptions of a Social Reality in Folklore," *Asian Folklore Studies*, 49, 2.

———, 1994. *The Veiled Women: Shifting Gender Equations in Rural Haryana 1880–1990*, Oxford University Press.

Chowdhury, Anwarullah, 1982. *Agrarian Social Relations and Rural Development in Bangladesh*, Oxford and IBH Publishing Co.

———, ed., 1985. *Pains and Pleasures of Fieldwork*, National Institute of Local Government.

Chowdhury, Momen, n.d. "Use of Folklore in Population Control," unpublished.

Chowdhury, Rafiqul Huda, 1974. "Labour Force and Fertility," *Bangladesh Development Studies*, 2, 4.

Chung, Betty Jamie and Ng Shui Meng, 1977. "The Status of Women in Law: A Comparison of Four Asian Countries," Institute of Southeast Asian Studies Occasional Paper No. 49.

Churairat, Chandhamrong, 1982. "Change and Kinship Organization in Rural Thailand," Malaysian National Commission for Unesco.

Cobwell, E. B., ed., 1957. *The Jataka Stories: Stories of Buddha's Former Births*, Pali Text Society.

Cohen, Paul, n.d. "The Cult of the Lineage Spirits in Northern Thailand," unpublished.

——— and Gehan Wijeyewardene, eds., 1984. "Spirit Cults and the Position of Women in Northern Thailand," special issue of *Mankind*, 14, 4.

Cohn, Bernard S., 1961. "Chamar Family in a North Indian Village: A Structural Contingent," *Economic Weekly*, 13.

———, 1970. "Society and Social Change under the Raj," *South Asian Review*, 4.

Collier, Jane Fishbourne and Sylvia Junko Yanagisako, eds., 1987. *Gender and Kinship: Essays Towards a Unified Analysis*, Stanford University Press.

Colson, Elizabeth, 1980. "The Resilience of Matrilineality: Gwembe and Plateau Tonga Adaptations," in Linda S. Cordell and Stephen Beckerman, eds., *The Versality of Kinship*, Academic Press.

Commission on Women (International Union of Anthropological and Ethnological Sciences), Research Committee 32, "Women in Society" (International Sociological Association), and Indian Association for Women's Studies, 1985. Collected papers, Regional Conference for Asia on Women and the Household, unpublished.

Condominas, Georges, 1975. "Phiban Cults in Rural Laos," in G. W. Skinner and A. T. Kirsch, eds., *Change and Persistence in Thai Society: Essays in Honor of Lauriston Sharp*, Cornell University Press.

Conklin, George H., 1968. "The Family Formation Process in India: An Overview," *Journal of Family Welfare*, 14.

Cordero, Felicidad and Isabel Panopio, 1969. *General Sociology: Focus on the Philippines*, College Professions Publishing Corporation.

Cormack, M., 1961. *The Hindu Woman*, Asia Publishing House.

Couillard, Marie-Andree, 1986. "A Brief Exploration into the Nature of Men–Women Relations among Pre-Colonial Malayan People," in Bruce Matthews and Judith Nagata, eds., *Religion, Values and Development in Southeast Asia*, Institute of Southeast Asia Studies.

176

CUSRI, 1985. *Traditional and Changing Thai World View*, Chulalongkorn University Social Research Institute.

Dabla, Basheer A., 1992. "Muslim Working Women in Kashmir," in Mohini Anjum, ed., *Muslim Women in India*, Radiant Publishers.

Dacca University, 1977. *Nutritional Survey of Rural Bangladesh 1975–76*, Institute of Nutrition and Food Sciences.

Darroch, Russell K. et al., 1981. *Two Are Enough: The Value of Children to Javanese and Sundanese Parents*, East–West Population Institute Paper No. 60-D.

Darunee, Tantiwiramanand and Shashi Pandey, 1987. "The Status and Role of Thai Women in the Pre-Modern Period: A Historical and Cultural Perspective," *Sojourn*, 2, 2.

Das, Man Singh, ed., 1991. *The Family in the Muslim World*, M. D. Publications.

—— and Panos D. Bardis, eds., 1978. *The Family in Asia*, Allen & Unwin.

Das, Veena, 1973. "The Structure of Marriage Preferences: An Account from Pakistani Fiction," *Man*, 8, 1.

——, 1975. "Marriage among Hindus," in Devaki Jain, ed., *Indian Women*, Publications Division, Government of India.

——, 1976a. "Indian Women: Work, Power and Status," in B. R. Nanda, ed., *Indian Woman: From Purdah to Modernity*, Vikas Publishing House.

——, 1976b. "Masks and Faces: An Essay on Punjabi Kinship," *Contributions to Indian Sociology*, 10, 1.

——, 1979. "Reflections on the Social Construction of Adulthood," in Sudhir Kakar, ed., *Identity and Adulthood*, Oxford University Press.

——, 1988. "Femininity and the Orientation to the Body," in Karuna Chanana, ed., *Socialisation, Education and Women: Explorations in Gender Identity*, Nehru Memorial Museum and Library and Orient Longman.

Das Gupta, M., 1987. "Selective Discrimination against Female Children in Rural Punjab, India," *Population and Development Review*, 13, 1.

Davis, Richard, 1973. "Muang Matrifocality," *Journal of the Siam Society*, 61, 2.

——, 1984. *Muang Metaphysics: A Study of Northern Thai Myth and Ritual*, Pandora Studies in Thai Anthropology 1.

De La Paz, D. R. and E. A. De Guzman, 1977. "The Filipino Family: Today and Tomorrow," University of the Philippines.

Derne, Steve, 1994. "Arranging Marriages: How Fathers' Concerns Limit Women's Educational Achievements," in Carol C. Mukhopadhyay and Susan Seymour, eds., *Women, Education and Family Structure in India*, Westview Press.

Desai, Neera and Maithreyi Krishna Raj, eds., 1987. *Women and Society in India*, Ajanta Publications.

Dewey, A. G., 1962. *Peasant Marketing in Java*, The Free Press.

Dey, Jennie, 1985. "Women in Rice Farming System Network: Country Profile on Bangladesh," unpublished.

Dhruvarajan, Vanaja, 1989. *Hindu Women and the Power of Ideology*, Vistar Publications.

Dizon, Jesse A. N., Jr., 1973. "Modern Filipino Kinship: The Manila Corporation Manager as a Case in Point," *Philippine Sociological Review*, 21.

Djajadiningrat-Nieuwenhuis, Madelon, 1987. "Ibuism and Priyayization: Path to Power?" in Elsbeth Locher-Scholten and Anke Niehof, eds., *Indonesian Women in Focus*, Foris Publications.

Djmour, Judith, 1959. *Malay Kinship and Marriage in Singapore*, University of London, Athlone Press.

———, 1960. *The Muslim Matrimonial Courts in Singapore*, Athlone Press.

Dobby, E. H. C., 1976. *Southeast Asia*, University of London Press.

Doherty, Victor S., 1974. "The Organizing Principles of Brahman Chetri Kinship," *Contributions to Nepalese Studies*, 2.

Donnan, Hastings, 1988. *Marriage among Muslims: Preference and Choice in Northern Pakistan*, Hindustan Publishing Corporation.

Dornsife, Cinnamon and Adnan Mahmoed, 1986. *An Evaluation of Pathfinder's Early Marriage Education Program in Indonesia*, Pathfinder Fund Working Paper No. 4.

D'Souza, Stan, Abbas Bhuiya, and Mizanur Rahman, 1980. "Socioeconomic Differentials in Mortality in a Rural Area of Bangladesh," International Centre for Diarrhoeal Disease Research Scientific Report No. 40.

D'Souza, Victor S., 1976. "Kinship Organization and Marriage Customs among the Moplahs on the South-west Coast of India," in I. Ahmad, ed., *Family, Kinship and Marriage among Muslims in India*, Manohar Book Service.

Dube, Leela, 1956. "The Gond Woman," Nagpur University Ph.D. thesis.

———, 1969a. *Matriliny and Islam: Religion and Society in the Laccadives*, National Publishing House.

———, 1969b. "Inheritance of Property in a Matrilineal Society," paper for All-India Sociological Conference, New Delhi.

———, 1974. *Sociology of Kinship: An Analytical Survey of Literature*, Popular Prakashan.

———, 1978. "Caste Analogues among the Laccadive (Lakshadweep) Muslims," in Imtiaz Ahmad, ed., *Social Stratification among Muslims in India*, Manohar Publications.

———, 1980. *Studies on Women in Southeast Asia*, Unesco.

———, 1983a. "Misadventures in Amniocentesis," *Economic and Political Weekly*, 28, 8.

———, 1983b. "Dowry: Victims of Kinship Morality," *Economic Times*, Sunday 20 March.

———, 1986. "Seed and Earth: The Symbolism of Biological Reproduction and Sexual Relations of Production," in Leela Dube, Eleanor Leacock, and Shirley Ardener, eds., *Visibility and Power: Essays on Women in Society and Development*, Oxford University Press.

———, 1988a. "On the Construction of Gender: Hindu Girls in Patrilineal India," *Economic and Political Weekly*, 23, 18.

———, 1988b. "Socialisation of Hindu Girls in Patrilineal India," in Karuna Chanana, ed., *Socialisation, Education and Women: Explorations in Gender Identity*, Nehru Memorial Museum and Library and Orient Longman.

———, 1988c. "The Nature of Bounded Groups and the Management of Female Sexuality: The Khasi and the Nayar," paper for 12th International Congress of Anthropological and Ethnological Sciences, Zagreb.

———, 1991a. "In the Mother's Line: Aspects of Structure and Change in Lakshadweep," unpublished.

———, 1991b. "Reconsidering the Matrilineal Puzzle: Gender Relations in Kalpeni, a Lakshadweep Island," unpublished.

178

————, 1992. "Women in a Matrilineal Muslim Community," in Mohini Anjum, ed., *Muslim Women in India*, Radiant Publishers.

————, 1993. "Who Gains from Matriliny? Men, Women and Change on a Lakshadweep Island," *Sociological Bulletin*, 42, 1&2.

————, 1994. "Conflict and Compromise: Devolution and Disposal of Property in a Matrilineal Muslim Society," *Economic and Political Weekly*, 29, 21.

————, 1996. "Caste and Women," in M. N. Srinivas, ed., *Caste: Its Twentieth Century Avatar*, Viking, Penguin.

———— and Rajni Palriwala, eds., 1990. *Structures and Strategies: Women, Work and Family*, Sage.

————, Eleanor Leacock, and Shirley Ardener, eds., 1986. *Visibility and Power: Essays on Women in Society and Development*, Oxford University Press.

Dube, Saurabh, 1993a. *Caste and Sect in Village Life. Satnamis of Chhattisgarh 1900–1950. Occasional Paper 5, Socio-Religious Movements and Cultural Networks in Indian Civilisation*, Indian Institute of Advanced Study, Shimla.

————, 1993b. "Idioms of Authority and Engendered Agendas: The Satnami Mahasabha, Chhattisgarh, 1925–50," *Indian Economic and Social History Review*, 30, 4.

————, 1995. "Paternalism and Freedom: The Evangelical Encounter in Colonial Chhattisgarh, Central India," *Modern Asian Studies*, 29, 1.

————, 1996a. "Colonial Law and Village Disputes: Two Cases from Chhattisgarh," in Satish Saberwal and N. Jayaram, eds., *Social Conflict. Oxford in India Readings in Sociology and Social Anthropology*, Oxford University Press.

————, 1996b. "Telling Tales and Trying Truths: Entitlements and Legalities in Village Disputes, Late Colonial Central India," *Studies in History*, 12, 2.

————, forthcoming. *Untouchable Pasts. Religion, Identity and Power among a Central Indian People, 1780–1950*, State University of New York Press.

Dube, S. C., 1951. *The Kamar*, Universal Publishers.

————, 1953. "Token Pre-puberty Marriage in India," *Man* (O.S.), 53.

————, 1955. *Indian Village*, Routledge & Kegan Paul.

————, 1963. "Men's and Women's Roles in India: A Sociological View," in B. E. Ward, ed., *Women in the New Asia*, Unesco.

Duff-Cooper, A., 1985a. "An Account of the Balinese 'Person' from West Lombok," *Bijdragen*, 141, 1.

————, 1985b. "The Family as an Aspect of the Totality of the Balinese Form of Life in Western Lombok," *Bijdragen*, 141, 2–3.

————, 1985c. "Ethnographical Notes on Two Operations of the Body among a Community of Balinese on Lombok," *Journal of the Anthropological Society of Oxford*, 16, 2.

Dumont, Jean-Paul, 1981. "Lost Relatives: Social Amnesia in a Visayan Setting," *Philippine Quarterly of Culture and Society*, 9.

Dumont, Louis, 1957. *Hierarchy and Marriage Alliance in South Indian Kinship*, Royal Anthropological Institute.

————, 1961. "Marriage in India: The Present State of the Question, I – Marriage Alliance in South-East India and Ceylon," *Contributions to Indian Sociology*, 5.

————, 1964. "Marriage in India: The Present State of the Question, II – Marriage and Status: Nayar and Newar," *Contributions to Indian Sociology*, 7.

————, 1966. "Marriage in India: The Present State of the Question, III – North India in Relation to South," *Contributions to Indian Sociology*, 9.

————, 1970. *Homo Hierarchicus: The Caste System and Its Implications*, Weidenfeld & Nicolson.

Dunham, David, 1982. "Politics and Land Settlement Schemes: The Case of Sri Lanka," *Development and Change*, 13.

Eglar, Zekiya, 1966. *A Punjabi Village in Pakistan*, Columbia University Press.

Ellickson, J., 1975. "Rural Women," in *Women for Women*, Dacca University Press.

Embree, John, 1950. "Thailand: A Loosely Structured Social System," *American Anthropologist*, 52.

Epstein, T. Scarlett, 1960. "Economic Development and Peasant Marriage in South India," *Man in India*, 40.

————, 1973. *South India: Yesterday, Today and Tomorrow*, Macmillan.

———— and R. A. Watts, eds., 1981. *The Endless Day: Some Material on Asian Rural Women*, Pergamon Press.

Errington, Frederick K., 1984. *Manners and Meaning in West Sumatra: The Social Context of Consciousness*, Yale University Press.

Esterik, John van, 1982. "Women Meditation Teachers in Thailand," in Penny van Esterik, ed., *Women in Southeast Asia*, Northern Illinois University Occasional Paper No. 9.

Esterik, Penny van, 1982a. "Introduction," in Penny van Esterik, ed., *Women in Southeast Asia*, Northern Illinois University Occasional Paper No. 9.

————, 1982b. "Laywomen in Theravada Buddhism," in Penny van Esterik, ed., *Women in Southeast Asia*, Northern Illinois University Occasional Paper No. 9.

————, ed., 1982c. *Women in Southeast Asia*, Northern Illinois University Occasional Paper No. 9.

Evers, Hans-Dieter, ed., 1969. *Loosely Structured Social Systems: Thailand in a Comparative Perspective*, Yale University Press.

Fazalbhoy, N., 1988. *The Health Status of Indian Women: A Reader*, Tata Institute of Social Sciences.

Ferro-Luzzi, Gabriella Eichinger, 1974. "Women's Pollution Period in Tamilnadu," *Anthropos*, 69.

Fett, Ione, 1983. "Land Ownership in Negri Sembilan, 1900–1977," in Lenore Manderson, ed., *Women's Work and Women's Roles*, Australian National University.

Firth, Rosemary, 1966. *Housekeeping among the Malay Peasants*, The Athlone Press.

Flavia, Agnes, 1988. "Violence in the Family: Wife Beating," in Rehana Ghadially, ed., *Women in Indian Society: A Reader*, Sage.

Fox, R., 1961. "Filipino Family and Kinship," *Philippine Quarterly*, 2, 1.

————, 1963. "Men and Women in the Philippines," in Barbara E. Ward, ed., *Women in the New Asia*, Unesco.

Freeman, J. D., 1961. "On the Concept of the Kindred," *Journal of the Royal Anthropological Institute*, 91.

Friedl, E., 1967. "The Position of Women: Appearance and Reality," Anthropological Quarterly, 40, 3.

Fruzzetti, Lina, 1980. "Ritual Status of Muslim Women in Rural India," in Jane I. Smith, ed., *Women in Contemporary Muslim Societies*, Bucknell University Press.

———— and Akos Ostor, 1976. "Seed and Earth: A Cultural Analysis of Kinship in a Bengali Town," *Contributions to Indian Sociology*, 10, 1.

Fuller, C. J., 1976. *The Nayars Today*, Cambridge University Press.

———, 1980. "The Divine Couple's Relationship in a South Indian Temple: Minakshi and Sundereswara at Madurai," *History of Religions*, 19.

Furer-Haimendorf, C. von, 1956. "Elements of Newar Social Structure," *Journal of the Royal Anthropological Institute*, 86, 2.

———, 1979. *The Gonds of Andhra Pradesh*, Vikas Publishing House.

Ganesh, Kamala, 1982. "The Kottai Pillaimar of Srivaikuntam: A Socio-historical Study," University of Bombay Ph.D. thesis.

———, 1985a. "Women's Seclusion and the Structure of Caste," paper for Regional Conference for Asia on Women and the Household, New Delhi.

———, 1985b. "State of the Art in Women's Studies," *Economic and Political Weekly*, 20, 16.

———, 1988. "Family and Kinship in India: Implications for Women," unpublished.

———, 1993. *Boundary Walls: Caste and Women in a Tamil Community*, Hindustan Publishing Corporation.

Gardezi, Fauzia, 1990. "Islam, Feminism and the Women's Movement in Pakistan 1981–1991," *South Asia Bulletin*, 10, 2.

Geertz, Hildred, 1961. *The Javanese Family: A Study of Kinship and Socialization*, The Free Press of Glencoe.

——— and Clifford Geertz, 1975. *Kinship in Bali*, Chicago University Press.

Germain, Adrienne, 1976. *Women's Roles in Bangladesh Development: A Program Assessment*, The Ford Foundation.

Ghadially, Rehana and Pramod Kumar, 1988. "Bride-burning and Psycho-social Dynamics of Dowry Deaths," in Rehana Ghadially, ed., *Women in Indian Society: A Reader*, Sage.

Girling, John L. S., 1981. *Thailand: Society and Politics*, Cornell University Press.

Go, Stella P., 1992. "The Filipino Family in the Eighties: A Review of Research," in *The Changing Family in Asia*, Unesco.

———, L. T. Postrado, and P. R. Jimenez, 1983. *The Effects of International Contract Labour*, Volume 1, De La Salle University.

Good, Anthony, 1991. *The Female Bridegroom*, Oxford University Press.

Goody, J., 1973. "Bridewealth and Dowry in Africa and Eurasia," in J. Goody and S. Tambiah, eds., *Bridewealth and Dowry*, Cambridge University Press.

———, 1975. *The Character of Kinship*, Cambridge University Press.

———, 1989. *The Oriental, the Ancient and the Primitive: Systems of Marriage and the Family in the Pre-industrial Societies of Eurasia*, Cambridge University Press.

——— and S. Tambiah, eds., 1973. *Bridewealth and Dowry*, Cambridge University Press.

Goonatilake, Hema, 1979. "Women in Creative Arts and Mass Media," in *Status of Women in Sri Lanka*, University of Colombo.

Gopalan, C., 1985. "The Mother and Child in India," *Economic and Political Weekly*, 20, 4.

Gore, M. S., 1968. *Urbanization and Family Change*, Popular Prakashan.

Gough, Kathleen, 1955. "Female Initiation Rites on the Malabar Coast," *Journal of the Royal Anthropological Institute*, 85.

———, 1956. "Brahman Kinship in a Tamil Village," *American Anthropologist*, 8.

———, 1959. "The Nayars and the Definition of Marriage," *Journal of the Royal Anthropological Institute*, 89, 1.

———, 1961. "Nayars: Central Kerala," in D. M. Schneider and Kathleen Gough, eds., *Matrilineal Kinship*, University of California Press.

———, 1971. "Nuer Kinship: A Re-examination," in T. O. Beidelman, ed., *The Translation of Culture: Essays for E. E. Evans-Pritchard*, Tavistock.

———, 1975. "Changing Households in Kerala," in D. Narain, ed., *Explorations in the Family and Other Essays*, Thacker and Company.

———, 1979. "Dravidian Kinship and Modes of Production," *Contributions to Indian Sociology*, 13, 2.

Gould, Harold A., 1960. "The Micro-demography of Marriage in a North Indian Area," *Southwestern Journal of Anthropology*, 16.

———, 1961. "A Further Note on Village Exogamy in North India," *Southwestern Journal of Anthropology*, 17.

———, 1968. "Time Dimension and Structural Change in an Indian Kinship System: A Problem of Conceptual Refinement," in Milton Singer and Bernard Cohn, eds., *Structure and Change in Indian Society*, Wenner-Gren Foundation for Anthropological Research.

Government of India, 1974. *Towards Equality: Report of the Committee on the Status of Women in India*, Department of Social Welfare.

———, 1983. *Survey on Infant Mortality 1979*, Office of the Registrar General.

Gray, John N., 1982. "Chetri Women in Domestic Groups and Rituals," in Michael Allen and S. N. Mukherjee, eds., *Women in India and Nepal*, Australian National University Monographs on South Asia No. 8.

———, 1989. "The Household in Nepal: Social and Experiential Crucible of Society," in John N. Gray and David J. Mearns, eds., *Society from the Inside Out: Anthropological Perspectives on the South Asian Household*, Sage.

——— and David J. Mearns, eds., 1989. *Society from the Inside Out: Anthropological Perspectives on the South Asian Household*, Sage.

Guhathakurta, Meghna, 1985. "Gender Violence in Bangladesh: The Role of the State," *Journal of Social Studies*, 30.

Gulati, Leela, 1975. "Occupational Distribution of Working Women," *Economic and Political Weekly*, 10, 43.

———, 1981. *Profiles in Female Poverty: A Study of Five Poor Working Women in Kerala*, Hindustan Publishing Corporation.

———, 1986. "The Impact on the Family of Male Migration to the Middle East: Some Evidence from Kerala, India," in F. Arnold and N. Shah, eds., *Asian Labour Migration: Pipeline to the Middle East*, Westview Press.

Gupta, Giri Raj, 1974. *Marriage, Religion and Society: Pattern of Change in an Indian Village*, Vikas Publishing House.

———, 1976. *Family and Social Change in Modern India*, Vikas Publishing House.

Gupta, Jayoti, 1990. "Class Relations, Family Structure and Bondage of Women," in Leela Dube and Rajni Palriwala, eds., *Structures and Strategies: Women, Work and Family*, Sage.

Guthrie, G. M. and P. J. Jacobs, 1967. *Child Rearing and Personality Development in the Philippines*, Pennsylvania State University Press.

Guthrie, G. M. et al., 1983. "Water, Waste and Well-being in the Rural Philippines," *Philippine Quarterly of Culture and Society*, 11.

Hafner, Annemarie, 1985. "Working Women, Their Problems and Trade Unions in India," *Journal of Social Studies*, 30.

Hainsworth, Geoffrey B. et al., eds., 1981. *Southeast Asia: Women, Changing Social Structure and Cultural Continuity*, University of Ottawa Press.

Haksar, Nandita, 1986. *Demystification of Law for Women*, Lancer Press.

Hale, Ann, 1974. "The Search for a Jural Rule: Women in Southeast Asia – The Northern Thai Cults in Perspective," *Mankind*, 14, 4.

Hanchett, S., 1975. "Hindu Potlaches: Ceremonial Reciprocity and Prestige in Karnataka," in Helen Ullrich, ed. *Competition and Modernization in South Asia*, Abhinav Publications.

———, 1985. "The Ambiguous Role of Women in the South Indian Family," paper for Regional Conference for Asia on Women and the Household, New Delhi.

Hang, Evelyn, ed., 1983. *Malaysian Women: Problems and Issues*, Consumers' Association of Penang.

Hanks, Jane R., 1963. *Maternity and Its Rituals in Bang Chan*, Cornell University Southeast Asia Program Data Paper No. 51.

Hanks, Lucien M., 1962. "Merit and Power in the Thai Social Order," *American Anthropologist*, 64.

———, 1966. "The Corporation and the Entourage: A Comparison of Thai and American Social Organization," *Catalyst*, 2.

Hannan, Ferdouse H. and Nazrul Islam, 1986. *Women in Agriculture: An Annotated Bibliography*, Bangladesh Academy for Rural Development.

Hara, Tadahiko, 1967. "Paribar and Kinship in a Muslim Rural Village in East Pakistan," Australian National University Ph.D. thesis.

Harper, E. B., 1959. "A Hindu Marriage Pantheon," *Southwestern Journal of Anthropology*, 15, 3.

———, 1963. "Spirit Possession and Social Structure," in B. Ratnam, ed., *Anthropology on the March: Recent Studies of Indian Beliefs, Attitudes and Social Institutions*, Madras Social Sciences Association.

———, 1964. "Ritual Pollution as an Integration of Caste and Religion," *Journal of Asian Studies*, 23.

———, 1969. "Fear and the Status of Women," *Southwestern Journal of Anthropology*, 25.

Harris, Grace, 1975. "Furies, Witches and Mothers," in Jack Goody, ed., *The Character of Kinship*, Cambridge University Press.

Harris, M., 1974. *Cows, Pigs, Wars and Witches: The Riddles of Culture*, Random House.

Harris, Olivia, 1981. "Households as Natural Units," in Kate Young, Carol Wolkowitz, and R. McCullagh, eds., *Of Marriage and the Market: Women's Subordination in International Perspective*, CSE Books.

Harriss, Barbara, 1986. "The Intrafamily Distribution of Hunger in South Asia," unpublished.

Hart, Don V., Phya Hanuman Rajadhon, and Richard J. Conghlin, 1965. *Three Studies in Human Reproduction*, New Haven Human Relations Area Files.

Hartman, Betsy and James R. Boyce, 1983. *A Quiet Violence: View from a Bangladesh Village*, Zed Press.

Hassan, Sharifah Zaleha Syed, 1986. "Women, Divorce and Islam in Keddah," *Sojourn: Social Issues in Southeast Asia*, 1, 2.

Heltige, S. T., 1984. *Wealth, Power and Prestige: Emerging Patterns of Social Inequality in a Peasant Context*, Ministry of Higher Education, Sri Lanka.

Hershman, Paul, 1974. "Hair, Sex and Dirt," *Man*, 9, 2.

———, 1977. "Virgin and Mother," in I. Lewis, ed., *Symbols and Sentiments*, Academic Press.

———, 1981. *Punjabi Kinship and Marriage*, Hindustan Publishing Corporation.

Hetler, Carol B., 1984. "Rural and Urban Female-headed Households in Java: Results of a Village Study in Central Java," unpublished.

———, 1990. "Survival Strategies, Migration and Household Headship," in Leela Dube and Rajni Palriwala, eds., *Structures and Strategies: Women, Work and Family*, Sage.

Heyzer, Noeleen, 1986. *Working Women in South-east Asia: Development, Subordination and Emancipation*, Open University Press.

———, ed., 1985. *Missing Women: Development Planning in Asia and the Pacific*, Asian and Pacific Development Centre.

Hirschon, Renée, ed., 1984. *Women and Property, Women as Property*, Croom Helm.

Hitchcock, J., 1956. "The Rajputs of Khalapur: A Study of Kinship, Social Stratification and Politics," Cornell University Ph.D. thesis.

Hobart, P. M., 1985a. "Is God Evil?" in D. J. Parkin, ed., *The Anthropology of Evil*, Blackwell.

———, 1985b. "Anthropos through the Looking Glass: Or How to Teach the Balinese to Bark," in J. Overing, ed., *Reason and Morality*, Tavistock Publications.

Hobson, Sarah, 1978. *The Family Web: A Story of India*, John Murray.

Hollnsteiner, Mary Racelis, 1981. "Modernization, Changing Roles of Women and Expectations from Development in Southeast Asia," in Geoffrey B. Hainsworth et al., eds., *Southeast Asia: Women, Changing Social Structure and Cultural Continuity*, University of Ottawa Press.

———, ed., 1979. *Society, Culture and the Filipino*, Institute of Philippine Culture.

Hooker, M. B., 1972. *Adat Laws in Modern Malaya: Land Tenure, Traditional Government and Religion*, Oxford University Press.

———, ed., 1970. *Readings in Malay Adat Laws*, Singapore University Press.

Hossain, Mahabub, 1985. *Credit for the Rural Poor: The Grameen Bank in Bangladesh*, Bangladesh Institute of Development Studies.

Hossain, Rokeya Sakhawat, 1988. *Sultana's Dream and Selections from The Secluded Ones*, The Feminist Press.

Howe, L. E. A., 1985. "Caste in Bali and India: Levels of Comparisons," in R. H. Barnes et al., eds., *Contexts and Levels: Anthropological Essays on Hierarchy*, JASO Occasional Paper No. 4.

Hsu, Francis L. K., 1963. *Clan, Caste and Club*, D. Van Nostrand.

Huda, Sigma, n.d. "Achievements in Law," unpublished.

Hull, Terence, 1976. *The Influence of Social Class on the Need and Effective Demand for Children in a Javanese Village*, Gadjah Mada University Population Institute Working Paper No. 7.

———, 1977. *A Review of Research on the Price, Cost and Value of Children in Indonesia*, Gadjah Mada University Population Institute Working Paper No. 12.

Hull, Valerie, 1976. *Women in Java's Rural Middle Class: Progress or Regress?* Gadjah Mada University Population Institute Working Paper No. 3.

184

————, 1979. *A Woman's Place...: Social Class Variations in Women's Work Patterns in a Javanese Village*, Gadjah Mada University Population Studies Centre Working Paper No. 21.

Huq, Jahanara et al., eds., 1983. *Women in Bangladesh: Some Socio-economic Issues*, Women for Women.

Hussain, Sheikh Abrar, 1976. *Marriage Customs among Muslims in India: A Sociological Study of the Shiah Marriage Customs*, Sterling.

Hyder, Qurratulain, 1975. "Muslim Women in India," in Devaki Jain, ed., *Indian Women*, [New Delhi].

Ibrahim, Ahmad, 1965a. "The Status of Muslim Women in Family Law," Malayan Law Journal, Ltd.

————, 1965b. *Islamic Law in Malaya*, Malaysian Sociological Research Institute Ltd.

————, 1981. "Islamic Law in Malaysia," *Journal of Malaysian and Comparative Law* – Jernal Undang Undang.

————, Sharon Siddique, and Yasmin Hussain, comp., 1986. *Readings on Islam in Southeast Asia*, Institute of Southeast Asian Studies.

Ichimura, Shinichi, ed., 1977. *Southeast Asia: Nature, Society and Development*, University Press of Hawaii.

Illo, Jeanne Frances I., 1990. "Working and Living for Family: Gender, Work and Education," paper for Workshop on Changing Family Patterns and Gender Roles in Asia, New Delhi.

————, 1992. "Who Heads the Households? Women in Households in the Philippines," in K. Saradamoni, ed., *Finding the Household: Conceptual and Methodological Issues*, Sage.

———— and Jaime B. Polo, 1990. *Fishers, Traders, Farmers, Wives: The Life Stories of Ten Women in a Fishing Village*, Women's Work and Family Strategies Monograph 1, Ateneo de Manila University.

Inden, Ronald B. and Ralph Nicholas, 1977. *Kinship in Bengali Culture*, University of Chicago Press.

Irshad Ali, A. N. M., 1976. "Kinship and Marriage among the Assamese Muslims," in Imtiaz Ahmad, ed., *Family, Kinship and Marriage among Muslims in India*, Manohar.

Ishwaran, K., 1974. "The Interdependence of Elementary and Extended Family," in G. Kurien, ed., *Family in India: A Regional View*, Mouton.

Islam, M. Shafiqul and Stan Becker, 1981. "Interrelationships among Certain Socio-economic Variables in a Rural Population of Bangladesh," International Centre for Diarrhoeal Disease Research Working Paper No. 18.

Islam, Mahmuda, 1980. *Folk Medicine and Rural Women in Bangladesh*, Women for Women.

————, 1984. *Bibliography on Bangladesh Women with Annotation*, Women for Women.

————, 1985. *Women, Health and Culture: A Study of Beliefs and Practices Connected with Female Diseases in a Bangladesh Village*, Women for Women.

Islam, Rushidan, 1984. "The Situation of Employment and the Labour Market for Women in Bangladesh," unpublished.

Islam, Shamima, 1982. "Women's Education in Bangladesh: Needs and Issues," Foundation for Research on Educational Planning and Development.

————, 1989. "Rural Women and Childbirth in Bangladesh: The Social Cultural Context," in Maithreyi Krishna Raj and Karuna Chanana, eds., *Gender and the Household Domain: Social and Cultural Dimensions*, Sage.

———— and Jakia Begum, 1985. *Women: Victims of Violence 1975–84*, CWD.

Ismail, Kamariah, 1986. "Child Care Services for Working Women in Malaysia," in Hing Ai Yun and Rokiah Talib, eds., *Women and Employment in Malaysia*, University of Malaya.

Iyengar, Vishwapriya, 1990 and 1991. "The Library Girl," in Lakshmi Holstrom, ed., *The Inner Courtyard*, Virago and Rupa.

Jacob, Alice, 1986. "Equal Inheritance to Indian Christian Women of Kerala," *Journal of the Indian Law Institute*, 28.

Jacobson, Doranne, 1970. "Hidden Faces: Hindu and Muslim Purdah in a Central Indian Village," Columbia University Ph.D. thesis.

————, 1976. "The Veil of Virtue: Purdah and the Muslim Family in the Bhopal Region of India," in Imtiaz Ahmad, ed., *Family, Kinship and Marriage among Muslims in India*, Manohar.

————, 1977a. "Flexibility in Central Indian Kinship," in Kenneth David, ed., *The New Wind: Changing Identities in South Asia*, Mouton.

————, 1977b. "The Women of North and Central India: Goddesses and Wives," in Doranne Jacobson and Susan Wadley, eds., *Women in India: Two Perspectives*, Manohar.

————, 1978. "The Chaste Wife: Cultural Norm and Individual Experience," in Sylvia Vatuk, ed., *American Studies in the Anthropology of India*, American Institute of Indian Studies and Manohar Publications.

————, 1980. "Golden Handprints," in Nancy A. Falk and Rita M. Gross, eds., *Unspoken Words: Women's Religious Lives in Non-Western Cultures*, Harper & Row.

————, 1982. "Purdah and the Hindu Family in Central India," in Hanna Papanek and Gail Minault, eds., *Separate Worlds: Studies of Purdah in South Asia*, Chanakya Publications.

Jacobson, Helga E., 1981. "Women, Society and Change: Perspectives on the Division of Labour," in Geoffrey B. Hainsworth et al., eds., *Southeast Asia*, University of Ottawa Press.

Jahangir, B. K., 1986a. *Problematics of Nationalism in Bangladesh*, Centre for Social Studies, Dhaka University.

————, 1986b. "Women and Property in Rural Bangladesh," *Journal of Social Studies*, 34.

Jain, Devaki and Nirmala Banerjee, eds., 1985. *Tyranny of the Household: Investigative Essays on Women's Work*, Vikas Publishing House.

Jain, S. D. and G. S. Bhatt, 1974. "Changing Status of Woman in a Polyandrous Society – Jaunsar Bawar," Indian Council of Social Science Research.

Jain, Shobhita, 1986. "Sex Roles and Dialectics of Survival and Equality: A Case Study of Women Workers on a Tea Plantation in Assam," in Leela Dube, Eleanor Leacock, and Shirley Ardener, eds., *Visibility and Power: Essays on Women in Society and Development*, Oxford University Press.

Jansen, Eirik G., B. K. Jahangir, and Bodil Maal, 1983. "Dilemmas Involved in Defining and Delimiting Household Units in Rural Surveys in Bangladesh," *Journal of Social Studies*, 21.

Javillonar, G. V., 1978. "The Filipino Family," in Man Singh Das and P. D. Bardis, eds., *The Family in Asia*, Allen & Unwin.

Jay, R. R., 1969. *Javanese Villagers: Social Relations in Rural Modjokuto*, M.I.T. Press.

Jayaraman, R., 1981. *Caste, Class and Sex: The Dynamics of Inequality in Indian Society*, Hindustan Publishing Corporation.

Jayawardena, Kumari, 1975. "Women of Sri Lanka: Oppressed or Emancipated?" *Economic Review*, 1, 3, Colombo People's Bank.

———, 1980a. "Some Aspects of the Status of Women in Sri Lanka," Asian and Pacific Centre for Women and Development.

———, 1980b. "The Traditional Concept of Woman and Its Persistence Today," *Voice of Women*, 1.

———, 1986. *Feminism and Nationalism in the Third World*, Zed Books.

——— and Swarna Jayaweera, 1985. "The Integration of Women in Development Planning: Sri Lanka," in Noeleen Heyzer, ed., *Missing Women*, Asian and Pacific Development Centre.

Jayaweera, Swarna, 1988. "Class and Gender: Education and Employment," paper prepared for the United Nations University.

Jeffrey, P., 1978 and 1979. *Frogs in a Well: Indian Women in Purdah*, Zed Press and Vikas.

———, 1981. "Women's Private Work: The Social Organisation of Childbearing and Childrearing in a Muslim Village in Delhi," unpublished.

———, Roger Jeffrey, and Andrew Lyon, 1989. *Labour Pains and Labour Power: Women and Childbearing in India*, Zed Books.

Jeffrey, Roger and Patricia M. Jeffrey, 1993. "Traditional Birth Attendants in Rural North India: The Social Organization of Childbearing," in Shirley Lindenbaum and Margaret Lick, eds., *Knowledge, Power and Practice: The Anthropology of Medicine and Everyday Life*, University of California Press.

Jetley, Surinder, 1984. "India: Eternal Waiting," in *Women in the Villages, Men in Towns*, Unesco.

———, 1987. "Impact of Male Migration on Rural Females," *Economic and Political Weekly*, 22, 44.

Jocano, F. Landa, 1969. *Growing up in a Philippine Barrio*, Holt, Rinehart & Winston.

———, 1972. *The Filipino Family: Two Kinship Systems*, University of the Philippines Institute of Mass Communication.

———, 1979. "Childhood in a Philippine Barrio," in M. R. Hollnsteiner, ed., *Society, Culture and the Filipino*, Institute of Philippine Culture.

Jones, Rex L. and Shirley Kurz Jones, 1976. *The Himalayan Woman: A Study of Limbu Women in Marriage and Divorce*, Mayfield Publishing Company.

Joseph, M. J., 1993. "Gendered Justice," *Economic and Political Weekly*, 28, 50.

Josselin de Jong, P. E. de, 1985a. "The Comparative Method in Southeast Asia: Ideal and Practice (Rejoinder to Barnes)," *Journal of the Anthropological Society of Oxford*, 16, 3,.

———, ed., 1985b. *Unity in Diversity*, Verhandelingen van het Koninklijk Instituut.

Kabeer, Naila, 1985a. "Organizing Landless Women in Bangladesh," *Community Development Journal*, 3.

———, 1985b. "Do Women Gain from High Fertility?" in Haleh Afshar, ed., *Women, Work and Ideology in the Third World*, Tavistock Publications.

Kahn, Joel S., 1980. *Minangkabau Social Formations: Indonesian Peasants and the World-Economy*, Cambridge University Press.

Kakar, Sudhir, 1978. *The Inner World: A Psychoanalytic Study of Childhood and Society in India*, Oxford University Press.

———, ed., 1979. *Identity and Adulthood*, Oxford University Press.

Kalpagam, U., 1985. "Women and the Household: What the Indian Data Sources Have to Offer," paper for Regional Conference for Asia on Women and the Household, New Delhi.

———, 1986. "Gender in Economics: The Indian Experience," *Economic and Political Weekly*, 21, 43.

Kamarazuman, Kamah Ainiah, 1986. "The Legal Status of Women in Islam, with Special Reference to the Islamic Family Law in West Malaysia," University of Kent M.Phil. thesis.

Kandiyoti, Deniz, 1988. "Bargaining with Patriarchy," *Gender and Society*, 2, 3.

Kapadia, K. M., 1955. *Marriage and Family in India*, Oxford University Press.

Kaplan, Marion A., 1985a. "For Love or Money: The Marriage Strategies of Jews in Imperial Germany," in Marion A. Kaplan, ed., *The Marriage Bargain: Women and Dowries in European History*, The Haworth Press.

———, ed., 1985b. *The Marriage Bargain: Women and Dowries in European History*, The Haworth Press.

Karim, Wazir-Jahan, 1980. "Children of the Garden: Concepts of Size, Space and Time in Child Socialization among the Ma' Betisek and the Malays," *Federation Museums Journal*, 25.

———, 1987. "The Status of Malay Women in Malaysia: From Culture to Islam and Industrialization," *International Journal of Sociology of the Family*, 17, 1.

———, n.d. "Women's Contributions to Culture: Malay Women in Adat and Islam," manuscript.

Karkal, Malini, 1987. "Differentials in Mortality by Sex," *Economic and Political Weekly*, 22, 32.

Karlekar, Malavika, 1986. "A Study of Balmiki Women in Delhi," in Leela Dube, Eleanor Leacock, and Shirley Ardener, eds., *Visibility and Power: Essays on Women in Society and Development*, Oxford University Press.

Karve, Irawati, 1961. *Hindu Society: An Interpretation*, Deccan College.

———, 1963. "A Family through Six Generations," in Bala Ratnam, ed., *Anthropology on the March*, Book Centre.

———, 1965. *Kinship Organization in India*, Asia Publishing House.

Kassim, Azizah, 1984. "Women and Divorce among the Urban Malays," in Hing Ai Yun, Nik Safiah Karim, and Rokiah Talib, eds., *Women in Malaysia*, Pelanduk Press.

———, 1986. "The Squatter Women and the Informal Economy," in Hing Ai Yun and Rokiah Talib, eds., *Women and Employment in Malaysia*, University of Malaya.

Kato, Tsuyoshi, 1982. *Matriliny and Migration: Evolving Minagkabau Traditions in Indonesia*, Cornell University Press.

Katona-Apte, J., 1978. "Urbanisation, Income and Socio-cultural Factors Relevant to Nutrition in Tamilnadu," in A. de Souza, ed., *The Indian City*, Manohar Publications.

Kaufman, Howard K., 1960. *Bangkhuad: A Community Study in Thailand*, J. J. Augustin.

Kazi, Shahnaz and Bilquees Raza, 1990. "The Duality in Female Employment in Pakistan," *South Asia Bulletin*, 10, 2.

Keddie, Nikki, 1987. "Islam and Society in Minangkabau and in the Middle East," *Sojourn*, 2, 1.

Kemp, Jeremy H., 1970. "Initial Marriage Residence in Rural Thailand," in Tej Bunnag and M. Smithies, eds., *In Memoriam Phya Anuman Rajadhon*, Siam Society.

———, 1975. "Kin Groups in a Thai-Lao Community," in G. W. Skinner and A. T. Kirsch, eds., *Change and Persistence in Thai Society*, Cornell University Press.

———, 1976. "The Social Organization of a Hamlet in Phitsanulok Province, North-Central Thailand," University of London Ph.D. thesis.

———, 1978. "Cognatic Descent and the Generation of Social Stratification in Southeast Asia," *Bijdragen*, 134, 1.

———, 1981. "Legal and Informal Land Tenures in Thailand," *Studies*, 15, 1.

———, 1982. *Towards a Comparative Analysis of Thai Kinship*, University of the Saar.

———, 1983. "Kinship and the Management of Personal Relations: Kin Terminologies and the Axiom of Amity," *Bijdragen*, 139, 1.

———, 1984. "The Manipulation of Personal Relations: From Kinship to Patron–Clientage," in Han ten Brummelhuis and Jeremy H. Kemp, eds., *Strategies and Structures in Thai Society*, Anthropological-Sociological Centre, University of Amsterdam.

Kessinger, T. G., 1974. *Villayatpur, 1848–1968: Social and Economic Change in a North Indian Village*, University of California Press.

Keyes, Charles F., 1967. "Baan Nooing Tyyn, A Central Isan Village," unpublished.

Khan, Nighat S., 1985. "Women in Pakistan: Position, Status and Movement," *Journal of Social Studies*, 30.

Khan, Zarina Rahman, 1985. "Women's Economic Role: Insights from a Village in Bangladesh," *Journal of Social Studies*, 30.

Khare, R. S., 1983. "From Kanya to Mata: Aspects of the Cultural Language of Kinship," in Akas Ostor, Lina Fruzzetti, and Steve Barnett, eds., *Concepts of Person: Kinship, Caste and Marriage in India*, Oxford University Press.

Khera, P. D., 1969. "The Family in the Indian Census," University of Delhi M.Litt. thesis.

Khongphai, B. L., 1970, 1974. *Principles of Khasi Law*, the author.

Kim, Khoo Kay, 1977. "Traditional and Modern Social Justice in Malaysia," in Nancy Chng, ed., *Questioning Development in Southeast Asia*, Select Books.

Kingshill, Conrad, 1960. *The Red Tomb: A Village Study in Northern Thailand*, Chiengmai Prince Royal's College.

Kirsch, A. Thomas, 1967. "Phu Thai Religious Syncretism: A Case Study of Thai Religion and Society," Harvard University Ph.D. thesis.

———, 1975. "Economy, Polity and Religion in Thailand," in G. William Skinner and A. Thomas Kirsch, eds., *Change and Persistence in Thai Society: Essays in Honor of Lauriston Sharp*, Cornell University Press.

———, 1977. "Complexity in the Thai Religious System: An Interpretation," *Journal of Asian Studies*, 36.

————, 1982. "Buddhism, Sex Roles and the Thai Economy," in Penny van Esterik, ed., *Women in Southeast Asia*, Northern Illinois University Occasional Paper No. 9.

Kisango, R. H., 1985. "The Legal Profession, Pluralism and Public Interest Litigation," *Ethnic Studies Report*, 3, 1.

Knappert, J., 1985. "The Myth of the Rice Goddess in Java," *Orientalia Lovanesia Periodica*, 16.

————, 1986. "Islam in Indonesia and Malaysia," in P. Auchterlonie, ed., *Middle East and Islam: A Bibliographical Introduction*, IDC AG.

Knodel, John et al., 1984. "Marriage Patterns in Thailand: A Review of Demographic Evidence," in C. Apichart, ed., *Perspectives on the Thai Marriage*, Mahidol University.

Koentjaraningrat, 1957. *A Preliminary Description of the Javanese Kinship System*, Yale University Press.

————, 1985. *Javanese Culture*, Oxford University Press and Institute of Southeast Asian Studies.

Kolenda, Pauline, 1967. "Regional Differences in Indian Family Structure," in R. I. Crane, ed., *Regions and Regionalism in South Asian Studies*, Duke University Program in Comparative Studies on South Asia, Monograph No. 5.

————, 1968. "Region, Caste and Family Structure: A Comparative Study of the Indian 'Joint' Family," in M. Singer and B. S. Cohn, eds., *Structure and Change in Indian Society*, Aldine.

————, 1970. "Family Structure in Village Lonikand, India: 1819, 1958 and 1967," *Contributions to Indian Sociology*, 4.

————, 1983. "Widowhood among 'Untouchable' Chuhras," in Akos Ostor, Lina Fruzzetti, and Steve Barnett, eds., *Concepts of Person: Kinship, Caste and Marriage in India*, Oxford University Press.

————, 1984. "Woman as Tribute, Woman as Flower: Images of Woman in Weddings in North and South India," *American Ethnologist*, 11, 3.

————, 1987a. *Regional Differences in Family Structure in India*, Rawat Publications.

————, 1987b. "Marked Regional Differences in Family Structure in India," in P. Kolenda, *Regional Differences in Family Structure in India*, Rawat.

————, 1989. "The Joint Family Household in Rural Rajasthan: Ecological, Cultural and Demographic Conditions for Its Occurrence," in John N. Gray and David J. Mearns, eds., *Society from the Inside Out: Anthropological Perspectives on the South Asian Household*, Sage.

————, 1990. "Untouchable Chuhras through Their Humour: Equalizing Marital Ties through Teasing, Pretense and Farce," in Owen Lynch, ed., *Divine Passions: The Social Construction of Emotions in India*, Oxford University Press.

Komin, Suntaree, 1985. "The World View through Thai Value Systems," in *Traditional and Changing Thai World View*, Chulalongkorn University Social Research Institute.

Kondos, Vivienne, 1989. "Subjection and the Domicile: Some Problematic Issues Relating to High Caste Nepalese Women," in John N. Gray and David Mearns, eds., *Society from the Inside Out: Anthropological Perspectives on the South Asian Household*, Sage.

————, 1991. "Subjection and the Ethics of Anguish: The Nepalese Parbatiya Parent–Daughter Relationship," *Contributions to Indian Sociology*, 25, 1.

Korson, J. H., 1965. "Age and Social Status at Marriage: Karachi, Pakistan, 1961–64," *Pakistan Development Review*, 5, 4.

———, 1967. "Dower and Social Class in an Urban Muslim Community," *Journal of Marriage and the Family*, 29.

———, 1968. "The Roles of Dower and Dowry as Indicators of Social Change in Pakistan," *Journal of Marriage and the Family*, 30.

———, 1971. "Endogamous Marriage in a Traditional Muslim Society: West Pakistan, A Study of Intergenerational Change," *Journal of Comparative Family Studies*, 2.

——— and Michelle Maskiell, 1985. "Islamization and Social Policy in Pakistan: The Constitutional Crisis and the Status of Women," *Asian Survey*, 25.

Krishna Raj, Maithreyi, 1987. "Health: A Gender Issue in India," in Neera Desai and Maithreyi Krishna Raj, eds., *Women and Society in India*, Ajanta Publications.

———, 1989. "Introduction," Section I, in Maithreyi Krishna Raj and Karuna Chanana, eds., *Gender and the Household Domain: Social and Cultural Dimensions*, Sage.

———, 1992. "Women Craft Workers as Security for Family Subsistence," *Economic and Political Weekly*, 27, 17.

——— and Karuna Chanana, eds., 1989. *Gender and the Household Domain: Social and Cultural Dimensions*, Sage.

——— and Divya Pande, 1987. "Women's Work and Family Strategies among Cane Bamboo Workers in Sindhudurg," unpublished.

——— and Jyoti Ranadive, 1982. "The Rural Female Heads of Households: Hidden from View," unpublished.

Krishnaswamy, S., 1988. "Female Infanticide in Contemporary India: A Case Study of Kallars of Tamilnadu," in Rehana Ghadially, ed., *Women in Indian Society: A Reader*, Sage.

Krulfeld, Ruth, 1986. "Sasak Attitudes towards Polygyny and the Changing Position of Women in Sasak Peasant Villages," in Leela Dube, Eleanor Leacock, and Shirley Ardener, eds., *Visibility and Power: Essays on Women in Society and Development*, Oxford University Press.

Krygier, Jocelyn, 1982. "Caste and Female Pollution," in M. Allen and S. M. Mukherjee, eds., *Women in India and Nepal*, Australian National University Monographs on South Asia No. 8.

Kuchiba, Masou et al., eds., 1979. *Three Malay Villages: A Sociology of Paddy Growers in West Malaysia*, University Press of Hawaii.

Kurien, George, ed., 1974. *The Family in India: A Regional View*, Mouton Studies in the Social Sciences No. 12.

Kutty, A. R., 1972. *Marriage and Kinship in an Island Society*, National.

Kynch, J. and A. K. Sen, 1983. "Indian Women: Well-being and Survival," *Cambridge Journal of Economics*, 7.

Laderman, Carol, 1982. "Putting Malay Women in Their Place," in Penny van Esterik, ed., *Women in Southeast Asia*, Northern Illinois University Occasional Paper No. 9.

———, 1983. *Wives and Midwives: Childbirth and Nutrition in Rural Malaysia*, University of California Press.

Lambert, Ismail A., 1976. "Marriage among the Sunni Surati Vohras in South

191

Gujarat," in Imtiaz Ahmad, ed., *Family, Kinship and Marriage among Muslims in India*, Manohar.

Lambiri-Dimaki, Jane, 1985. "Dowry in Modern Greece: An Institution at the Crossroads between Persistence and Decline," in Marion A. Kaplan, ed., *The Marriage Bargain: Women and Dowries in European History*, The Haworth Press.

Leach, Edmund, 1961. *Pul Eliya, A Village in Ceylon: A Study of Land Tenure and Kinship*, Cambridge University Press.

———, 1975. "Complementary Filiation and Bilateral Kinship," in Jack Goody, ed., *The Character of Kinship*, Cambridge University Press.

———, 1984. "Glimpses of the Unmentionable in the History of British Social Anthropology," *Annual Review of Anthropology*, 13.

Leonard, Karen Isaksen, 1978. *Social History of an Indian Caste: The Kayasths of Hyderabad*, University of California Press.

Leslie, Julia, 1989. *The Perfect Wife: The Orthodox Hindu Woman According to the Stridharmapaddhati of Tryambakayajvan*, Oxford University Press.

Lessinger, Johanna, 1990. "Work and Modesty: The Dilemma of Women Market Traders in Madras," in Leela Dube and Rajni Palriwala, eds., *Structures and Strategies: Women, Work and Family*, Sage.

Lev, Daniel S., 1972. *Islamic Courts in Indonesia: A Study in Political Bases of Legal Institutions*, University of California Press.

Lewis, Oscar, 1965. *Village Life in Northern India*, Random House.

Liddle, Joanna and Rama Joshi, 1986. *Daughters of Independence: Gender, Caste and Class in India*, Zed Books and Kali for Women.

Lindenbaum, Shirley, 1974. "The Social and Economic Status of Women in Bangladesh," The Ford Foundation.

———, Manisha Chakraborty, and Mohammed Elias, 1985. "The Influence of Maternal Education on Infant and Child Mortality in Bangladesh," International Centre for Diarrhoeal Disease Research Special Publication No. 23.

Locher-Scholten, Elsbeth and Anke Niehof, eds., 1987. *Indonesian Women in Focus: Past and Present Notions*, Foris Publications.

Luschinsky, Mildred, 1962. "The Life of Women in a Village in Northern India: A Study of Role and Status," Cornell University Ph.D. thesis.

McCarthy, Florence E., 1981a. "Differential Family Characteristics as the Context for Women's Productive Activities," Ministry of Agriculture, Bangladesh, Study Paper No. 1.

———, 1981b. "Patterns of Involvement and Participation of Rural Women in Postharvest Processing Operations," Ministry of Agriculture, Bangladesh, Study Paper No. 2.

McGilveray, Denis, 1982. "Sexual Power and Fertility in Sri Lanka: Batticaloa Tamils and Moors," in Carol McCormack, ed., *Ethnography of Fertility and Birth*, Academic Press.

———, 1989. "Households in Akkaripattu: Dowry and Domestic Organization among the Matrilineal Tamils and Moors of Sri Lanka," in John N. Gray and David J. Mearns, eds., *Society from the Inside Out: Anthropological Perspectives on the South Asian Household*, Sage.

McKinley, Robert Hunter, 1975. "A Knife Cutting Water: Child Transfers and Siblingship among Urban Malays," University of Michigan Ph.D. thesis.

Mackintosh, Maureen, 1981. "Gender and Economics: The Sexual Division of Labour and the Subordination of Women," in Kate Young et al., eds., *Of Marriage and the Market*, CSE Books.

Madan, T. N., 1965. *Family and Kinship: A Study of the Pandits of Rural Kashmir*, Asia Publishing House.

———, 1981a. "The Ideology of the Householder among the Kashmiri Pandits," *Contributions to Indian Sociology*, 15, 1 and 15, 2.

———, 1981b. "Religious Ideology and Social Structure: The Muslims and Hindus of Kashmir," in Imtiaz Ahmad, ed., *Ritual and Religion among Muslims in India*, Manohar.

Maeda, Narifumi, 1975. "Family Circle, Community, and Nation in Malaysia," *Current Anthropology*, 16.

Maher, Vanessa, 1976. "Kin, Clients and Accomplices: Relationships among Women in Morocco," in Diana Leonard Barker and Shiela Allen, eds., *Sexual Divisions and Society: Process and Change*, Tavistock Publications.

———, 1984. "Work, Consumption and Authority within the Household: A Moroccan Case," in Kate Young, Carol Wolkowitz, and R. McCullagh, eds., *Of Marriage and the Market*, Routledge & Kegan Paul.

Mahtab, Nazmunnessa, 1989. "Health Education and Nutrition of Rural Women in Bangladesh: The Household Interface," in Maithreyi Krishna Raj and Karuna Chanana, eds., *Gender and the Household Domain: Social and Cultural Dimensions*, Sage.

Majumdar, D. N., 1962. *Himalayan Polyandry: Structure, Functioning and Culture Change, A Field Study of Jaunsar Bawar*, Asia Publishing House.

Maloney, Clarence, 1980. *People of the Maldive Islands*, Orient Longman.

——— et al., 1981. *Beliefs and Fertility in Bangladesh*, International Centre for Diarrhoeal Disease Research Monograph No. 2.

Mandelbaum, David G., 1938. "Polyandry in Kota Society," *American Anthropologist*, 40.

———, 1949. "The Family in India," in R. Anshen, ed., *The Family: Its Function and Destiny*, Harper & Brothers.

———, 1972. *Society in India*, University of California Press.

———, 1988. *Women's Seclusion and Men's Honour: Sex Roles in North India, Bangladesh and Pakistan*, University of Arizona Press.

Manderson, Lenore, ed., 1983. *Women's Work and Women's Roles: Economics and Everyday Life in Indonesia, Malaysia and Singapore*, Australian National University.

Maneevone, M. F. R., 1974. "The Socialization of the Rural Thai Child in Family and School," Claremont Graduate School Ph.D. thesis.

Mani, Lata, 1989. "Contentious Traditions: The Debate on *Sati* in Colonial India," in Kumkum Sangari and Sudesh Vaid, eds., *Recasting Women: Essays in Colonial History*, Kali for Women.

Marasinghe, Lakshman, 1986. "The Use of Customary Law in Development in Southeast Asia," in Bruce Matthews and Judith Nagata, eds., *Religion, Values and Development in Southeast Asia*, Institute of Southeast Asian Studies.

Marriott, McKim, 1955. "Social Structure and Change in a U.P. Village," in M. N. Srinivas, ed., *India's Villages*, Asia Publishing House.

Mascarenhas-Keyes, Stella, 1990. "Migration, 'Progressive Motherhood' and Female

Autonomy: Catholic Women in Goa," in Leela Dube and Rajni Palriwala, eds., *Structures and Strategies: Women, Work and Family*, Sage.

Mather, Celia, 1985. "'Rather Than Make Trouble, It's Better Just to Leave': Behind the Lack of Industrial Strife in the Tangerang Region of West Java," in Haleh Afshar, ed., *Women, Work and Ideology in the Third World*, Tavistock Publications.

Matthews, Bruce and Judith Nagata, eds., 1986. *Religion, Values and Development in Southeast Asia*, Institute of Southeast Asian Studies.

Mayer, Adrian C., 1960. *Caste and Kinship in Central India*, Routledge & Kegan Paul.

Mehta, R., 1975. *The Divorced Hindu Woman*, Vikas Publishing House.

———, 1976. "From Purdah to Modernity," in B. R. Nanda, ed., *Indian Women: From Purdah to Modernity*, Vikas Publishing House.

———, 1982. "Purdah among the Oswals of Mewar," in Hanna Papanek and Gail Minault, eds., *Separate Worlds: Studies of Purdah in South Asia*, Chanakya Publications.

Meillassoux, Claude, 1973. "Are There Castes in India?" *Economy and Society*, 3.

Mencher, Joan, 1962. "Changing Familial Roles among South Malabar Nayars," *Southwestern Journal of Anthropology*, 18.

——— and Deborah D'Amico, 1986. "Kerala Women as Labourers and Supervisors: Implications for Women and Development," in Leela Dube, Eleanor Leacock, and Shirley Ardener, eds., *Visibility and Power: Essays on Women in Society and Development*, Oxford University Press.

——— and K. Saradamoni, 1982. "Muddy Feet, Dirty Hands: Rice Production and Female Agricultural Labour," *Economic and Political Weekly*, 17.

Mendez, P. P. and F. L. Jocano, 1974. *The Filipino Family in Its Rural and Urban Orientation: Two Case Studies*, Centro Escolar University Research and Development Center.

———, 1979. *The Filipino Adolescent in a Rural and an Urban Setting: A Study in Culture and Education*, Centro Escolar University Research and Development Center.

Mernissi, Fatima, 1994. *Dreams of Trespass: Tales of a Harem Girlhood*, Addison-Wesley.

Mies, Maria, 1980. "Capitalist Development and Subsistence Reproduction: Rural Women in India," *Bulletin of Concerned Asian Scholars*, 12.

———, 1982. *The Lace Makers of Narsapur: Indian Housewives Produce for the World Market*, Zed Press.

Miller, Barbara D., 1980. "Female Neglect and the Costs of Marriage in Rural India," *Contributions to Indian Sociology*, 14, 1.

———, 1981. *The Endangered Sex: Neglect of Female Children in Rural North India*, Cornell University Press.

———, 1989a. "Son Preference, the Household and a Public Health Programme in India," in Maithreyi Krishna Raj and Karuna Chanana, eds., *Gender and the Household Domain: Social and Cultural Dimensions*, Sage.

———, 1989b. "Changing Patterns of Juvenile Sex Ratios in Rural India 1961–1971," *Economic and Political Weekly*, 24, 22.

Minturn, Leigh and John T. Hitchcock, 1963. "The Rajputs of Khalapur, India," in B. B. Whiting, ed., *Six Cultures: Studies of Childrearing*, John Wiley.

Minturn, Leigh and William W. Lambert, 1964. *Mothers of Six Cultures*, John Wiley.

Mizuno, Koichi, 1968. "Multi-household Compounds in Northeast Thailand," *Asian Survey*, 8, 10.

———, 1971. "Social System of Don Daeng Village: A Community Study in Northeast Thailand," Kyoto University Center for Southeast Asian Studies Discussion Paper.

———, 1977. "Thai Pattern of Social Organization: Notes on a Comparative Study," in Shinichi Ichimura, ed., *Southeast Asia: Nature, Society and Development*, University Press of Hawaii.

Molnar, Augusta, 1981. *The Kham Magar Women of Thabang*, Volume 2, Part 2 of *The Status of Women in Nepal*, Centre for Economic Development and Administration, Kathmandu.

Mueke, Marjorie, 1976. "Reproductive Success among the Urban Poor: A Micro-level Study of Infant Survival and Child Growth in Northern Thailand," University of Washington Ph.D. thesis.

———, 1981. "Changes in Women's Status Associated with Modernization in Northern Thailand," in Geoffrey B. Hainsworth et al., eds., *Southeast Asia*, University of Ottawa Press.

Muhammad, Khadijah Haji, 1976. "Kindreds and Task Groups in Malay Social Organization," unpublished.

Mukherjee, Prabhati, 1978. *Hindu Women: Normative Models*, Orient Longman.

Mukherjee, Ramkrishna, 1969. "Family in India: A Perspective," Indian Statistical Institute.

Mukhopadhyay, Carol Chapnick and Susan Seymour, eds., 1994. *Women, Education and Family Structure in India*, Westview Press.

Mukund, Kanakalatha, 1992. "Turmeric Land: Women's Property Rights in Tamil Society since Early Medieval Times," *Economic and Political Weekly*, 27, 17.

Mulder, Niels, 1980. *Mysticism and Everyday Life in Contemporary Java: Cultural Persistence and Change*, Singapore University Press.

Mumtaz, Khawar and Farida Shaheed, eds., 1987. *Women of Pakistan: Two Steps Forward, One Step Back*, Zed Books.

Muntemba, Shimwaani, 1982. "Women as Food Producers and Suppliers in the Twentieth Century: The Case of Zambia," *Development Dialogue: A Journal of International Development Cooperation*, 1–2.

Murdock, George P., 1960. "Cognatic Forms of Social Organization," in George P. Murdock, ed., *Social Structure in Southeast Asia*, Quadrangle Books.

Murray, Francis J., Jr., 1973a. "Lowland Social Organization I: Local Kin Groups in a Central Luzon Barrio," *Philippine Sociological Review*, 21.

———, 1973b. "Lowland Social Organization II: Ambilineal Kin Groups in a Central Luzon Barrio," *Philippine Sociological Review*, 21.

Nagata, Judith, 1976. "Kinship and Social Mobility among the Malays," *Man*, 11.

———, 1986. "The Impact of the Islamic Revival (Dakwah) on the Religious Culture of Malaysia," in Bruce Matthews and Judith Nagata, eds., *Religion, Values and Development in Southeast Asia*, Institute of Southeast Asian Studies.

Naher, Milu Shamsun, 1985. "Marriage Patterns: Customs and Changes in Rural Bangladesh," *Journal of Social Studies*, 30.

Nakamura, Hisako, 1983. *Divorce in Java: A Study of the Dissolution of Marriage among Javanese Muslims*, Gadjah Mada University Press.

Nakane, Chie, 1963. "The Nayar Family in a Disintegrating Matrilineal System," in John Mogey, ed., *Family and Marriage*, E. J. Brill.

———, 1968. *Garo and Khasi: A Comparative Study in Matrilineal Systems*, Mouton.

Nanda, B. R., ed., 1976. *Indian Women: From Purdah to Modernity*, Vikas Publishing House.

Nasir, Rohany, 1986. "Sex-role Attitudes of Malaysian Women: Implications for Career Development and Counselling," *Sojourn: Social Issues in Southeast Asia*, 1, 2.

Navbharat Times, 1994. "Soon There Will Be a Shortage of Women"; "Sex Identification Tests: Absence of Legal Measures"; and "India Too Is Going on the Path of China", 21 August (in Hindi).

Naveed-i-Rahat, 1981. "The Role of Women in Reciprocal Relations in a Punjabi Village," in T. S. Epstein and R. A. Watts, eds., *The Endless Day: Some Material on Asian Rural Women*, Pergamon.

———, 1990. *Male Outmigration and Matri-weighted Households: A Case Study of a Punjabi Village in Pakistan*, Hindustan Publishing Corporation.

Nazmul Karim, A. K., 1963. "Changing Patterns of an East Pakistan Family," in Barbara E. Ward, ed., *Women in the New Asia*, Unesco.

Neher, Clark D., 1982. "Sex Roles in the Philippines: The Ambiguous Cebuana," in Penny van Esterik, ed., *Women in Southeast Asia*, Northern Illinois University Occasional Paper No. 9.

Nelson, Nici, 1979. *Why Has Development Neglected Rural Women? A Review of South Asian Literature*, Pergamon Press.

Netzorg, Morton J., 1982. "Books for Children in the Philippines: The Late Spanish Period," *Philippine Quarterly of Culture and Society*, 10.

Ng, Cecilia, 1986. "Gender and the Division of Labour: A Case Study," in Hing Ai Yun and Rokiah Talib, eds., *Women and Employment in Malaysia*, University of Malaya.

——— and Maznah Mohamed, 1988. "Primary but Subordinated: Changing Class and Gender Relations in Rural Malaysia," in Bina Agarwal, ed., *Structures of Patriarchy: State, Community and Household in Modernising Asia*, Kali for Women.

Ngah, Mohd. Nor bin, 1985. "Islamic World-view of Man, Society and Nature among the Malays in Malaysia," in Mohd. Taib Osman, ed., *Malaysian World-View*, Institute of Southeast Asian Studies.

Nicholas, Ralph, 1965. "Economics of Family Types in Two West Bengal Villages," in *Seven Articles on Village Conditions*, Michigan State University Asian Studies Papers Reprint Series No. 1.

Nicolaisen, Ida, 1983. "Introduction," in Bo Utas, ed., *Women in Islamic Societies*, Curzon Press.

Nongbri, Tiplut, 1990. "Gender and the Khasi Family Structure: Some Implications of Meghalaya Succession to Self-Acquired Property Act," *Sociological Bulletin*, 37, 1&2.

Obeyesekere, G., 1963. "Pregnancy Cravings (dola-duka) in Relation to Social Structure and Personality in a Sinhalese Village," *American Anthropologist*, 65, 1.

———, 1967. *Land Tenure in Village Ceylon: A Sociological and Historical Study*, Cambridge University Press.

O'Brien, Leslie N., 1983. "Four Paces Behind: Women's Work in Peninsular Malaysia," in Lenore Manderson, ed., *Women's Work and Women's Roles*, Australian National University.

Omar, Asmah Haji, 1985. "Language and the World-view of the Malay Peasants," in Mohd. Taib Osman, ed., *Malaysian World-View*, Institute of Southeast Asian Studies.

Omvedt, Gail, 1975a. "Rural Origins of Women's Liberation in India," *Social Scientist*, 4, 4–5.

———, 1975b. "Caste, Class and Women's Liberation in India," *Bulletin of Concerned Asian Scholars*, 7.

———, 1978. "Women and Rural Revolt in India," *Journal of Peasant Studies*, 5.

———, 1980. *We Will Smash This Prison: Indian Women in Struggle*, Orient Longman.

———, 1982. *Land, Caste and Politics in Indian States*, Authors' Guild Publications.

Orenstein, Henry, 1961. "The Recent History of the Extended Family in India," *Social Problems*, 8.

———, 1965. "The Structure of Hindu Caste Values: A Preliminary Study of Hierarchy and Ritual Defilement," *Ethnology*, 4.

———, 1970. "Death and Kinship in Hinduism: Structural and Functional Interpretations," *American Anthropologist*, 72, 6.

Ortner, Sherry B., 1978. "The Virgin and the State," *Feminist Studies*, 4.

———, 1981. "Gender and Sexuality in Hierarchical Societies: The Case of Polynesia and Some Comparative Implications," in Sherry B. Ortner and Harriet Whitehead, eds., *Sexual Meanings: The Cultural Construction of Gender and Sexuality*, Cambridge University Press.

——— and Harriet Whitehead, eds., 1981. *Sexual Meanings: The Cultural Construction of Gender and Sexuality*, Cambridge University Press.

Osman, Mohd. Taib, ed., 1985. *Malaysian World-View*, Institute of Southeast Asian Studies.

Ostor, Akos, Lina Fruzzetti, and Steve Barnett, eds., 1983. *Concepts of Person: Kinship, Caste and Marriage in India*, Oxford University Press.

Palriwala, Rajni, 1990. "Production, Reproduction and the Position of Women in a Rajasthan Village," University of Delhi Ph.D. thesis.

———, 1991. "Transitory Residence and Invisible Work: A Case Study of a Rajasthan Village," *Economic and Political Weekly*, 26, 48.

———, 1994. "Changing Kinship, Family and Gender Relations: Processes, Trends and Issues," VENA, Leiden University.

Pandey, Raj Bali, 1969. *Hindu Samskaras*, Motilal Banarsidass.

Paneru, Sudha, ed., 1980. *Traditional and Prevailing Child-Rearing Practices among Different Communities in Nepal*, Tribhuvan University Press.

Panikkar, K. N., 1977. "Land Control, Ideology and Reform: A Study of the Changes in Family Organization and Marriage System in Kerala," *Indian Historical Review*, 4, 1.

Papanek, Hanna, 1982a. "Purdah in Pakistan: Seclusion and Modern Occupations for Women," in Hanna Papanek and Gail Minault, eds., *Separate Worlds: Studies of Purdah in South Asia*, Chanakya Publications.

———, 1982b. "Purdah: Separate World and Symbolic Shelter," in Hanna Papanek and Gail Minault, eds., *Separate Worlds: Studies of Purdah in South Asia*, Chanakya Publications.

————, 1989. "Family Status-Production Work: Women's Contribution to Social Mobility and Class Differentiation," in Maithreyi Krishna Raj and Karuna Chanana, eds., *Gender and the Household Domain: Social and Cultural Dimensions*, Sage.

————, 1991. "Socialization for Inequality: Entitlements, the Value of Women, and Domestic Hierarchies," unpublished.

———— and Gail Minault, eds., 1982. *Separate Worlds: Studies of Purdah in South Asia*, Chanakya Publications.

———— and Laurel Schwede, 1988. "Women Are Good with Money: Earning and Managing in an Indonesian City," in Daisy Dwyer and Judith Bruce, eds., *A Home Divided: Women and Income in the Third World*, Stanford University Press.

Parry, J. P., 1979. *Caste and Kinship in Kangra*, Routledge & Kegan Paul.

Parthasarathi, Vibha, 1988. "Socialisation, Women and Education: An Experiment," in Karuna Chanana, ed., *Socialisation, Education and Women: Explorations in Gender Identity*, Nehru Memorial Museum and Library and Orient Longman.

Partini, Dra. and Nancy Lee Peluso, 1977. "The Roles of Rural Women in the Family Economy: A Micro-study of Women Working outside of the Agricultural Sector in Rural Yogyakarta," unpublished.

Pastner, Carrol McC., 1971. "Sexual Dichotomization in Society and Culture: The Women of Panjgur, Baluchistan," unpublished Ph.D. dissertation, Department of Anthropology, Brandeis University.

————, 1972. "A Social Structural and Historical Analysis of Honour, Shame and Purdah," *Anthropological Quarterly*, 45.

————, 1974. "Accommodation to Purdah: The Female Perspective," *Journal of Marriage and the Family*, 36.

————, 1978. "The Status of Women and Property on a Baluchistan Oasis in Pakistan," in L. Beck and N. Keddie, eds., *Women in the Muslim World*, Harvard University Press.

————, 1979. "Cousin Marriage among the Zakri Baluch of Coastal Pakistan," *Ethnology*, 18.

————, 1982. "Gradations of Purdah and the Creation of Social Boundaries on a Baluchistan Oasis," in Hanna Papanek and Gail Minault, eds., *Separate Worlds: Studies of Purdah in South Asia*, Chanakya Publications.

Patel, Tulsi, 1991. "Population and Society in a Rajasthan Village (with Special Reference to Fertility Behaviour)," University of Delhi Ph.D. thesis.

Patel, Vibhuti, 1988. "Sex Determination and Sex Preselection Tests: Abuse of Advanced Technologies," in Rehana Ghadially, ed., *Women in Indian Society: A Reader*, Sage.

Pathak, Zakia and Rajeshwari Sunder Rajan, 1989. "Shahbano," *Signs*, 14, 3.

Pati, Biswamoy, 1993. "Faces of Dowry in Orissa," *Economic and Political Weekly*, 28, 21.

Paul, Kim, 1992. "Constituting Charan: An Ethnological Account of the Maru Charans of Jodhpur," Sydney University Ph.D. thesis.

Peiris, Kamala, 1983. *Tiny Sapling, Sturdy Tree: The Inside Story of Primary Education Reforms of the 1970s in Sri Lanka*, Universitetsforlaget.

Pettigrew, Joyce, 1975. *Robber Noblemen: A Study of the Political System of the Sikh Jats*, Routledge & Kegan Paul.

Phillips, Herbert, 1965. *Thai Peasant Personality*, University of California Press.

————, 1969. "The Scope and Limits of the Loose Structure Concept," in Hans-Dieter Evers, ed., *Loosely Structured Social Systems: Thailand in a Comparative Perspective*, Yale University Press.

Phongpaichit, Pasuk, 1982. "From Peasant Girl to Bangkok Masseuse," ILO.

Phutharaporn, Kobkul, 1985. "Country Folk Songs and Thai Society," in *Traditional and Changing Thai World View*, Chulalongkorn University Social Research Institute.

Piker, Steven, 1975. "The Post-peasant Village in Central Plain Thai Society," in G. W. Skinner and A. T. Kirsch, eds., *Change and Persistence in Thai Society: Essays in Honor of Lauriston Sharp*, Cornell University Press.

————, 1983. *Peasant Community in Changing Thailand*, Arizona State University Anthropological Research Paper No. 30.

Pinard, Leo W., 1975. "Courtship in an Urban Visayas Setting," *Philippine Quarterly of Culture and Society*, 3.

Pletz, Michael G., 1981. *Social History and Evolution in the Interrelationship of Adat and Islam in Rembau, Negri Sembilan*, Institute of Southeast Asian Studies Research Notes and Discussion Papers No. 27.

Podhisita, Chai, 1984. "Marriage in Rural Northeast Thailand: A Household Perspective," in C. Apichart, ed., *Perspectives on the Thai Marriage*, Mahidol University.

————, 1985. "Buddhism and Thai World View," in *Traditional and Changing Thai World View*, Chulalongkorn University Social Research Institute.

Poewe, Carla, 1979. "Women, Horticulture and Society in Sub-Saharan Africa: Some Comments," *American Anthropologist*, 81.

Pongsapich, Amara, 1985. "Introduction," in *Traditional and Changing Thai World View*, Chulalongkorn University Social Research Institute.

————, 1986. "Women's Social Protest in Thailand," paper presented at the Eleventh International Sociological Congress, New Delhi.

————, 1990. "Women Homeworkers in Rural Thailand," International Labour Office.

————, 1992. "Changing Family Pattern in Thailand," in *The Changing Family in Asia*, Unesco.

———— et al., 1988. "Enhancement of Household Capacity in Post-migration Phase of the Asian Regional Programme on International Migration," Chulalongkorn University Social Research Institute.

———— et al., 1990. *Women Homeworkers in Rural Thailand*, ILO.

Ponnambalam, Satchi, 1981. *Dependent Capitalism in Crisis: The Sri Lankan Economy, 1948–1980*, Zed Press.

Postel, Els, 1985. "Who Is the Head of the Household? Some Myths around the Nuclear Family," paper for Regional Conference for Asia on Women and the Household, New Delhi.

———— and Joke Schrijvers, eds., 1980. *A Woman's Mind is Longer than a Kitchen Spoon: Report on Women in Sri Lanka*, Research Project "Women and Development," Colombo and Leiden.

Postel-Coster, Els, 1987. "The Image of Women in Minangkabau Fiction," in Elsbeth Locher-Scholten and Anke Niehof, eds., *Indonesian Women in Focus: Past and Present Notions*, Foris Publications.

Potter, Jack M., 1976. *Thai Peasant Social Structure*, University of Chicago Press.

Potter, Sulamith Heins, 1977. *Family Life in a Northern Thai Village: A Study in the Structural Significance of Women*, University of California Press.

Pradhan, Bina, 1981. *The Newar Women of Bulu*, Volume 2, Part 6 of *The Status of Women in Nepal*, Centre for Economic Development and Administration, Kathmandu.

Pramualratana, A., N. Havanon, and J. Knodel, 1985. "Exploring the Normative Basis for Age at Marriage in Thailand: An Example from Focus Group Research," *Journal of Marriage and the Family*, 47, 1.

Prindiville, Joanne C. J., 1981. "The Image and Role of Minangkabau Women," in Geoffrey B. Hainsworth et al., eds., *Southeast Asia*, University of Ottawa Press.

———, n.d. "Food, Form and Forum: Minangkabau Women as Culinary Communicators," unpublished.

Provencher, Ronald, 1971. *Two Malay Worlds: Interaction in Urban and Rural Settings*, University of California Center for Southeast Asia Studies Research Monograph No. 4.

Quddus, M. A., M. Solaiman, and M. R. Karim, 1985. *Rural Women in Households in Bangladesh: With a Case Study of Three Villages in Comilla*, Bangladesh Academy for Rural Development.

Rahaman, M. Mujibur et al., 1980. "Utilisation of a Diarrhoea Clinic in Rural Bangladesh: Influence of Distance, Age and Sex on Attendance and Diarrhoeal Mortality," International Centre for Diarrhoeal Disease Research Scientific Report No. 37.

Raheja, Gloria Goodwin and Ann Grodzius Gold, 1996. "On the Uses of Irony and Ambiguity," in *Listen to the Heron's Words: Reimagining Gender and Kinship in North India*, Oxford University Press.

Rahman, Atiur, 1987. "The State and the Peasantry: The Bangladesh Case," *Journal of Social Studies*, 35.

Rahman, Makhlisur, 1978. "Parental Dependency on Children in Matlab, Bangladesh," Cholera Research Laboratory Working Paper No. 11.

Rahman, Rushidan Islam, 1985. "The Integration of Women in Development Planning: Bangladesh," in Noeleen Heyzer, ed., *Missing Women*, Asian and Pacific Development Centre.

Rajadhon, Phya Anuman, 1955. "The Rice Mother," *Journal of the Siam Society*, 43.

———, 1961. "Life and Ritual in Old Siam," New Haven Human Relations Area Files.

———, 1963. *Khwan and Khwan Ceremony Performing*, [Bangkok].

———, 1968. *Essays on Thai Folklore*, Social Science Association Press of Thailand.

Rajaram, Indira, 1983. "Economics of Bride-price and Dowry," *Economic and Political Weekly*, 18.

Ramirez, Mina, 1984. *Understanding Philippine Social Realities through Filipino Family: Phenomenological Approach*, Asian Institute Communication Center.

Ramu, G. N., 1977. *Family and Caste in Urban India: A Case Study*, Vikas Publishing House.

Randeria, Shalini and Leela Visaria, 1984. "Sociology of Bride-price and Dowry," *Economic and Political Weekly*, 19.

Rao, M. S. A., 1968. "Occupational and Joint Household Organization," *Contributions to Indian Sociology*, n.s. 2.

Rao, N. J. Usha, 1985. "Gaps in Definition and Analysis," paper for Regional Conference for Asia on Women and the Household, New Delhi.

Raymundo, C. M. and C. Ruiz, 1985. "Adolescent Fertility in the Regions," *Philippine Population Journal*, 1, 4.

Reynes, Josefina F., 1985. "Women in Transition: Patterns of Pre-natal Care in Semi-rural Philippines," *Journal of Southeast Asian Studies*, 16, 2.

Richards, A. I., 1950. "Some Types of Family Structure amongst the Central Bantu," in A. R. Radcliffe-Brown and C. D. Forde, eds., *African Systems of Kinship and Marriage*, Oxford University Press.

Rihani, May, 1978. *Development as if Women Mattered: An Annotated Bibliography with a Third World Focus*, Overseas Development Council.

Riley, James N., 1972. "Family Organization and Population Dynamics in a Central Thai Village," University of North Carolina Ph.D. thesis.

Risseeuw, Carla, 1980. *The Wrong End of the Rope: Women Coir Workers in Sri Lanka*, Research Project "Women and Development," Colombo and Leiden.

Rizvi, Najma, 1984. "Nutrition and Health of Women in Bangladesh," unpublished.

Robinson, Kathy, 1983. "Women and Work in an Indonesian Mining Town," in Lenore Manderson, ed., *Women's Work and Women's Roles*, Australian National University.

Robinson, Rowena, 1994. "Conversion and Catholicism in Southern Goa, India," University of Cambridge Ph.D. thesis.

Rogers, Barbara, 1980. *The Domestication of Women: Discrimination in Developing Societies*, Kogan Page.

Roy, Shibani, 1979. *Status of Muslim Women in North India*, B. R. Publishing Corporation.

Rudie, Ingrid, 1983. "Women in Malaysia: Economic Autonomy, Ritual Segregation and Some Future Possibilities," in Bo Utas, ed., *Women in Islamic Societies*, Curzon Press.

Ruzicka, L. T. and Chowdhury, A. K. M. A., 1978. *Demographic Surveillance System: Matlab*, Census 1974, Cholera Research Laboratory.

Saadawi, Nawal El, 1980. *The Hidden Face of Eve: Women in the Arab World*, Zed Press.

Safa, Helen and Eleanor Leacock, 1981. "Preface" to "Development and Sexual Division of Labour," *Signs: Journal of Women in Culture and Society*, special issue, 9.

Saifulla Khan, V., 1975. "Asian Women in Britain: Strategies of Adjustment of Indian and Pakistani Migrants," in A. de Souza, ed., *Women in Contemporary India*, Manohar.

Sairin, Sjafri, 1982. *Javanese Trah: Kin-Based Social Organization*, Gadjah Mada University Press.

Saiyed, A. R., 1976. "Purdah, Family Structure and the Status of Woman: A Note on a Deviant Case," in Imtiaz Ahmad, ed., *Family, Kinship and Marriage among Muslims in India*, Manohar.

———, 1992. "Muslim Women in India: An Overview," in Mohini Anjum, ed., *Muslim Women in India*, Radiant Publishers.

Sajogyo, Pudjiwati, 1981. "The Role of Women in the Family, Household and Wider Community in Rural Java: Two Case Studies in the District of Sukabumi and the District of Sumedang, West Java," Bogor Agricultural University Centre for Rural Sociological Research.

————, 1986. "Women's Studies in Rural Indonesia," in Bruce Matthews and Judith Nagata, eds., *Religion, Values and Development in Southeast Asia*, Institute of Southeast Asian Studies.

————, n.d. "Alternative Ways of Incorporating Women's Concerns in Farming Systems Research Sites," unpublished.

Salleh, Mohammed Haji, 1977. "Cultural Justice," in Nancy Chng, ed., *Questioning Development in Southeast Asia*, Select Books.

Sangari, Kumkum and Sudesh Vaid, 1981. "Sati in Modern India: A Report," *Economic and Political Weekly*, 16, 31.

————, eds., 1989. *Recasting Women: Essays in Colonial History*, Kali for Women.

Saradamoni, K., 1983. "Changing Land Relations and Women: A Case Study of Palghat," in Vina Mazumdar, ed., *Women and Rural Transformation*, Concept.

————, 1992a. "From Matriliny to Patriliny," *Indian Journal of Social Science*, 5, 1.

————, ed., 1992b. *Finding the Household: Conceptual and Methodological Issues*, Sage.

Saraswathi, T. S. and Ranjana Dutta, 1985. "Socialization of Children and Adolescent Girls among the Urban and Rural Poor," unpublished.

Saraswati, Baidya Nath, 1977. *Brahmin Ritual Tradition: In the Crucible of Time*, Indian Institute of Advanced Study.

Sarkar, Lotika, 1986. *Constitutional Guarantees: The Unequal Sex*, Centre for Women's Development Studies Occasional Paper No. 8.

Sathe, S. P., 1993. *Towards Gender Justice*, R.C.W.S., S.N.D.T. Women's University.

Sattar, Ellen, 1974. "Women in Bangladesh: A Village Study," Ford Foundation.

Schaffer, Teresita C., 1986. *Profile of Women in Bangladesh*, US Agency for International Development.

Schneider, D. M. and K. Gough, eds., 1961. *Matrilineal Kinship*, University of California Press.

Schneider, Jane, 1985. "Trousseau as Treasure: Some Contradictions of Late Nineteenth Century Change in Sicily," in Marion A. Kaplan, ed., *The Marriage Bargain: Women and Dowries in European History*, The Haworth Press.

Schrijvers, Joke, 1979. "Viricentrism and Anthropology," in G. Huizer and B. Mannheim, eds., *The Politics of Anthropology*, Mouton.

————, 1985. *Mothers for Life: Motherhood and Marginalization in the North Central Provinces of Sri Lanka*, Eburn.

————, 1988. "Blueprint for Undernourishment: The Mahaveli River Development Scheme in Sri Lanka," in Bina Agarwal, ed., *Structures of Patriarchy; State, Community and Household in Modernizing Asia*, Sage.

Schuster, Ilsa, 1983. "Anthropology and Women in Development: The Leiden Experiment," *Reviews in Anthropology*, 10, 4.

Schwede, Laurel Kathleen, 1986. "Family Strategies of Labor Allocation and Decision-making in a Matrilineal, Islamic Society: The Minangkabau of West Sumatra, Indonesia," Cornell University Ph.D. thesis, under revision.

————, 1989. "Male and Female Authority in Minangkabau," paper for American Anthropological Association Annual Meetings.

———, 1991. "Family Sustenance Strategies of Husband-Absent and Husband-Present Families in West Sumatra, Indonesia," unpublished.

Sen, A. and S. Sen Gupta, 1988. "Malnutrition of Rural Children and the Sex Bias," in N. Fazalbhoy, ed., *The Health Status of Indian Women: A Reader*, Tata Institute of Social Sciences.

Sen, Gita and Chiranjib Sen, 1985. "Women's Domestic Work and Economic Activity: Results from National Sample Survey," *Economic and Political Weekly*, 20.

Sen, Ilina, 1986. "Geography of Secular Change in Sex Ratio in 1981: How Much Room for Optimism?" *Economic and Political Weekly*, 21, 12.

Seneviratne, Maureen, 1969. *Some Women of the Mahavamsa*, Cave & Com.

Seymour, Susan, 1975. "Child Rearing in India: A Case Study in Change and Modernization," in T. R. Williams, ed., *Socialization and Communication in Primary Groups*, Aldine.

———, 1994a. "Women, Marriage and Educational Change in Bhubaneswar, India: A Twenty-five Year Perspective," in Carol C. Mukhopadhyay and Susan Seymour, eds., *Women, Education and Family Structure in India*, Westview Press.

———, 1994b. "College Women's Aspirations: A Challenge to the Patrifocal Family System?" in Carol C. Mukhopadhyay and Susan Seymour, eds., *Women, Education and Family Structure in India*, Westview Press.

Shah, A. M., 1964. "Basic Terms and Concepts in the Study of the Family in India," *Indian Economic and Social History Review*, 1, 3.

———, 1968. "Changes in the Indian Family: An Examination of Some Assumptions," *Economic and Political Weekly*, annual number.

———, 1973. *The Household Dimension of the Family in India: A Field Study in a Gujarat Village and a Review of Their Studies*, Orient Longman.

———, 1977. "Lineage Structure and Change in a Gujarat Village," in M. N. Srinivas et al., eds., *Dimensions of Social Change in India*, Allied.

———, 1988. "The Phase of Dispersal in the Indian Family Process," *Sociological Bulletin*, 37, 1&2.

Shaheed, Farida, 1985. "Legal Systems, Islam and Women in Pakistan," *Ethnic Studies Reports*, ICES, Colombo.

——— and Khawar Mumtaz, 1990. "The Rise of the Religious Right and Its Impact on Women," *South Asia Bulletin*, 10, 2.

Shaikh, M. A. Kashem, 1982. "Marriage and Marriage Dissolution in a Rural Area of Bangladesh," Australian National University M.A. thesis.

———, K. M. A. Aziz, and A. I. Chowdhury, 1986. "Differentials of Fertility between Polygynous and Monogamous Marriages in Rural Bangladesh," *Journal of Biosocial Sciences*, 19.

Sharma, S. P., 1973. "Marriage, Family and Kinship among the Jats and the Thakurs of North India: Some Comparisons," *Contributions to Indian Sociology*, 7.

Sharma, Ursula, 1975. "Purdah and Public Space," in A. de Souza, ed., *Women in Contemporary India*, Manohar.

———, 1978. "Segregation and Its Consequences," in P. Caplan and J. Bujra, eds., *Women United, Women Divided*, Tavistock Publications.

———, 1980. *Women, Work and Property in North-West India*, Tavistock Publications.

———, 1984. "Dowry in North India: Its Consequences for Women," in Renée Hirschon, ed., *Women and Property: Women as Property*, Croom Helm.

————, 1985. "Unmarried Women and the Household Economy: A Research Note," *Journal of Social Studies*, 30.

————, 1986. *Women's Work, Class and the Urban Household: A Study of Shimla, North India*, Tavistock Publications.

————, 1989. "Studying the Household: Individuation and Values," in John N. Gray and David J. Mearns, eds., *Society from the Inside Out: Anthropological Perspectives on the South Asian Household*, Sage.

————, n.d. "Women's Work in the Household: Family Status Production Work," unpublished.

Sharp, Lauriston and Lucien M. Hanks, 1978. *Bang Chan: Social History of a Rural Community in Thailand*, Cornell University Press.

Shatrughna, Veena, 1988. "The Girl Child: Health and Nutritional Aspects," paper for SAARC Workshop.

————, n.d. *Women and Health*, Current Information Series, 2, Research Unit on Women's Studies, S.N.D.T. Women's University.

Siegel, James T., 1969. *The Rope of God*, University of California Press.

Singer, Milton and Bernard S. Cohn, eds., 1968. *Structure and Change in Indian Society*, Aldine.

Singh, Andrea M., 1975. "The Study of Women in India: Some Problems in Methodology," in A. de Souza, ed., *Women in Contemporary India*, Manohar.

————, 1978. "Rural–Urban Migration of Women among the Urban Poor in India," *Social Action*, 28, 4.

————, 1980. "The Impact of Migration on Women and the Family: Research, Policy and Programme Issues in Developing Countries," *Social Action*, 30.

———— and Anita Kelles-Viitanen, eds., 1987. *Invisible Hands: Women in Home-Based Production*, Sage.

Singh, Jasbir Sarjit, 1986. "Industrialization and Urbanization: The Case of Women Workers in Malaysia," unpublished.

————, n.d. "Education and Social Equity in Peninsular Malaysia," unpublished.

Siraj, Mehrun, 1984. "Islamic Attitudes to Female Employment in Industrializing Economies: Some Notes from Malaysia," in *Women in the Urban and Industrial Workforce: Southeast and East Asia*, Australian National University Development Studies Centre Monograph No. 33.

Sirisambhand, Napat and Alec Gordon, n.d. "Agricultural Change, Rural Women and their Organizations: The Case Study of Thailand," unpublished.

Siwatibau, Suliana et al., 1985. "Women in Development Planning: Fiji," in Noeleen Heyzer, ed., *Missing Women*, Asian and Pacific Development Centre.

Skinner, B. William and A. Thomas Kirsch, 1975. *Change and Persistence in Thai Society: Essays in Honor of Lauriston Sharp*, Cornell University Press.

Smuckarn, Snit, 1976. *The Thai Family Kinship System*, Bannakot Trading Press.

————, 1985. "Thai Peasant World View," in *Traditional and Changing Thai World View*, Chulalongkorn University Social Research Institute.

Sobhan, Salma, 1978. *Legal Status of Women in Bangladesh*, Bangladesh Institute of Law and International Affairs.

Soedjatmoko, 1977. "Perceptions of Social Justice in Southeast Asia," in Nancy Chng, ed., *Questioning Development in Southeast Asia*, Select Books.

Soewondo, Nani, 1981. *Family Law in Indonesia*, Lawasia Family Law Series, Volume 2.

Souza, A. de, ed., 1975. *Women in Contemporary India*, Manohar.

Srinivas, M. N., 1942. *Marriage and Family in Mysore*, New Book Company.

————, 1966. "Sanskritization," in M. N. Srinivas, *Social Change in Modern India*, University of California Press.

————, 1976. *The Remembered Village*, Oxford University Press.

————, 1977. "The Changing Position of Women in India," *Man*, 12, 2.

————, 1984. *Some Reflections on Dowry*, Oxford University Press.

Srinivasan, Amrit, 1985. "Temple Prostitution and Community Reform: The Devadasi Case," paper for Regional Conference for Asia on Women and the Household, New Delhi.

Standing, Hilary, 1985. "Resources, Wages and Power: The Impact of Women's Employment on the Urban Bengali Household," in Haleh Afshar, ed., *Women, Work and Ideology in the Third World*, Tavistock Publications.

————, 1986. "The Effects of Women's Employment on the Urban Bengali Household," *Quarterly Journal of Social Affairs*, 2, 2.

———— and Bela Bandopadhyaya, 1985. "Women's Employment and the Household: Some Findings from Calcutta," *Economic and Political Weekly*, 20.

Stevenson, H. N. C., 1954. "Status Evaluation in the Hindu Caste System," *Journal of the Royal Anthropological Institute*, 84.

Stivens, Maila, 1984. "Women, Kinship and Capitalist Development," in K. Young et al., eds., *Of Marriage and the Market*, Routledge & Kegan Paul.

————, 1985a. "Women and Development in South-East Asia II," Centre for South-East Asian Studies, University of Kent, Occasional Paper No. 5.

————, 1985b. "The Fate of Women's Land Rights," in Haleh Afshar, ed., *Women, Work and Ideology in the Third World*, Tavistock Pulications.

Stoler, Ann, 1977. "Class Structure and Female Autonomy in Rural Java," in Wellesley Editorial Committee, ed., *Women and National Development: The Complexities of Change*, University of Chicago Press.

Stone, Linda S., 1976. "Illness, Hierarchy and Food Symbolism in Hindu Nepal," Brown University Ph.D. thesis.

Strange, Heather, 1981. *Rural Malay Women in Tradition and Transition*, Praeger.

Strathern, Marilyn, 1972. *Women in between: Female Roles in a Male World – Mount Hagen, New Guinea*, Seminar.

Strout, Alan M., 1985. "Managing the Agricultural Transformation on Java: A Review of the Survey Agro Ekonomi," *Bulletin of Indonesian Economic Studies*, 21, 1.

Sulaiman, Husna, 1986. "Rural Malaysian Women's Economic Contribution and Family's Level of Living," unpublished.

Sullivan, Norma, 1983. "Indonesian Women in Development: State Theory and Urban Kampung Practice," in Lenore Manderson, ed., *Women's Work and Women's Roles*, Australian National University.

Sundaram, Jomo Kwame, 1986. *A Question of Class: Capital, the State, and Uneven Development in Malaya*, Oxford University Press.

———— and Tan Pek Leng, 1985. "Not the Better Half: Malaysian Women and Development Planning," in Noeleen Heyzer, ed., *Missing Women*, Asian and Pacific Development Centre.

———— and Ishak Shari, 1986. *Development Policies and Income Inequality in Peninsular Malaysia*, Institute of Advanced Studies, University of Malaya.

Suratman, Suriani, 1986. "The Malays of Clementi: An Ethnography of Flat Dwellers in Singapore," Monash University M.A. thesis.

Swift, M. C., 1965. *Malay Peasant Society in Jelebu*, The Athlone Press.

Szanton, M. Cristina Blanc, 1982. "Women and Men: Iloilo, Philippines, 1903–1970," in Penny van Esterik, ed., *Women of Southeast Asia*, Northern Illinois University Occasional Paper No. 9.

———, 1990. "Gender and Inter-generational Resource Allocation among Thai and Sino-Thai Households," in Leela Dube and Rajni Palriwala, eds., *Structures and Strategies: Women, Work and Family*, Sage.

Tabari, Azar and Nahid Yeganeh, 1982. *In the Shadow of Islam: The Women's Movement in Iran*, Zed Press.

Tahir, Ungku Maimunah Mohd., 1986. "Women Fiction Writers and Images of Women in Modern Malay Literature," *Sojourn: Social Issues in Southeast Asia*, 1, 2.

Tambe, Kusum, 1991. "Nyaya," *Saptahik Hindustan*, 10 March (in Hindi).

Tambiah, S. J., 1968. "The Ideology of Merit and the Social Correlates of Buddhism in a Thai Village," in E. R. Leach, ed., *Dialectics in Practical Religion*, Cambridge University Press.

———, 1970. *Buddhism and the Spirit Cults in North-east Thailand*, Cambridge University Press.

———, 1973. "Dowry and Bridewealth, and the Property Rights of Women in South Asia," in J. Goody and S. J. Tambiah, eds., *Bridewealth and Dowry*, Cambridge University Press.

———, 1975. "From Varna to Caste through Mixed Unions," in J. Goody, ed., *The Character of Kinship*, Cambridge University Press.

———, 1976. *World Conqueror and World Renouncer*, Cambridge University Press.

———, 1989. "Bridewealth and Dowry Revisited: The Position of Women in Sub-Saharan Africa and North India," *Current Anthropology*, 30, 4.

Tan, Mely, 1973. *Social and Cultural Aspects of Food Habits in Five Rural Areas in Indonesia*, Leknas-Lipi.

———, n.d. "Changing Food Habits in Rural Households in Indonesia," unpublished.

Tanner, Nancy, 1974. "Matrifocality in Indonesia and Africa and among Black Americans," in M. Rosaldo and L. Lamphere, eds., *Women, Culture and Society*, Stanford University Press.

Taufik, Abdullah, 1966. "Adat and Islam: An Examination of Conflict in Minangkabau," *Indonesia*, 2.

Taylor, E. N., 1929. "Customary Law of Rembau," *Journal of the Royal Asiatic Society, Malayan Branch*, 7, 1; reprinted in M. B. Hooker, ed., *Readings in Malay Adat Laws*, Singapore University Press, 1970.

———, 1948. "Aspects of Customary Inheritance in Negari Sembilan," *Journal of the Royal Asiatic Society, Malayan Branch*, 21, 2; reprinted in M. B. Hooker, ed., *Readings in Malay Adat Laws*, Singapore University Press, 1970.

Thailand, 1976. *Civil and Commercial Code, Book V: Family*.

Thitsa, Khin, 1983. "Nuns, Mediums and Prostitutes in Chiengmai: A Study of Some Marginal Categories of Women," Centre for South-East Asian Studies, University of Kent, Occasional Paper No. 1.

—— and S. Howell, 1983. "Women and Development in South-East Asia I," Centre for South-East Asian Studies, University of Kent, Occasional Paper No. 1.

Thomas, John Byron, 1980. "The Nemonuito Solution to the Matrilineal Puzzle," *American Ethologist*, 7, 3.

Thomas-Lycklama a Nijeholt, Geertje, 1980. "The Household, a Woman's Cage? A Policy Perspective," in C. Presvelou and S. Spijkers-Zwart, eds., *The Household, Women and Agricultural Development*, H. Veenman en Zonen B. V.

Tidalgo, Rosa Linda P., 1985. "The Integration of Development and Philippine Development Planning," in Noeleen Heyzer, ed., *Missing Women*, Asian and Pacific Development Centre.

Tonkin, Elizabeth, 1982. "Rethinking Socialization," *Journal of the Anthropological Society of Oxford*, 13, 3.

Torres, Amaryllis T. et al., 1986. *An Anthology of Studies on the Filipino Woman*, Unesco.

Trautmann, Thomas R., 1974a. "Cross-cousin Marriage in Ancient North India?" in Thomas R. Trautmann, ed., *Kinship and History in South Asia*, Michigan Papers on South and Southeast Asia No. 7.

——, ed., 1974b. *Kinship and History in South Asia*, Michigan Papers on South and Southeast Asia No. 7.

——, 1981. *Dravidian Kinship*, Cambridge Studies in Social Anthropology No. 36.

Tsubouchi, Yoshihiro, 1977. "Islam and Divorce among Malay Peasants," in Shinichi Ichimura, ed., *Southeast Asia: Nature, Society and Development*, University Press of Hawaii.

Turton, Andrew, 1978. "The Current Situation in the Countryside," in Andrew Turton, ed., *Thailand: Roots of Conflict*, Spokesman Books and Bertrand Russell House.

——, 1984a. "Limits of Ideological Domination and the Formation of Social Consciousness," *Senri Ethnological Studies*, 13.

——, 1984b. "People of the Same Spirit: Local Matrikin Groups and Their Cults," in P. Cohen and G. Wijeyewardene, eds., *Spirit Cults and the Position of Women in Northern Thailand*, special issue of *Mankind*, 14, 4.

Uberoi, Patricia, 1993. *Family, Kinship, and Marriage in India*, Oxford University Press.

Unesco, 1982. *Rural Families with Dislocated Males: Effects of Urban Male Migration on Female Members Left in the Village*.

Unicef, 1984. *Statistics on Children in Unicef Countries*.

United Nations World Food Council, 1984. *The World Food and Hunger Problem: Changing Perspectives and Possibilities, 1974–1984*.

Unni, K. R., 1956. "Visiting Husbands in Malabar," *Journal of the M.S. University of Baroda*, 5.

Upadhyay, Carol B., 1990. "Dowry and Women's Property in Coastal Andhra Pradesh," *Contributions to Indian Sociology*, 24, 1.

Utas, Bo, ed., 1983. *Women in Islamic Societies: Social Attitudes and Historical Perspectives*, Curzon Press.

Vaddhanaphuti, Chayan, 1984. "Cultural and Ideological Reproduction in Rural Northern Thai Society," Stanford University Ph.D. thesis.

Vaid, Sudesh and Kumkum Sangari, 1991. "Institutions, Beliefs, Ideologies: Widow Immolation in Contemporary Rajasthan," *Economic and Political Weekly*, 26, 17.

Vallibhotama, Srisakra, 1983. "Study on Spirit Cults in Thailand," *Journal of the Thai-Australian Technological Services Centre*, 1, 1.

Vatuk, Sylvia, 1969. "Reference, Address and Fictive Kinship in North India," *Ethnology*, 8, 3.

———, 1971. "On a System of Private Savings among North Indian Village Women," *Journal of African and Asian Studies*, 6.

———, 1972. *Kinship and Urbanization: White Collar Migrants in North India*, University of California Press.

———, 1975. "The Ageing Woman in India: Self-perceptions and Changing Roles," in A. de Souza, *Women in Contemporary India*, Manohar.

———, 1982. "Purdah Revisited: A Comparison of Hindu and Muslim Interpretations of the Cultural Meaning of Purdah in South Asia," in Hanna Papanek and Gail Minault, eds., *Separate Worlds: Studies of Purdah in South Asia*, Chanakya Publications.

———, 1989. "Household Form and Formation: Variability and Social Change among South Indian Muslims," in John N. Gray and David J. Mearns, eds., *Society from the Inside Out: Anthropological Perspectives on the South Asian Household*, Sage.

———, 1990. "'To Be a Burden on Others': Dependency Anxiety among the Elderly in India," in Owen Lynch, ed., *Divine Passions: The Social Construction of Emotion in India*, Oxford University Press.

———, 1994. "Schooling for What? The Cultural and Social Context of Women's Education in a South Indian Muslim Family," in Carol C. Mukhopadhyay and Susan Seymour, eds., *Women, Education and Family Structure in India*, Westview Press.

Veen, Klass van der, 1972. *I Give Thee My Daughter: A Study of Marriage and Hierarchy among the Anavil Brahmins of South Gujarat*, Van Gorcum.

Venkatramani, S. K., 1986. "Born to Die: Female Infanticide," *India Today*, 15 June.

Vimochana, n.d. "The Quest for a Uniform Code: Some Dilemmas, Some Issues," Vimochana Women's Forum, Bangalore.

Visaria, Leela, 1985. "Infant Mortality in India: Level, Trends and Determinants," *Economic and Political Weekly*, 20, 32/34.

Visaria, Pravin and Leela Visaria, 1985. "Indian Households with Female Heads; Their Incidence, Characteristics and Level of Living," in Devaki Jain and Nirmala Banerjee, eds., *Tyranny of the Household: Investigative Essays on Women's Work*, Vikas Publishing House.

Vishwanath, L. S., 1969. "Female Infanticide in India during the British Period," University of Delhi M.Litt. thesis.

———, 1973. "Female Infanticide and the Lewa Kanbis of Gujarat in the Nineteenth Century," *Indian Economic and Social History Review*, 10.

———, 1976. "Changes in Kinship and Society in Two Selected Areas in India: A Study Based on Female Infanticide Records during the Nineteenth Century," University of Delhi Ph.D. thesis.

Visvanathan, Susan, 1989. "Marriage, Birth and Death: Property Rights and Domestic Relationships of the Orthodox/Jacobite Syrian Christians of Kerala," *Economic and Political Weekly*, 24.

————, 1993. *The Christians of Kerala: History, Belief and Ritual among the Yakoba*, Oxford University Press.

Vreede-de Stuers, Cora, 1959. *Emancipation de la Femme Indonesienne*, Mouton.

————, 1968. *Parda: A Study of Muslim Women's Life in Northern India*, Humanities Press.

Wadley, Susan S., ed., 1980. *The Powers of Tamil Women*, Syracuse University Press.

————, 1988. "Women and the Hindu Tradition," in Rehana Ghadially, ed., *Women in Indian Society: A Reader*, Sage.

———— and Bruce W. Derr, 1988. "Karimpur Families over Sixty Years," *South Asian Anthropologist*, 9, 2.

Wakil, P., 1970. "Explorations into the Kin Networks of the Punjabi Society: A Preliminary Statement," *Pakistan Sociological Writings 1*, University of Punjab.

————, 1972. "Zat and Qaum in Punjabi Society: A Contribution to the Problem of Caste," *Sociologus*, 22.

————, 1991. "Marriage and the Family in Pakistan," in Man Singh Das, ed., *The Family in the Muslim World*, M. D. Publications.

Wallace, Ben J., 1985. "The Invisible Resource: Women's Work in Rural Bangladesh," unpublished.

Wanasundera, Leelangi, 1986. *Women of Sri Lanka: An Annotated Bibliography*, Centre for Women's Research.

Ward, Barbara Elsie, ed., 1963. *Women in the New Asia: The Changing Social Roles of Men and Women in Southeast Asia*, Unesco.

Weiner, A. B., 1976. *Women of Value, Men of Renown: New Perspectives in Trobriand Exchange*, University of Texas Press.

————, 1979. "Trobriand Kinship from Another View: The Reproductive Power of Women and Men," *Man*, 14, 1.

————, 1980. "Stability in Banana Leaves: Colonization and Women in Kiriwina, Trobriand Islands," in M. Etienne and E. Leacock, eds., *Women and Colonization: Anthropological Perspectives*, Praeger.

Westergaard, Kirsten, 1983. *Pauperization and Rural Women in Bangladesh: A Case Study*, Bangladesh Academy for Rural Development.

————, n.d. *Boringram: Economic and Social Analysis of a Village in Bangladesh*, Rural Development Academy.

White, Benjamin, 1976. "The Economic Importance of Children in a Javanese Village," in David J. Banks, ed., *Changing Identities in Modern Southeast Asia*, Mouton.

————, 1980. "Rural Household Studies in Anthropological Perspective," in Hans P. Binswanger et al., eds., *Rural Household Studies in Asia*, Singapore University Press.

Whyte, Robert Orr and Pauline Whyte, 1982. *The Women of Rural Asia*, Westview Press.

Wijeyewardene, Gehan, 1967. "Some Aspects of Rural Life in Thailand," in T. H. Silcock, ed., *Thailand: Social and Economic Studies in Development*, Australian National University Press.

————, 1984. "Northern Thai Succession and the Search for Matriliny," *Mankind*, 14, 4.

209

Wilder, W. D., ed., 1986. *Wealth and Poverty in Contemporary Southeast Asia*, special issue of *Southeast Asian Journal of Social Science*, 14, 1.

Williams, Thomas Rhys, 1969. *A Borneo Childhood: Enculturation in Dasun Society*, Holt, Rinehart & Winston.

Wilson, Constance, n.d. "Thai and Western Approaches to the Study of Thai History: Interaction and Growth," unpublished.

Winslow, Deborah, 1980. "Rituals of First Menstruation in Sri Lanka," *Man*, 15, 4.

Women for Women, 1979. *Situation of Women in Bangladesh, 1979*, Women for Women and Unicef.

Wong, Aline, 1977. "Perceptions of Social Justice and the Status of Women in Singapore," in Nancy Chng, ed., *Questioning Development in Southeast Asia*, Select Books.

Woodcroft-Lee, Carlien Patricia, 1983. "Separate but Equal: Indonesian Muslim Perceptions of the Role of Women," in Lenore Manderson, ed., *Women's Work and Women's Roles*, Australian National University.

Woodtikarn, Kruatas, n.d. "Some Socio-linguistic Implications of Traditional Northern Thai Courtship Language," unpublished.

World Health Organization, 1980. *Health and the Status of Women*, WHO, Division of Family Health.

Yalman, Nur, 1963. "On the Purity of Women in the Castes of Ceylon and Malabar," *Journal of the Royal Anthropological Institute*, 93, Part 1.

———, 1967. *Under the Bo Tree: Studies in Caste, Kinship and Marriage in the Interior of Ceylon*, University of California Press.

Yaspar, Md. Salleh, 1985. "The World-view of Peninsular Malaysian Folk-tales and Folk Dramas," in Mohd. Taib Osman, ed., *Malaysian World-View*, Institute of Southeast Asian Studies.

Young, Kate, Carol Wolkowitz, and Roslyn McCullagh, eds., 1984. *Of Marriage and the Market: Women's Subordination in International Perspective*, Routledge & Kegan Paul.

Yun, Hing Ai and Rokiah Talib, eds., 1986. *Women and Employment in Malaysia*, Department of Anthropology and Sociology, University of Malaya.

Yun, Hing Ai, Nik Safiah Karim, and Rokiah Talib, eds., 1984. *Women in Malaysia*, Pelanduk Press.

Yunus, Muhammad, ed., 1984. *Jorimon of Beltoil Village and Others: In Search of a Future*, Bangladesh Grameen Bank.

Zakariah, Mazidah and Nik Safiah Karim, 1986. "Women in Development: The Case of an All-women Youth Land Development Scheme in Malaysia," in Leela Dube, Eleanor Leacock, and Shirley Ardener, eds., *Visibility and Power: Essays on Women in Society and Development*, Oxford University Press.

Index

adoption, 104–5
amniocentesis, 143–44
Atjehnese, 46–47, 100–101, 126
autonomy: of women in South Asia, 7–8; of women in South-East Asia, 6–7, 8, 43, 47, 62

Bangladesh: economic roles of women in, 45; food consumption patterns in, 139–40; kinship structures in, 23–24, 35, 96; marriage in, 34–35, 110, 121, 122; postnuptial residence in, 23; property rights in, 24, 41; seclusion practices in, 62
Bants, 15
bilateral kinship, 2, 6–7, 26–29, 35–36, 47, 101, 102–3, 127, 157–58; in the Philippines, 29–30
bride-price, 120, 132, 133
burqa (veil), 61, 63, 65

caste, 54–56, 66–67, 74
Catholic families: in India, 18–19, 40
chadar (cloak), 63–64
childbirth, 70, 72–73, 75, 80–81
children: allocation of following divorce, 24, 28, 53–54, 98, 104, 118, 125, 130; care of, 19, 20, 30, 47, 101; gender preference for, 80, 81–82; relative value of in South Asia, 81–82, 145, 146, 148; relative value of in South-East Asia, 82, 145, 148–49, 150

Christians: in India, 17–19, 40; in the Philippines, 29, 109, 131, 153
conception, 76–79
courtship, 110–111

descent groups: membership of, 34–38, 156
Dhunds, 25
divorce, 122–23, 124, 126–27, 128, 129, 130, 131–32, 153–54
dowry, 19, 38, 39, 40, 41, 91, 122, 132–36, 145

education, 7–8, 146; content of, 149–50; and gender, 146–47, 148–50
entitlement, 5, 6
extended families: in India, 12, 14, 21; in Nepal, 22; in the Philippines, 30. *See also* joint families

families: break-up of, 11, 13, 19, 20, 93; composition of, 3; organization of among Hindus, 10–14, 15, 37. *See also* joint families; nuclear families
foeticide, 137, 143, 144

Garos, 17, 37, 83, 99, 100
gender roles, 2, 45, 138–39, 140, 141
Goa: Catholic families of, 18, 40

health care, 142